THE RITUAL MADNESS OF ROCK & ROLL

AN INQUIRY INTO AESTHETICS

KEEGAN KJELDSEN

Black Rose Writing | Texas

©2024 by Keegan Kjeldsen
All rights reserved. No part of this book may be reproduced, stored in a retrieval system or transmitted in any form or by any means without the prior written permission of the publishers, except by a reviewer who may quote brief passages in a review to be printed in a newspaper, magazine or journal.

The author grants the final approval for this literary material.

First printing

The author has tried to recreate events, locales and conversations from his/her memories. In order to maintain anonymity in some instances, the author may have changed the names of individuals and places. The author may have changed some identifying characteristics and details such as physical properties, occupations and places of residence.

ISBN: 978-1-68513-413-6
PUBLISHED BY BLACK ROSE WRITING
www.blackrosewriting.com

Printed in the United States of America
Suggested Retail Price (SRP) $23.95

The Ritual Madness of Rock & Roll is printed in Garamond Premier Pro

*As a planet-friendly publisher, Black Rose Writing does its best to eliminate unnecessary waste to reduce paper usage and energy costs, while never compromising the reading experience. As a result, the final word count vs. page count may not meet common expectations.

Dedicated to Amberly Pierson, Steve Colca,
Penny Turner, Nick Coffman, and Jeff Klein.
Thank you to our drivers Alex & Davide,
and Doc, Luca, Alex and Andrea in Hell Obelisco.
Much love to Messa, & The Great Electric Quest.
Thank you to Karl Nord & Jeff Klein for notes with first draft revisions,
and Amberly Pierson for help with further revisions.
Thank you to John Hunt for all the love and support.

doom metal:

/do͞om ˈmedl/

noun; a style of heavy metal music distinguished by high-volume amplification, slow tempos, low guitar tunings, long compositions, and lyrical content involving tragedy & melancholia

e.g. "For the last seven years, I toured the United States in a doom metal band."

THE RITUAL MADNESS
OF
ROCK & ROLL

"I am haunted by the need to dance. It is the purest expression of every emotion, earthly and spiritual. It is happiness."
– Anna Pavlova (1881 – 1931)

"If you have to ask what jazz is, you'll never know."
– Louis Armstrong (1901 – 1971)

PREFACE

We'll begin with a joke. A musician is someone who loads five thousand dollars' worth of equipment into a five-hundred-dollar car to drive a hundred miles to a fifty-dollar gig. Underground bands can't expect much from venues while touring in the United States, and often rely on fans for a couch or spare bed. How many nights we played for two free beers apiece, and a hundred from the door! How many times had the venue not paid us at all!

But it was different in Europe – everyone said so. They said that if a band could foot the bill of crossing the Atlantic, the rewards were great. The venues treated the bands well. They paid better, provided a meal and accommodations. The fanaticism towards music, especially for rock and heavy metal, was more intense in Europe. Even if your band was entirely unknown, Europe was the place to be.

It was 2019, and we had just released a record with an independent record label from Italy. They'd offered us their support for a tour in Europe. We'd met bands from Europe when they were on tour in the United States, and befriended American bands who had played Europe. The groundwork was laid. The label started booking it. One night while playing a road show in Baton Rouge, our drummer yelled out that he'd found a good deal online, and we all took the leap of faith. We purchased our airfare.

Seven years of touring in the United States didn't count for nothing. Our friendships had been tested time and again. If there is any tension between you and a fellow band member, it will erupt to the surface on tour. You're all occupying the same spaces day-in and day-out, but the van is hardly bigger than a prison cell. Instead of one cellmate, you have three. You have to share sleeping arrangements, make group decisions to find food and shelter. Roommates, business partners, siblings – all of these describe the relationship between touring bandmates, which is nevertheless something more than merely the sum of these parts.

If things really went wrong – if we got in a wreck, if someone got arrested, if we lost our passports, were robbed of all our gear, or whatever other nightmare – then we would be solely in the hands of an indie record label. To put it another way, we were entrusting ourselves to a couple of Italian guys we'd met on the internet. As it turned out, they were not the most reputable people to begin with, though we didn't know it at the time.

This is not a book of advice. It is not a series of salacious tales about sex and drugs. It is not a how-to guide, nor a story of artists touring in fame and luxury. This is because I have no advice to give, we never had time for such things, and I'd never recommend our actions as anyone else's blueprint. When it comes to all the usual reasons one might want to read a tour memoir, you will find none of them here. This is a book written for those who wish to understand themselves and their place in the world. I cannot claim this book will help you do any of that either, but it is a love letter – from me, to all of those who feel as strangers to themselves.

This is the story of a somewhat foolish endeavor: a doom metal band from Austin, Texas called Destroyer of Light hitting the road in Europe with an Italian band. We found ourselves moving from gig to gig at breakneck speed, on an outing planned by people who didn't know what they were doing. The experience was so punishing that I began to question why I was doing this in the first place. What exactly was it that I was pursuing in pursuing the musician's life? Why would I willingly do this to myself? What is the point of all the stress and privation? What is the point of being a musician at all? Familiar questions followed me through an unfamiliar land, but for the first time demanded an answer, and not merely a provisional one. All at once, we explored the upper limits of frustration and fulfillment. This tour was a mitigated disaster. It was one of the most exhilarating and frustrating events of my life.

CHAPTER ONE
JFK

Silhouettes of skyscrapers and sickly fog. I could barely see the city. A guy in a neon, reflective rain jacket hauled his way up the orange, metal stairs leading from the tarmac, a guitar in each hand. I recognized mine in his left, the pink tag with its final destination dangling from the neck of the case, and reached for it. He handed it to me, and I thanked him. I ran my fingers over the little beads of water on the guitar case. He handed the other guitar to Steve and went back down for Nick's bass.

A light drizzle blew in on the humid air, and the smell of jet fuel wafted inside. We both stood off to the side to make room while the other passengers hurriedly disembarked. I studied their faces as we waited. Some bounded onto the terminal, grinning, eager to be free of the constriction of the airplane. Others had sour looks on their faces.

The bagman came back up with Nick's guitar. I glanced down the walkway. Penny had taken a head-start on the long walk to the terminal. He was well ahead of us.

"Where you playing?" the bagman asked. Small talk. I suppose he'd finally delivered all the gate-checked luggage and had a moment to spare.

"Italy." I said.

He stared at me, saying nothing for a few long moments.

"Little Italy?" he asked, yelling over the noise from the tarmac.

"No, Italy," I said.

"Milan," Steve added.

The baggage man didn't say anything, he didn't nod or even acknowledge the answer. He just stared for a few seconds, blinked, then went back down the stairs for more luggage. It was like it didn't register, and of course it didn't. Who were we, to be playing in Italy?

JFK International Airport was a monstrosity. We hurried our way through throngs of people, all in their own little hurries. It was the toughest for Penny, who walked slower than the rest of us. His injury happened when he was eighteen. At the time, the accident had threatened to leave him a quadriplegic. His doctors initially thought he would never recover. He once told me how he'd determined that he was going to walk out of those hospital doors – and, over a year later, did just that. "It wasn't pretty, but I did it". All of that was years before I knew him.

The massive, glowing monolith in the center of the terminal displayed all the information about arriving and departing flights; around it, the people gathered, studied, and pointed. We walked briskly to the tram, then clung to the metal post for balance as it whisked us to the adjacent terminal. With multiple terminals connected by tramline, if your connection is in a different terminal form the one you landed in, you have to re-enter through airport security once more upon arriving. That was another hour, maybe two. I checked the time nervously as we waited in line, but we eventually made it through the security gauntlet with time to spare.

"It's a fully booked flight," the woman at the gate said. She was polite enough, but her body language and the exasperated sigh revealed everything. She glanced back and forth between us and the gate. "Go ahead and take the guitars onboard. A stewardess will meet you and find a place for your luggage."

The stewardesses aboard an Emirates flight are dressed as though they're from a bygone decade. The beige suit, red cap and white scarf was the outfit. There is even a uniform color palette for lipstick and make-up, and a uniform hairstyle (a smart, tight bun).

Onboard, the stewardess fretted for a moment, then brought over a second stewardess, and then she consulted with a third. I started to feel uncomfortable. Four bearded men in T-shirts and jeans, waited on by the concierge. Did we deserve this special consideration? The feeling of being undeserving is apparently common, even among successful musicians. They call it imposter syndrome. Still a better problem than the alternative: having a huge ego while touring as an underground musician. No one has time for that shit.

We managed to fit two guitars into the miniscule closets, but had to check the bass guitar, due to the length of its case. Nick was probably anxious at the prospect, without the relative peace of mind that Steve and I now had, but the passengers had mostly boarded by now and everything had to be stowed quickly before lift-off. There was nothing else for it, and he handed off his instrument. Finally, we were through with all the variables of JFK airport. Things always seem to work out somehow. We took our seats – all in the same row near the back of the plane, in the center column flanked by two aisles.

Steve Colca was our singer and the other guitarist besides myself. Steve's long, wavy brown hair flowed out from beneath his trucker hat bearing the logo of the eighties hair metal band, Ratt. When I first met him, his hairy arms bore maybe one or two tattoos, but he'd adorned himself with more and more pieces over the years. His left arm was covered with famous movie monsters and villains – the Creature from the Black Lagoon, Lo Pan, the Chatterbox Cenobite, the Thing. On his other arm, Teen Wolf air-guitared in full glory. Steve had a deep voice, and spoke little. I suppose we were all like that with one another. Over the years, we'd all mostly run out of things to say to one another. He was an ideal frontman for a metal band, with his large, captivating eyes and the deep, dark circles into which they were set.

Penny Turner, our drummer, had a long, unkempt, bushy beard that would not have been out of place in a grainy, sepia-tone photograph from the 19th century. The only member taller than myself, at about six foot four. He was lanky, with a metabolism that seemed to retain virtually nothing. In conversation, he could be blunt to a fault. He was pretty funny in many respects. Especially when he was flying into a rage about a shitty driver, or other moments of stupidity we witnessed around us. He said what he felt and didn't usually put any effort toward sugarcoating things. He was also one of the most competent people I knew.

By the time of this tour, Nick Coffman had played bass in Destroyer of Light for two years. Nick was the closest to my age of all the other members of the band. We shared much in common. We both had an interest in philosophy, in classic literature, in absurd and depressing authors. We both liked Nietzsche, Cioran, La Rochefoucauld. I could sometimes become quiet and pensive, but I was an amateur compared to Nick, who remained withdrawn almost all the time. I knew more about Nick than most people in the Austin music scene did, but I felt I still knew relatively little about him. He didn't exactly dress formally, often content to wear blue or black jeans and a dark button-down. Let us say that his appearance was more fashionable than Steve or myself.

And then there was me: Keegan. The protagonist. The six-foot-two, long, blonde-haired, bearded American Viking, hauling his book bag around on his shoulder. I must, to some extent, serve as a cipher for you, the reader, so I will refrain from being too indulgent in my description of myself – and will refrain from breaking the fourth wall, for that matter – so that you may forget about me and become the protagonist yourself if you so please.

There was a certain comfort in occupying a whole middle row of four seats, despite being surrounded by strangers. Normally, being on a plane made me a bit claustrophobic. It's easier for me when I don't have to worry about my elbows touching someone I don't know. None of us had much of a personal space bubble with one another after the years spent in close quarters in the tour van.

The lights dimmed. Sleep seemed both highly desirable and also insurmountably difficult. If you don't manage to sleep on a flight across the Atlantic, the jet-lag will completely ruin your circadian rhythm. Determined as I was to pass out, this only made it more difficult. I only managed to dip my toes in the shallow end of unconsciousness for a few precious minutes, here and there. Maybe even for an hour or so. Sleep from relaxation was impossible, but occasionally sheer fatigue overwhelmed my whirling thoughts and held me under for a few moments. It never lasted. I remained in a pained, perpetual twilight of consciousness. I was cramped and sweaty, and felt myself stick to the increasingly uncomfortable chair. My right knee panged with soreness; it always got that way when it had to stay constantly bent.

How was it that my own actions had conspired to put me here? Nothing about it made sense. No financial motivator existed; there is no practical motive to get involved with the arts. Why become wrapped up in something so quixotic? Why did I have this longing so foolish, this love for music that only a few people understood? And the arrogance to cross the ocean with it?

What is served by the performance of art? The appreciation of beauty? Do people really talk about art that way anymore? What good is 'beauty', and why should it be that humans care about it? And what about when art is ugly – challenging, horrifying, illustrative of brutal realities, tragedies, and suffering?

I'd seen terrifying and abrasive musical performances over the years. I'd heard people describe guitar riffs as "stupid disgusting" – and mean it as a compliment. How could that be called "beautiful"? Is that really what we're doing when we make art, creating beauty? What would such a thing even mean? I had first-hand experience with those "artistic motivations": with the urge to make art, to engage in creative expression, to share my art with the world. And yet, I felt I had no greater understanding of the desire now than I did when we first started touring seven years before.

As musicians, we try to connect our music to more fans than before. And yet, many musicians will turn about and tell you that they don't give a damn what their audience thinks. There are those artists who claim that their art is incredibly personal, that they have no care for how it will be received. And yet, what were we doing by flying over to Europe? Seeking a new audience, seeking to expand the existing audience? What is the value of expanding one's art to more people, if art is such a personal endeavor? Why is it that, in the domain of art, we paradoxically have an ethos of disregarding the will of the audience, whilst simultaneously hoping to appeal to it? Why do these godforsaken questions wait to bombard me until the plane is in the air?

CHAPTER TWO
MILAN - BOLOGNA

We arrived at Malpensa in the early afternoon, which was strange, since we'd departed America in late afternoon. The customs agents of Italy gradually admitted travelers, one stamp at a time. There had been some kind of problem with the computers, and there was no express entry for E.U. or U.S. citizens. Everyone stood in one long line.

Steve did double-duty as both frontman and the band manager, and he had set up the arrangement with Argonauta Records. Steve worked his ass off for years. He'd become a booking agent, and worked with bands in the Austin metal scene, in addition to booking all of our own tours. It was a stressful and often thankless job, and we were all happy to have found a label to take care of this task for him, and diminish some of that stress. That way, Steve could focus more on being a guitarist and singer. Now we were in the hands of others.

Steve had already heard from Alex via text, who'd arrived early. The label had sent him to take us from the airport to Bologna. We met him at baggage claim. He was unmistakably a metalhead, with long, wavy hair in a ponytail, wearing a black band tee and jeans.

"Destroyer of Light!" Alex exclaimed and flashed the metal horns. He was relieved to see us, having had while we stood in the customs line.

"Alex, buongiorno. Nice to meet you," Steve said, and shook his hand.

"Sorry we're late," Penny said.

We explained about the ticket counter.

"That is Italy for you," Alex said.

He helped us with our checked items. Penny's cymbals, Nick's pedalboard as well as mine, and our checked luggage. Steve had opted to carry his pedalboard as a carry-on item, and used up his checked baggage in order to bring more gear. He had nothing for personal effects except a backpack with his clothes and a single book. I admired his dedication to the cause, but I still checked my luggage and brought a personal bag as carry-on, consisting of my notebooks, several philosophy books, pens and pencils. After lugging the bag around on my shoulder at airports all day, I'd begun to wonder if I'd packed too many books. It was heavier now than it had felt before.

Outside of the airport, Alex led us through the parking lot to the van. The vehicle was full of the rented gear. Drums and drum hardware – Penny added his Paiste cymbals and kick drum pedal to the pile – two Marshall speakers, a Marshall amplifier and a Hi-Watt amplifier, and the Ampeg bass rig. We squeezed our luggage into the back of the van, then our guitars and pedalboards. The three of us packed into the back seat: Steve, Nick and myself. Penny rode shotgun. It was as cramped as the airplane. After the hours of claustrophobic travel, the thought of continuing in close quarters for a few hours more was terrible.

It was a two-hour drive to Bologna, the first show. For most of the tour, we would join forces with the Italian band, Hell Obelisco, based in Bologna. After the kick-off show, we'd part ways with Alex. The second driver, a friend of Hell Obelisco, was scheduled to pick us up the following day. The planned route was two and a half weeks, and five countries. After twelve days with Hell Obelisco and their driver, we would part ways with them, and Alex would return to take us the rest of the way. The tour would conclude with four additional days in Italy. During those last shows, we were scheduled to meet up with two bands we already knew. The first was a band from America, The Great Electric Quest. They would link up with us for three days. Then, a final show with the Italian band Messa, somewhere in the Dolomites. After that, the journey home.

The complexity of it all was daunting to my anxious mind. Suppose our first driver arrives, but the second driver is late, or doesn't show up? Unlikely, but worse things had gone wrong for us before. The language barrier with the record label hadn't helped to assuage my doubts. I got the impression from some of their responses to Steve that they didn't fully understand the questions we were asking. Too late to have misgivings now.

***

Alex shot onto the highway and took us outside of Milan. There were billboards and factories and houses and businesses visible from the highway in the metropolitan area, just like in any country. But once we got a little into the countryside, one could see all these old, very old farmhouses, roofed by red terra cotta shingles and in various states of disrepair. The straight, pillar-like cypresses buttressed the open sky. There is something regal, something Ancient Roman about those cypresses, arrayed in little rows as they always were.

Alex covered enough ground to take us away from the hustle and bustle of Milan. After about twenty minutes, Alex said he needed something to eat. We were all hungry too. He pulled off, into the parking lot of an Autogrill.

"Autogrill!" I shouted in excitement.

"Been to Italy before?" Alex asked.

"I came here about ten years ago," I said. "Just backpacking, for a couple months. I only spent a couple weeks in Italy. I'm interested to see what's changed since I last visited."

"Nothing has changed," he said, without missing a beat. "Italians live at a doom metal pace. Very slow."

I thought of the term in musical notation – in Italian, of course, as all the classical notations of tempo – for the slowest possible tempo: *gravé*. The cognate with the English adjective 'grave' was apropos. A composition played at a *gravé* pace is tragic and solemn. This is the tempo of dirges and laments.

Such a tempo didn't seem to fit with the stereotype of Italians as jovial and animated – as people who love life and savor its finest things to the highest degree. A slow pace in music is always associated with sadness and tragedy. Slow music is music for sad people. This certainly holds true in doom metal: the subject matter is typically sad, even nihilistic. Is Italy's pace of life really the equivalent of a "doom metal pace"?

Perhaps it is because Italians are very traditional people. There is an innate bittersweetness that comes with a love of tradition, because tradition is always becoming irrelevant. It's always crumbling, falling away, being forgotten by the youth; who, from their immature and energetic temperament, don't understand the solemnity of tradition, the importance of respect for bygone things. Perhaps there is a hidden sadness behind the veil of Italian culture. Not a hysterical, weeping sadness... but a quiet, nostalgic sentimentality, a love for the past that of course carries with it the understanding that the past is dead and is never really coming back.

The store inside offered pasta, cheese, cured meat, fruit, Italian snacks and baked goods, and of course Nutella and L'acqua frizzante. There was still junk food, candy, and processed footstuffs, but the norm in Europe seems to indicate a preference for quality and authenticity, even at the gas station. At the counter, there was an espresso bar, the staple of Italian life – a shot is one euro, *always* – and women at the counter offered a selection of hot sandwiches.

I realized that I had no European money, as we hadn't stopped to convert our currency or make any withdrawals. I only had my card, which I didn't want to use excessively and incur all sorts of fees. My stomach rumbled. *Fuck it. Need nourishment.* I got an espresso, a caprese sandwich and a San Pellegrino.

I met Alex outside. He was sitting at a picnic table with a Whopper and a Coke from the neighboring Burger King. The rest of the band soon joined us outside. It seemed everyone had an Italian sandwich, an espresso, and a sparkling water.

"It's like you're the Italians and I'm the American," Alex said.

We spent about twenty or thirty minutes eating and making small talk. None of us could speak Italian, but his English was perfectly adequate, marinated in those melodious Italian inflections. Sometimes he had to ask one of us to repeat something, but other than that we had no problem communicating.

***

Two hours later, we stopped somewhere in the Bologna metropolitan area. It was the early twilight hours. Alex parked illegally; he said we'd be fine if we remained only for a short while. Just across the street and down the block was a guitar store there that Alex found on the GPS. Guitar pedals require power. The type of power supply we normally used for our pedalboards wasn't compatible with European voltage.

The quaint, little shop wouldn't have been out of place back home in Austin. But it was a bit cramped. One of the first things you notice is that everything is tighter over in Europe. There was a beautiful array of acoustic guitars, electrics of all the popular models lined the walls. There was a single drum kit. A few older musicians, with long white hair worn in wispy ponytails, spoke cordially but incomprehensibly with the clerk. All sorts of designer pedals sat in the glass display cases.

Steve, as Alex translated for him, inquired about a pedal power supply. The clerk pulled out a box marked with the price of fifty euros.

"Fifty euros?" I exclaimed.

"What is that in American?" Penny asked.

I made some rough calculations with my phone.

"About seventy bucks," I said.

I glanced at Nick and he glanced back at me. We weighed the options as Steve did the transaction.

"Do you think it's worth it?" I asked.

"I have no clue," Nick replied. "But I am a bit tight on funds myself."

"Me too," I said. "I just got a new Voodoo Labs power supply, damnit."

"I told you it wasn't going to work over here," Penny said.

"I didn't believe you," I said.

I'd worn my last pedalboard to shit over the years on the road. I'd just spent hundreds on a brand-new board, a new power supply, and a metal case for my pedals. I could technically afford the power supply, but it was more money I hadn't planned on spending that wasn't in my budget.

"Maybe if we just get a different plug," I suggested. "I'm sure there's somewhere we can get a detachable cable for a power supply. Just plug that into our pedalboards."

"You're gonna blow your shit up," Penny said.

"I think it would be fine," Nick said. "Let's do that."

"Can we stop at an electronics store or something?" I asked Alex.

"I'll look for one," he said, and took out his phone.

By the time we reached the strip mall Alex found, we'd been awake for about twenty hours. I was exhausted, sticky, and we all probably stank terribly, but the chance for a change of clothes was nowhere in the immediate future. I can't imagine what the clerks at the electronics store thought of us. Unfortunately, our foolish plan didn't work out. There were no such power cables for sale. We didn't have time to try another store. They were all closing by now.

"The best place to look for such a thing is not in Bologna," Alex said, shrugging his shoulders. "Probably not even in Italy."

"So... what is our best option, then?" I wondered aloud.

"Batteries," Nick said.

We each grabbed two packs of nine volts in each hand, enough for four pedals each. Once again, I swiped the card and tried to just forget about whatever fees the bank would charge. I spent over twenty euros on batteries.

It was almost sundown when we walked out of the store. Alex pointed out a bar in the same shopping center, a short walk away. It had been such a rush getting to Bologna that the thought of tying one on hadn't even crossed our minds. Technically, we were supposed to be at the club in less than a half hour.

"We have time," Alex assured us. "Things won't begin until later."

The bar was very modern. White leather couches, sharply-dressed bartenders, expensive bottles arrayed on the back wall. The prices weren't half bad, but I didn't want to debit my account again. Steve offered to buy me a drink. I wasn't sure if I should drink. I might collapse from fatigue after a single drink. Maybe if I ate something. The sandwich I had for... what meal was that? Lunch, dinner, breakfast? Anyway, that was hours ago. There were free tapas on the bar for anyone who was drinking: bread with pesto, bruschetta. Steve bought me a drink and I thanked him.

Alex suggested Negronis, a preparatory drink for a night out. I tried some. It was bitter, but not repulsive. Steve loved it. I had mixed feelings about the drink. The Italians had many drinks for many different purposes, to be imbibed at certain times. There were drinks for the early evening, and drinks for the end of the night. There were drinks to be had with food, before food, and after food. Coffee, Alex explained – or rather, espresso – was typically after a meal, not during. After the meal, it was mixed with grappa.

I found a common spirit with the Italian culture immediately on two points. For one, coffee is consumed at all hours of the day. The typical manner of consumption is the espresso shot; if one asks for American coffee, you'll get an espresso shot with hot water poured in to dilute it. This is a great metaphor for describing the American version of most things.

Second, I also began to perceive that Italian culture had roughly the same views on punctuality that I do. Punctuality is an onerous curse, visited upon western society by the British. The Americans certainly helped to universalize this caustic ideology. Punctuality is key to squeezing every last penny out of every day, which American business has refined to a veritable science. But it is deeply unnatural to divide up the day into not only hours, minutes and seconds, but into micro- and milli-seconds. Time-keeping exists for the instrumental purposes of doing business, making money, running efficient systems, coordinating human activities. But beyond this usefulness to us, all our little designations of units of time are fictional and arbitrary. We've reified the time conventions of western society. These units of time are not real, but we act as though they are, and, what's more, force each other to act as though they are. This is what happens when you create a category, give it a name, and bring it into the public consciousness.

The Italians manage to run their own businesses, institutions and systems, yet they still maintain a blasé attitude towards punctuality in their personal life. They respect and value the present moment, especially insofar as one is spending it with friends or family. I suppose the downside is the long lines at the airport.

***

We drove into Bologna's downtown. Laundry hung from the balconies, flowing lazily in the wind; it was nearing sundown and a few residents were out, unclipping their garments and bringing them inside. The tires rumbled against the cobblestone beneath us. The streets were all so narrow here. Alex turned right. The road took us beneath an underpass, decorated with colorful, chaotic graffiti. We entered a small neighborhood near the railways. The road circled around the building in the center. If any of surrounding businesses were still in operation, they were all closed for the day. Freakout club was located in the central building. Directly across from the venue was a building under construction, skeletal rebar protruding from it, looming in its disarray over the scene.

The van slowed to a halt, and Alex parked. There was no sidewalk, and no traffic, no other vehicles. It was an urban cul-de-sac. There were a couple of old men sitting in cheap plastic chairs a few feet away, in front of a graffiti-covered building with faded yellow paint, chatting and smoking between a dirty, white plastic table stained with overlapping rings, from bottles of beer or soda or espresso.

The club owner met us out front. He and Alex shook hands and started talking in Italian. The two old men quietly observed us as we piled out of the van, puffing on their cigarettes. I smiled at them, and they politely smiled back.

The owner's English was less fluent, so he relied on Alex to translate. Alex told us that we could load our gear directly onto the stage. Since we would share gear for the duration of the run, we didn't have to worry about backlining two sets of speaker cabinets. We were the only two bands that night, and didn't have to wait for anyone else to load-in. *Great*, I thought. *Let's get this over with*. The fatigue was crushing by this point, and getting out of the vehicle was a struggle. I had almost no sense of expectation for the show any longer and was now so tired that the show had simply become another obstacle before sleep was possible.

After load-in, there was still the mental, logistical labor to attend to. All of our pedalboards needed attention. Steve replaced his power supply. I asked the bar, through Alex, for a screwdriver. They gave me one. Nick and I began opening up guitar pedals and plugging batteries into them. There was a small room next to the room with the bar and stage. I set my pedalboard down on the table, where I figured that the doorguy probably collected the cover.

I collapsed onto the chair next to it and began unscrewing my Orange Two-Stroke pedal. There was an adjacent room. There were vinyl records stacked on shelves inside. It looked like a mini record shop. The sense of relief from sitting down was seductive, and dangerous. It wasn't the most comfortable chair, but I had to fight the urge to close my eyes.

A half an hour later, Hell Obelisco, arrived. They were a sludge band, a genre related to doom. In comparison to our material, they played music that was rougher, angrier, dripping with grease. They certainly looked the part. If our aesthetic was denim, theirs was leather.

They were mostly older than we were. I think their youngest was about as old as Penny, who was our eldest member. We were scattered throughout our thirties – the youngest being myself, at exactly thirty years of age. I sized them up as scattered throughout their forties. They were all bearded, as we were. Not one smooth face on this tour.

Their drummer was also named Alex, which would have been confusing for the sake of this narrative had Alex the driver been our driver for the entirety of the tour. Thankfully, this was the only time the two Alexes were together. Alex the drummer was bald and bearded, and I think their oldest member. He had a bandana hanging from his back pocket, and a chain from his belt. He spoke the least English, and so I got to know him least well.

The rest of the members of Hell Obelisco were mostly fluent. The vocalist was Andrea, the largest among them, in terms of height and girth. He was the toughest looking, and completely bald, just as Alex was. In actuality, I'd learn over the coming week or so that he was not only very kind, but hilarious. He had a raucous sense of humor. His vocal style was one of the aspects that set Hell Obelisco apart from us. While we had experimented with some harsh vocals on our early recordings, we'd phased it out almost entirely. Andrea's style consisted entirely of guttural screams and mid-range shrieks.

There was no bassist, only the two guitar players. Luca usually stood on stage left. He was quiet, seemed a bit older, and had those darkened sockets that Steve had. I realized in comparison to the other Italians just how Italian Steve looked. Then there was Daniele on stage right, always wearing a cap. He went by "Doc", and had a certain confident swagger to him. He could talk shit or be self-deprecating, but always seemed at ease.

Doc dealt with the managerial duties of the band: doing the booking, sending the emails, making the tours happen. Steve was the equivalent in Destroyer of Light. When it came to talking business, which on this tour would mean calculating our share of the joint expenses, such as gas and tolls, and dividing up the pay-out, the men in charge were Steve and Doc.

The two bands didn't interact so much as we set about preparing our gear. Partially it was because there was too much to do. Tonight we were in Hell Obelisco's hometown, so they were headlining. We'd be headlining on the other dates, but tonight it would be smarter for us to open. The audience was more likely to stick around for the locals.

I'd have to get accustomed to the gear I was using. In the States, we played on Orange amplifiers. I used Orange cabinets, Steve used both Orange and Worshipers. While touring America, we played at an unapologetically loud volume. While we might occasionally have a disagreement with a soundguy over volume, it was the exception and not the rule. I'd heard mixed things about playing at loud volumes in a club setting over in Europe. I'd need to dial in the Marshall amp, find the right tone.

We finished setting up and spent about forty minutes on stage. First, sound checking, then, getting the closest facsimile of our tone that was possible. We asked the club if we could rehearse, in so many words, and they allowed it. We finally got our tone as close as we could get it. We left everything on stage. We had an hour or so to relax before the doors opened. This was not so much a blessing as a curse, since any moment I felt like I could doze off.

The most exciting part of the night was opening the box of CDs. Alex had brought all the European merch we'd printed up, which included the compact disc of the new album. We'd figured we'd save on shipping, and planned our tour so that we could just collect the album upon arrival. It was beautiful.

And yet, as I flipped over one of the CDs, to my horror, I noticed a typo. It was as though the last couple letters on one of the lines of text had been clipped off during the formatting. It wasn't a terribly important couple of letters – it was just the credit to the violinist who performed on three tracks. The last track she'd performed on was entitled, "Eternal Death", and but on the back of the CD, in the middle of the paragraph, the line abruptly ended with, "Eternal Dea". The T and H were missing.

The label had sent us proofs. How the hell could they have fucked up the formatting? I took a deep breath. It was a minor thing. Yeah, a minor thing. But then again, no. No it wasn't! This typo was on all the hundreds of CDs that had been printed up. It wasn't the worst mistake that could have been made, but it marred every copy of the album we'd just received.

I pointed it out to Steve. I just pointed to the typo, and didn't say anything. He looked at it, then looked at me, then back to the typo.

"Well, that sucks."

"What?" Penny asked.

"Typo," I said, showing him. Penny examined the back of the CD.

"Yeah, it *does* suck," Penny said, shaking his head and glaring at Steve.

Steve shrugged. He was in rock n' roll mode. It was the beginning of tour. Steve always wanted to stay positive and keep looking forward. I guess I'm not even sure what I wanted out of him. Maybe the acknowledgement that this was a serious fuck-up. But Steve wasn't going to go there, especially not in front of Alex. I dropped the subject. What the hell could we do about it anyway?

It wasn't the first sign that this Italian record label wasn't the most professional outfit. They'd told us a few weeks before the tour began that the vinyl pressing had taken considerably longer than the CD pressing. We then learned that we wouldn't receive the records until the end of the tour. That really sucked. We'd hoped to have the records to sell for our European shows. We still had a handful of vinyl records from previous releases that we'd brought with us on the flight, stuffed in with personal effects and clothing in Penny's luggage. The new shirts looked good, at least. They depicted a grotesque, screaming hellscape, with the band logo at the bottom. We'd also reprinted some past designs. Our merch table wasn't as impressive as it looked when we toured America. But it was something.

The staff laid out a giant bowl of pasta, and some bread on a plate next to it. The beer was free. It was a lot of carbohydrates – a thought I'd often have about our meals in the coming days. It disappeared much faster than seemed possible. Nine men can lay waste to huge quantities of food.

I was now on the verge of delirium. Still trapped inside this never-ending day. I repeated to myself that sleep was not an option. I rubbed my eyes as I picked up my second pint glass. I sat next to Nick, on an uncomfortable wooden bench against the wall.

"Did you sleep at all on the flight?" I asked.

"I tried my damndest," Nick said. He smirked. The situation suddenly felt funny. Probably because of the delirium.

"Jesus christ," I said, rubbing my eyes again.

"I'm not sure I realized how long today was going to be when I woke up this morning."

"Yesterday morning?" I asked.

"No, no," Nick shook his head.

"An entire day has passed."

"That was a false day."

I decided that more beer was the answer, and continued drinking. Alcohol can be both a stimulant and depressant, or so I've heard. Best to try and get into the spirit of things.

The metalheads began to file in. They look the same in every country. Black shirts, blue or black jeans, leather and denim vests adorned with patches, spikes, tattoos, long hair (though there are always some baldies). Mostly people went inside for a drink, then came outside and congregated in front of the club while they smoked cigarettes. The alleyway that had seemed so lifeless, ugly and remote this afternoon now seemed vibrantly alive.

After all these years, and all these hundreds or thousands of shows we've played, I'd long since stopped feeling stage fright. But now, I was anxious. It was our first ever gig in Europe. The crowd was not warmed up – we would have to warm them up. I wasn't sure *I* was warmed up. In my jet-lagged, sleep-deprived state, I lingered behind the black curtains to the side of the stage.

It was time. I flipped the little switch from 'Standby' to 'On'. The amps hummed on. The delicious, low, warm vibrations of feedback. I stood in front of the amplifier and held the guitar aloft. I aimed the headstock at the amp. The vibrations swelled. I began to synthesize my guitar tone with Steve's. Feedback, when done well, is sonic alchemy, something only doom and drone musicians can really understand. Eventually, the howling drone of your guitar tones blend into one.

My eyes were about to droop out of my skull from fatigue. Everything was rippling. The soundwaves danced across the bizarre waking dreamscape of my reality. Penny kicked into the driving rhythm of the first song. My body began to move again. My blood once again became liquid. I headbanged myself out of my stupor.

I missed most of Hell Obelisco's show; I caught a song or two. But I was in a daze after we played, now not only fatigued but physically exhausted, and I'd have plenty more chances to witness their set. Paradoxically, I wanted to socialize with the people around me whom I couldn't talk to, and wanted to collapse into sleep on a bed that wasn't there. I was still brimming with sweat from the performance and savored the feeling of the night air, which felt wonderful on my skin, in contrast to the stuffiness of the venue.

Alex – driver Alex, not drummer Alex – was standing outside the venue. He had a date with him, someone he'd invited out to the show. I didn't know anyone else, and I didn't know if anyone else spoke English, so I mostly stuck to talking to Alex. I bummed a cigarette from him. Smoking, like eating meat, was not something I did when I wasn't on tour. I still had my consumptive habits back home, but I'd just quit smoking cigarettes altogether and hadn't intended to pick it up again. But I just wanted to smoke. As I lit and inhaled the damned thing, I remembered how good a cigarette feels at the end of a show.

Alex's date spoke almost no English. Alex could speak to both of us, but really only to one of us at a time. I suppose we made the most of it. Alex attempted to teach me to say, "nice to meet you" in Italian.

"Piacere di conoscerti," he repeated. Italians tend to speak quickly.

"Picere... de..."

"Di."

"Di... cono sherdi?"

His date laughed. Maybe she found it endearing, maybe she thought it was pathetic, I'm not sure. After a while, Alex hinted that he needed to be going. The reasons seemed rather obvious, as his date hung from his arm. So this was it: we'd be without a vehicle. It's hard to explain how this made me feel. On tour, your van is not just a van. It's a home, or the closest thing to it. It is a shared space between you and your bandmates, and it is the one place that is just for the band and for no one else. If anyone else enters, it's because they are invited. When you need to retreat from the venue, and be in quietude for a little while, then the van is that place of retreat. You need those retreats when you're at a music venue every single night of the week. There isn't always a green room.

I'd known that this van was only a temporary home, but here was the real feeling of vulnerability. Without the van, there would be no sanctuary. Alex was our guide and translator since we'd gotten here. Now, we'd have to entrust our gear to the Freakout club, and trust that the next driver would show up tomorrow. And who knew what he would be like?

We unloaded our luggage – the last personal articles left inside the van – and moved it into the gear area to the side of the stage. Alex told me that we were staying at the owner's apartment that night. We shook hands with Alex, thanked him, and said our goodbyes.

"I'll see you at the end," he said. "When you get back to Italy."

The van's brakelights disappeared behind the underpass; Alex departed. The owner of Freakout locked up for the night, then drove us to his apartment. He maneuvered through the narrow alleyways with dispassionate ease. Some of the little avenues didn't seem quite wide enough even for the tiny car into which the five of us had somehow managed to cram ourselves. We whipped around corner after corner, and finally pulled into a snug, angled parking space.

We followed our host upstairs. Two cats rolled around the floor, wrestling with each other quite viciously, and paid no heed to us as we came inside. He led us down a hallway into a bunkroom, cordoned off as an Airbnb. There were three bunk beds, a small table by the window, plenty of outlets to charge our phones – though with our one power converter we could do a maximum of three at a time. He said we could use the washer and dryer in the bathroom just outside the bunkroom if we needed to do laundry. It was the first day, and none of us needed to. He told us that we weren't to let the cats inside, then went to sleep.

The four of us picked our beds and settled in. A shower had sounded nice earlier, but now I was too tired. Gravity fought me as I clambered up to one of the top bunks, then pinned me down immediately after I collapsed. I struggled out of my jeans and shoved them into the corner of the bunk with my leg. I calculated the total number of hours we'd been awake, around twenty-seven. Suddenly, it was almost as if my system had given up on sleep and sprung back into being alert. My mind ached with fatigue, but I was indefatigably awake. Goddamn jet lag.

CHAPTER THREE
BOLOGNA

I roused in the morning light, having slept perhaps four hours. My first thought was to text Amberly and tell her good morning, which I always did when touring America, but I remembered that it was the middle of the night in Austin. I supposed she'd text me when she woke up, which would be the early afternoon over here in Europe. I decided to remain in bed a little while longer, and wait for the pain behind my eyes to go away, along with the dull soreness in my neck and my joints, from the plane ride and the show afterwards. It was usually tough on the muscles at the beginning of tour.

Nick was gone already, his bunk empty. He always kept to his schedule of physical and mental exercise. Anywhere and everywhere that we traveled on tour, Nick would go for his daily jog. There was hardly anything that could stop him – except of course the false day we had just endured, during which there was absolutely no time to spare. I admired his discipline in this, as well as in his reading. He rarely allowed himself to get sucked into his phone on our longer drivers, preferring to read, or to drive himself. In the earlier days of touring, when I didn't even possess a phone with the capacity to browse the internet, it had been easy to stick to my reading. Sadly, it was not so easy for me any longer. Thankfully, none of our phones worked very well. Browsing the internet while in transit would likely be difficult, if not impossible.

Penny was still snoozing soundly in the adjacent bunk. Penny would always sleep for as long as he could manage. He never slept to the point of delaying us, supposing we had to depart early. But it was his habit to arise at the last possible minute. If we had a late drive, he would sleep as late as one or two in the afternoon if he could. Owing to this, as well as his long, fuzzy beard and his general manner – of grumpiness, albeit sometimes endearing grumpiness – his nicknames over the years alternated between "grandpa" and "the cat". Eventually, Sara, our old tour manager, combined both nicknames and took to calling him, "grandpa kitty." Cats sleep around sixteen hours per day.

Steve woke up just around the same time I did.

"I'm going to go look for a Bancomat and a coffee," he said, tying his shoes. A coffee sounded nice. But I didn't have it in me to get dressed and go for a walk.

"Nah," I said. "I'm still out of it."

Steve was almost the polar opposite of Penny in terms of his sleeping habits. He always tried to make the most of his time with fans and other musicians; we often had to peel him away from the bar at the end of the night. He was usually the last one in the venue, partying with the staff and the local musicians. He'd wake first out of all of us, after staying up later than everyone else. He'd really been looking forward to Italy. He was Italian-American, after all; this was his old country. He already loved it here, and wanted to soak as much of it in as possible. He said goodbye and the door shut behind him.

I dragged my corpse down to the floorboards, and into the shower. The steamy water peeled off the stench of the long journey. I dried off, stepping around the cat's litter boxes. I remembered it was pretty warm the afternoon before, so I picked out a sleeveless shirt. When I returned to the bunk room, Penny was still asleep. I felt hungry. Maybe I could have used that espresso and a bite to eat, but I wasn't going to wander off alone. I plugged my phone into the power converter.

I sat by the window and watched the street below. There wasn't much activity. I watched a tree with the pink flowers swaying in the breeze. A few passersby walked to and fro. The novelty of the scene wore off. After a while, I was simply staring into space.

Questions crept into my mind again. Here I am, in Europe, touring with a doom metal band. Trying to reach a new audience. Why? Last night, at the end of the impossibly long day, the show had been like a resurrection for me. Now, after awakening from the night's rest, I was weary and disoriented.

Obviously, a grand tour of Europe is on the wish list of most Americans, but we were not here for an expensive vacation. At one city per day, we would have virtually no time for recreation. We were here as musicians: music was the only purpose and justification for our time here. What made it a source of rejuvenation? What made its propagation a goal so worthy of having brought our music with us across the ocean?

I was alone with myself, aside from Penny who was fast asleep. What a rarity for the first day of tour! People, ideas, and the connections between swirled around in my brain. I had a book of the Platonic dialogues that I'd brought along. In one of those dialogues, *Ion*, Socrates had used a metaphor that now tugged at my memory – a metaphor about a magnetic stone. I reached for my bag and fished around for the book, and for my notebook and pen. I started scribbling.

I. Art is Irrational

Philosophy 101, the first day. The professor went down the list of all the various branches of philosophy. He gave us a general outline of each, in the order we would cover them over the course of the semester.

"First," he began, "we'll look at epistemology, which concerns the questions of how we know what it is we claim to know.

"Then, philosophy of religion – the various arguments for and against the existence of God, and the extent to which we can possess knowledge about metaphysics, or the divine will.

"Then, ethics. This is the study of morality, which is the school of philosophy concerned with human action, and standards for human behavior.

"Then, there is political philosophy. This branch of philosophy concerns itself with the questions of how man ought to govern, and be governed. The questions of rights and freedoms, as well as the role of the state.

"Then, there is aesthetics, the philosophy of art," he concluded. He cleared his throat. "We won't be covering that one so much."

As a matter of fact, I don't recall that we talked about aesthetics at all. If we did, none of it was memorable.

We studied the dialogues of Socrates, of course, as students in every introductory philosophy course do. Some of these dialogues involved the questions of what was beautiful, but Socrates' ideas of beauty seemed to be a cipher for his conception of The Good – the life of virtue at which all Socratic philosophy aims. As expressed by Socrates, The Beautiful seemed a thing so abstract, so removed from any discussion of the experience of art: it was beauty considered from the eye of the logician, not the artist. After we read Plato's Republic, we talked about the artistic censorship that Socrates calls for. His attitude towards art and poetry treated it as something dangerous and manipulative, a perspective that we students, as modern people, experienced as alien. Thus, the discussion of aesthetics in my first philosophy class was a thoroughly inartistic discussion.

Perhaps unsurprisingly, then, the general attitude towards aesthetics among my classmates was dismissive. Aesthetics simply wasn't as interesting as any of the deep questions about ethics, religion or metaphysics. And besides, how could one come to some sort of philosophical conclusion about what is beautiful? Isn't that subjective? In our discussions at the philosophy club, no one ever wanted to talk about aesthetics.

Aesthetics appeared useless to us. This is in keeping with the prejudices of academic philosophy following the ascendance of analytical philosophy, around the turn of the 20th century. Analytical philosophy represented a revolution in philosophical thinking. The new type of philosopher held that the role of philosophy was merely to inform the sciences, and to clarify questions of logic. They accordingly began to philosophize by means of mathematical formulae.

For examples, we might consider the philosophers of language, led by Wittgenstein, and the logical positivists of the Vienna Circle. The logical positivists held that aesthetic questions are simply statements of preference. Wittgenstein considered all philosophical thinking to be contained within the domain of what was expressible with language – and it is difficult, if not impossible, to express in language what we mean by 'beautiful'. That of which we cannot speak, we must remain silent – this was Wittgenstein's famous dictum from his early period. If you cannot express the idea clearly, in a coherent and non-contradictory manner, then you are not doing philosophy. This leaves little room for a philosophy of aesthetics.

In the post-positivist world, ethics became a mere statement of approval or disapproval – nothing that could be proven by logical argument. Politics became a task assigned to the political scientists. Aesthetics, as a branch of philosophy, then seems the most disagreeable of all. Not that aesthetics was ever held in high regard: not even in antiquity, nor during the glory days of continental philosophy. Can one make a clear linguistic statement clarifying what beauty means? If not, then we must remain silent – and so we have, in the popular consciousness.

The distinction between the old continental style and the new analytical style of philosophy is wearing thin, it is true, even in the academy today. Even though analytical philosophy once saw itself as an entirely new chapter in the philosophical endeavor, it seems that they may just be another branch on the philosophical tree. The logical positivists have mostly been rejected these days. Influential as they were, we now recognize the fatal flaw in their central point: if we are to say that a philosophical argument is valuable only so long as we can subject it to verification by experiment, how can we verify this very same principle? There is no experiment that can verify it. The philosophers who railed against irrational, preferential axioms in philosophy have still to rely on an irrational, preferential axiom in order to justify their whole project.

But the positivist mode of thought will remain relevant so long as it represents the habitual thinking of the contemporary intellectual – and I would argue that it still does. Whether or not we find the arguments of the positivists to be logically valid, this is how we moderns tend to think about these questions. Ethics, politics and aesthetics *are* subjective, in the popular view – aside from a few insistent moral realists, and the lingering influence of religious thought. We should at least remember that this theory of their innate subjectivity is a relatively new outlook. Go back in time a few hundred years, and all of the most educated people in Europe would be walking around at the Church-funded universities speaking sincerely about absolute moral standards, arguing about the most virtuous forms of governance, the correct metaphysics, and yes, objective standards of aesthetics.

Furthermore, rather than this subjectivity opening the way for a myriad of possibilities, we often deploy the designation 'subjective' as a means of dismissing the question from our minds. I do not disagree that these questions – "what is good?"; "what is the best form of government?"; "what is beautiful?" – are ultimately subjective. Questions about objective facts, or about the external world, are handled by the sciences these days. It is an innovation and not a misstep to create the division between philosophy and natural philosophy (the sciences). But discussing whether something is beautiful or not is surely no more subjective than discussing whether an action is good or not. Ethics is not any more of a hard science than aesthetics. No experiment can reveal to us what the ideal form of government might be. And yet, political and ethical debates have not been relegated to the dustbin of philosophical importance, as aesthetics has. These debates are all the rage on campuses these days, just as they have always been.

My classmates admitted as much, when pressed on the issue. I got into the same argument a handful of times. I would express an interest in aesthetics, and a classmate would tell me that it was simply subjective. Usually, I could get them to concede: sure, ethics is just as subjective as aesthetics. But then, in one phrasing or another, they'd admit that the real issue is that art is just not that important to them. Morality, politics and religion seem to be weighty, consequential areas of study. Politics can affect every aspect of our lives. Religion and metaphysics address themselves to the questions of meaning, the spiritual questions that consume whole lives and gnaw at the souls of so many. Ethics is nothing less than the quest to determine how man ought to live.

On the other hand, most people never develop a need for the proper understanding of aesthetics. People have the art they like, the art they don't like, and their opinions on popular art and culture. Art is basically for entertainment, and they want to be entertained. For most, that is where it ends.

I found myself unsatisfied with these notions. Aesthetics intrigued me for years, but it wasn't obvious to me why. There seemed to be a chasm between myself and others. I observed that people chose to spend their free time engaging in aesthetic pleasures, but they mostly saw any reflection on this activity as basically unimportant.

Nevertheless, for a long while, I could not find a philosopher with whom I found agreement on aesthetic ideas. Perhaps the popular relationship to art as simply subjective held some appeal for me as well. What good could someone else's opinion on art or beauty do me? I was playing guitar in a metal band. I was certain that neither Plato, nor Hegel, nor the other continental philosophers, would have approved of my chosen form of artistic expression. Consulting the philosophical opinions of antiquity had not brought me any closer to understanding art. I was certain of one thing: I was not making any kind of music that the ancients would call "beautiful". So what was I looking for, anyway? Eventually, I filed these questions away, somewhere in the back of my mind, and tried to forget about them. I dropped out of college and pursued a career in music. Destroyer of Light formed in 2012, we went out on our first short tours that same year, then began to tour regularly from that point onward. I stopped thinking about art, and started doing art.

***

Steve and Nick returned to our little apartment. By now we had only a half hour or so before we had to return to the venue. Steve entered the room with a huge grin on his face, and regaled us with tales of his morning.

"This homeless guy comes up to me, and asks me if I have five euro," he began. "I told him that I didn't have any money. He didn't believe me. I said, I really have no money, and as proof, I told him I was on the way to the Bancomat to get some…And he said, 'Okay, then get me *fifty euro!*' So, I shook him off. Then, I was walking through the square. And right in the middle of the walkway, there's two women fighting, yelling at each other. And there's this guy in the middle of them, with one woman on each arm, fighting over him! They're both pulling him in different directions, cursing at each other!"

I asked Nick about his run. He said only a few words. He described the architecture briefly as magnificent. We marveled at the majesty of the city's age. Said he jogged across some beautiful bridges. It is sometimes said that, to Europeans, a hundred miles is a long distance, and to Americans, a hundred years is a long time. We are used to wide open spaces and a loose population density that is quite the opposite of the situation in Europe. Americans lack the historical sense that comes with long traditions reaching back millennia and living among the standing relics of ancient times. Europeans, on the other hand, live with the intuitive understanding that they inhabit a culture built upon the edifices of an unimaginably distant past. I felt somewhat regretful for not seeing much of Bologna, but I knew plenty of other sights awaited me. I was grateful for the morning's relative solitude besides.

The owner drove us back to the venue. It was early afternoon by then, and hot when standing in direct sunlight. We set to work moving all the gear out of the bar and into the alleyway, in anticipation of the second driver's arrival.

Hell Obelisco arrived shortly after we did. Steve called me over to their group. As I walked up, he said that Hell Obelisco had brought breakfast. Not having eaten anything that morning, this piqued my interest. Andrea walked over, and presented me with a spliff, holding it up with a smirk on his face.

"Breakfast," he said.

Combining weed and tobacco is the typical European convention. The pure marijuana cigarette is somewhat uncommon here, though it is the norm in America. After sharing a spliff between so many parties, the buzz was somewhat light, but welcome.

The sun was beating down by then. It was not nearly as hot nor as humid as Texas that time of year, but it was hot enough to be unpleasant. Despite the fact that I'd lived in Austin my entire life, I always perspired easily. I suppose it is my pale, Scandinavian complexion. We'd have to wait outside for a good while.

We moved all of our gear out of the venue. The owner informed us that he had to close up and leave again. He went and grabbed a tarp from inside; in case it rained, we could throw it over our gear while it sat in the alleyway. It was thoughtful of him, though rain did not seem likely. We left the tarp folded and off to the side. The owner left.

"He will be here soon," Doc said, referring to the driver, checking his phone for updates.

Once again, at the mercy of others. Touring is not for control freaks. I tried to relax. There was nothing to do but wait, for as long as we had to.

We migrated over to the shade cast by the building opposite the Freakout club. Our rented gear and the guitars that had made the trip across the Atlantic sat alongside our luggage, baking on the hot concrete. The two bands made small talk for a time. Eventually, we just clustered back into little groups with our own band members. It was just easier to converse that way, in our own native languages. Besides, we didn't know each other very well yet.

"He is now twenty minutes away," Doc announced.

Twenty minutes later, he was ten minutes away.

Ten minutes later, he was five minutes away.

***

Over the years, the questions of art began to emerge at the peripheries of my attention once again. While I had abandoned my degree in philosophy, I did not stop reading philosophy books. Touring gave me ample time to read and write, on the long drives in between destinations.

The first book to bring the issue to the forefront for me once more was *The Birth of Tragedy*, by Friedrich Nietzsche. I'd read some of his other, more famous works, in college and in the years immediately afterwards. But *The Birth of Tragedy*, his first and very unpolished work, concerned itself not with the questions of value, or the death of God, or the grandiose ideas of Nietzsche's later career. *The Birth of Tragedy* was almost solely concerned with art.

Nietzsche later described himself as a "godless anti-metaphysician", as "an immoralist", and as someone whose politics were based on force and the law of nature rather than high-flying idealism. Here was a man who had overcome the same, old, metaphysical prejudices that the analytical philosophers had overcome, and many decades before them. He recognized the indelible subjectivity of moral and religious beliefs, their irreducible perspectivism, and their natural and human origin – rather than a divine or supernatural origin.

And yet, Nietzsche predicted that the abandonment of the sacred values of society – the same values that he himself rejected – would cause havoc for society. Once these values were abandoned *en masse*, mankind would fall into nihilism, finding no transcendent meaning for any of the events or actions of human life. Nietzsche's solution to this problem changed throughout his career. But here, in his first book, he located the answer in, of all places, dramatic tragedy – art. Through art, mankind could find redemption. Nietzsche's most famous sentence from that work: "It is only as an aesthetic phenomenon that existence and the world are eternally justified."

There was something intuitively appealing to me about aesthetics as the redemption of the world. But, helpful as Nietzsche's book was, it did not resolve the core contradictions rattling around in my mind. At this period in time, I didn't fully understand the book. If anything, it simply raised more questions. I continued my autodidactic studies, and against all odds, the questions of aesthetics became the most important.

Why was this the case? It was the unprofitability of my life as a musician, coupled with the conviction that this life was worthwhile. How could these two things be true at the same time? How could something bring no discernible benefit, and yet be held in the highest value?

Touring is not easy, although it is an adventure. In my time on the road, I saw most of the country, met hundreds – no, thousands – of musicians, promoters, fans. I would do it all again in a heartbeat. But it is stressful, expensive, and emotionally demanding. What was it all for?

I am proud to say that, without the backing of a record label for almost our whole career, and entirely on our own gumption, we made enough money to make the band self-sustaining, even if it did not produce a profit. We made sales in merchandise that we designed and had printed ourselves; we made sales in albums that we conceived, recorded, and pressed with our own money; and we made money at the door for our live performances. After a successful tour, we'd return home with enough money to pay for the whole recording, mixing and mastering process of the next project; sometimes with enough to pay for the artwork, the album pressing, the distribution. We made enough money to pay people to go on the road with us, selling merchandise and helping load gear. When necessary, we paid ourselves from the band fund in order to cover expenses and bills that a given member might not be able to pay due to our touring schedule. I was paid out in this manner once; as was more than one of our bassists, over the years.

The individual members of the band, however, had never made enough money to pay their bills from the band's revenue. From what I understand, you only reach this level once you're playing small arenas. Oftentimes, we'd pay money out of our own pockets to finance some venture – usually, the cost of more merch. Over the years, the band fund would sometimes dwindle, and we would borrow money. Sometimes as a bank loan, sometimes from relatives. Penny's wife, Merriet, was our financier for many ventures. In the middle years, we racked up a considerable debt to her. We paid it down whenever we could. If it weren't for my wife, I wouldn't have known any degree of financial stability.

As ill-advised as this all sounds, we were still more successful than the vast majority of bands to ever exist. This says less about us and our individual case than it does about the cutthroat world of the music industry as a whole. Hunter S. Thompson once said, "The music business is a cruel and shallow money trench, a long plastic hallway where thieves and pimps run free, and good men die like dogs. There's also a negative side."

The chances of success are so slim that young and upcoming artists who did get noticed by the industry are treated like whores, and many are willing to fulfill this role, and do anything to prostitute themselves, out of the knowledge that success is so unlikely. The record industry doesn't care so much about artistic value as they do about financial value, and it is therefore a profit motive that drives the industry. There is more access than ever when it comes to releasing and distributing one's own music – with the advent of the internet, as well as home recording equipment and software. But it is still mostly impossible to compete with the large record labels in terms of their ability to push an artist into the public spotlight. Money buys attention. The new music industry is therefore not so different from the old. The attention market is thus cornered by large firms, just as it was during the old days.

My intention in stressing this point is to emphasize that the material benefit of being in an underground band is virtually nonexistent. In fact, it is a drain on your material wealth. And yet, I still did it, year after year. There was always another tour, another record.

One explanation for why someone might do such a thing would be that it is a gambler's approach to life. The artist is a gambler because he knows that there is a chance, however tiny, that he will come into fame and fortune. The arts are all alike in this respect. There are a few great actors, authors, musicians, who have the lion's share of fans, revenue, and influence. In contrast, there is a crowd of zeroes at the bottom, who are so numerous they cannot even be counted. The arts are perhaps the most brutally meritocratic industry, with the worst income inequality amongst themselves out of any profession. The successful in the arts are outlandishly successful, and the unsuccessful cannot even feed themselves with the revenue from their art. They're forced to expend resources they earn from other, profitable jobs in order to support their artistic habit.

But most artists aren't really satisfied with this answer. I think most of them would object. This isn't about the money – it's not even about the potential, long-term financial gain, however distant, unlikely and absurd such a prospect may be. "It's all about the music," a touring musician might say. Or, "It's just rock n' roll, man!" "It's punk rock!"

Let us look down upon humanity, as though we were aliens. What conclusions would we come to, regarding the human activity of art? Would we even understand it? What is it that the archetypal starving artist is getting out of his lifestyle that compels him to continue in it, in spite of the continued drain on his resources? What is it that drives the artist? Why do we want to make art?

The inevitable conclusion of my life experience was that aesthetics was not unimportant. Not at all. How could something to which we artists sacrifice everything be thought unimportant? People toil at soul-crushing jobs in order to continue to make art. Artists ruin their personal relationships in the pursuit of art. People spend their savings on it.

All of the labor and exertion that characterizes everyday life in America is punctuated by the enjoyment of art: whether in the form of a TV show at the end of the day, or a book, or a film. Whatever one's opinion may be of the quality of contemporary American television, for example, it is undoubtedly art. The creation and appreciation of art seems to be what most people would prefer to occupy themselves with, since that is what they do when they're not compelled to do anything else. Therefore, *art is the end to which everything else in the artistic person's life is only a means*. I am not saying that art is necessarily of the highest value to all people. Rather, I offer the simple observation that, in the normal rhythm of life, we exert ourselves towards material or pragmatic ends – in our occupations and daily work – then take our rest and recreation in the arts. Work wears the soul thin, and art restores it to its former vitality.

Some devote their lives to meaningful and lofty causes, such as the sciences, or political movements. Some derive real satisfaction from the world of business. There are those to whom their family is everything, or to whom religion is everything. Perhaps it is only to the strange and artistic types that aesthetics redeems the world. But we all experience the joy of art, and the re-creation of our energy that occurs within it. Some are more or less susceptible. These descriptions of different types could be true to a greater or lesser degree in different people.

What concerned me, when the questions of aesthetics gripped me again by force, was not discovering a universal explanation for all people, but first and foremost an explanation for myself – for my own type: the starving artist, the touring musician, the troubadour who lives on the charity of others, and who travels in the service of his artform, because he considers his art to be of chief importance, worthy of sacrificing everything else in order to further it. Again, this is not a complaint, *but a riddle*. If there is no material value in it for me to do art, and in fact art requires the sacrifice of material resources, a strain on my personal relationships, and requires me to sacrifice my time and deal with inconveniences and privations, then it must be of great value indeed. But there was no consistent story about the nature of that value that I could find.

There is an arbitrariness to art. This is the next in the series of dismissive impulses towards examining the question. If we have defined art as an ends and not as a means, as I have said above, then there is a tendency to conclude that we shall have to think no more of it. Art is simply "creativity for its own sake", one might argue. Art is an end unto itself, therefore its value is also unto itself. Art justifies itself. *"It's just rock n' roll!"*

All of these statements are basically just different phrasings of the idea that the impulse to do art cannot be explained rationally. I think people are impelled to give such answers because they think that a philosophy of art would be about coming up with some objective standard of beauty, or some rational explanation of art's value: they are filtering the question through the analytical mindset. We have designated art as subjective, and dogmatically resist any objective claims about it. Then, because no clear answer presents itself, as we have made all clear answers regarding art impossible within this mode of thinking, we are reduced to such meaningless truisms as "art for art's sake". Once again, we wish to dismiss the question from our minds.

The question is further complicated by the fact that there are so many different kinds of art. We don't even have an understanding of why we conflate all of these experiences under a single word. What we might say makes a song beautiful are not the same terms we'd use to explain what makes a painting beautiful. What does a Cannibal Corpse song have to do with a Rembrandt? Both are designated as forms of "art", but what do they have in common?

Even the suggestion that "beautiful" as a description could apply to both a painting – a physical object, occupying space, which we experience and describe visually – and a song – not an object, but a pattern of waveforms, which do not occupy space in any meaningful way, and which we experience and describe aurally – therefore suggests that the quality we call "beautiful" can't have anything to do with the actual visual appearance of a thing, since the song has no appearance. Nor can it have anything to do with the aural experience of hearing a thing, since the painting has no sound. The word "beautiful" is ultimately empty of any descriptive characteristics. The word does not refer to an objective quality that the beautiful object has.

This is like trying to define "love". You can come up with a physiological definition: love is a surge of dopamine and other chemical reactions in one's brain, which brings about certain emotional states, etc. You can put forward a totally unfalsifiable spiritual definition of love, and construe it as a divine and ineffable thing. One could have existential notions about the significance of love, and wax poetic about the irreducibly complex sum of causes and conditions that nevertheless contrived to bring two lovers to a greater understanding of their individuality, and so on. But ultimately, love is experienced as a feeling. No rational-cognitive explanation of love will suffice for the understanding of the feeling. For better or worse, it is indescribable unless one has themselves experienced it. This means that the feeling is untranslatable. There is no one commonality we can find to describe all the different types of love.

It is the same fundamental problem that beguiles us when trying to define love that we meet when attempting to understand art, or beauty. Coming to an objective standard of what should be designated as beautiful might be as absurd as coming to an objective standard of who is worthy of love. This is why people object to the whole discipline of aesthetics on an intuitive level: as an exercise in binding to the objective what ought to be pure subjectivity.

The techniques of art are learned; they are developed by application of the rational, problem-solving aspect of the intellect. One can also use the intellect to engage in art criticism and deep analysis of a work of art. But the artistic expression itself is not contained in technique, is not founded on reason, and cannot be justified by reason. The fact that so many types of art exist is proof of this: each with their own different techniques, none of which offer us any insight into art as such.

What is for certain is that art is of the passions, and the way that art resists rational analysis tempts us to the conclusion that *the extent to which something is artistic is the extent to which it is irrational.* Art is irrational, and is in fact constituted by irrationality. Therefore, philosophizing about art has always been a sort of contradiction, in the time of both Socrates and the analytical philosophers. If the questions of art cannot be clarified logically, and art is inexorably irrational, then what place can aesthetics have in philosophy?

My years of creative ventures, to no profit to myself, were not *reasonable* in any pragmatic sense. On the contrary, my creative ventures were themselves *the point* of all my pragmatic exertion. Working various jobs, saving money, making time for rehearsals – these activities were in fact a rational means to an irrational end. We might argue over the most rational way to pursue a goal. But, in the most fundamental sense, the goal cannot be obtained by the use of reason. What one loves, what one values, what one finds beautiful – these feelings can't be reasoned with. *Reason is what we use to get what we desire, not to determine what to desire.*

This threatens to place art in the domain of the most flighty, metaphysical concepts that we have – with love, with God, with "the meaning of life". This is the danger every time we declare something as simply a matter of the heart. We throw up our hands and say that it is an unresolvable question. To each his own God, to each his own sense of beauty. Always, we wish to dismiss these questions.

But why? Why should the admitted irrationality of art prevent us from looking further at the question? There might still be a natural, physiological, or psychological context for the artist's un-reason.

How can one explain, in rational terms, what is itself beyond reason? The continental tradition tells me to search myself: to look within for an answer. My advantage in this inquiry into aesthetics is that I am an artist first, and a philosopher second. I therefore possess the necessary subject for my study: myself. My own experience.

***

Thirty minutes later, Davide Stracchione turned the corner and his van appeared in view. This was the vehicle that would be our home for the next week and half. It was a forest green Sprinter. These are taller than most passenger vans and common in Europe. Our van back home was a 15-seat Ford passenger van: a bigger vehicle, shared by less people – four or five at the most. In that arrangement, each person can have an entire row to himself, where he can spread out, sleep, and have his personal space, along with ample room for luggage. Our Ford seemed like a palatial estate in comparison to Stracchione's Sprinter van. The roadways in Europe are smaller than America, and the vehicles accordingly more compact. A Sprinter can generally fit anywhere from eight to ten people, but it's a tight fit. The reality of these travel arrangements was somewhat jarring.

Davide had a long, black beard – perhaps the only beard on par with Penny's – and almost always wore a black cap under which he hid his long black hair, tied back in a ponytail. Hell Obelisco knew him already, and they exchanged hugs. We Americans shook his hand and introduced ourselves.

He opened up the back doors. We began to pile the gear inside. This was the old game of Tetris that was very familiar to us, from the days before we'd bought our own trailer and no longer had to cram gear and personal luggage into such limited space. The gear barely fit, not to mention the added cargo of all of our luggage – the bags of nine people now – and the merchandise for both bands. It took about a half hour to stuff everything into place.

As we jostled and shifted the speakers and pedalboards into the modest cargo hold, a large stuffed bear fell out. Davide caught it just before it hit the street.

"What's the bear's name?" I asked, because surely the bear had a name.

"Ryoko," Davide said. He returned the bear into an overhead compartment above the back storage area.

There were three rows of seats, into which we filed, three people in each row, even in the front row, with two passenger seats to the right of the driver. We packed in, shoulder-to-shoulder. I tried to relax, but of course the seats did not recline and there was no way to rest my head. The fatigue was already setting in, the midday nod caused by the jet lag. This was going to be a hell of a tour.

CHAPTER FOUR - GENOA

The road to Genoa was mountainous and winding. We passed through small towns, through tunnels carved into the ranges, through wooded hills and clouds of mist. After a couple hours, it started raining. I generally find mountain drives to be beautiful, but they are also somewhat nerve-wracking, especially when you're on a two-lane highway and the roads are slick. I looked down at the cliffside that was only a short distance and a flimsy bit of metal railing away.

Driving in the rain reminded me of the accident – the worst car accident I'd ever had. I was going eighty miles per hour on I-10 on my way from Houston to Austin in heavy rain. My front, passenger-side tire blew out. I spiraled across the two lanes and crashed into the median. I avoided being struck head-on by the traffic behind me by mere seconds. The accident felt like so long ago, but it had left its mark on me.

We hadn't spent any substantial amount of time on the road with Davide yet. I had no idea how safe this vehicle would be in a collision, or how likely such an event would be. Given the blasé driving of most Italians and the fact that any wreck on this road would surely send us tumbling down the side of a cliff, I decided that any accident would be lethal. I shoved down the anxious thoughts and buried them somewhere in the pit of my stomach.

I turned my focus to the trees and crags. I studied the little stone-built hovels on the mountainsides, always with those red, terra cotta roof tiles. I wondered how a human being could even make it up to some of those houses – but sure enough, occasionally I would spot a little figure on the mountainside, attending to their precariously planted vineyard or garden. Some other houses looked as if no human had dwelt there for some time. Some were nothing more than ruins.

I watched the focused expression in Davide's eyes in the rearview mirror. He seemed patient and serious. We remained at the speed of about one hundred kilometers per hour – or around sixty miles per hour. This was something of a maximum uphill speed for the van, weighted down with all the gear and nine passengers.

I leaned my face against the foggy window. I was suddenly deathly tired, in the middle of the day. It would have been perfect, if sleeping in this vehicle were a possibility. It didn't seem likely. I purposefully shut my eyes and tried to relax my neck muscles, but relaxation didn't find me. I gave up, and rifled through my book bag looking for the dialogues of Plato once more. I returned to the passage in *Ion*, and starting scribbling again.

II. Divine Madness

As is the case with most other philosophical questions, Socrates weighed in on the issue of art thousands of years before most other philosophers were born. Plato's account of Socrates' dialogue with Ion concerns itself with the topic of dramatic poetry. In this dialogue, Socrates gives his most important discourse on art, and particularly on the relationship between dramatic poetry and art. It is also the shortest Socratic dialogue. Why is it the shortest? Perhaps because art is something problematic and undesirable to Socrates, and he would like to dispense with it as promptly as possible.

We philosophers tend to like Socrates, the avatar of philosophy. He is unshakable in his devotion to logic. He stands for skepticism and rational inquiry, and against dogmatism and mystical thinking. He is the first true philosopher and is the advocate for reason *par excellence*. We should pay close attention to how this ancient philosopher regarded art, because it reveals something about ourselves. Socrates remains a perennial influence on modern, scientific thought.

In *Ion*, Socrates debates with the eponymous rhapsode named Ion. A rhapsode is a profession for which we have no modern equivalent. In Ancient Greece, the rhapsode performed poetry, but this profession was distinct from that of the poet, the person who wrote the poetry. The rhapsode was not himself the poet, but the orator, who dramatized the poetic verses. To understand Ion's role as a rhapsode, we may characterize him as a sort of narrator and actor rolled into one. Modern-day performers that are similar to rhapsodes are the performing musician, the actor in a musical, or perhaps even a politician, dramatizing a speech that someone else wrote. All these modern figures perform some form of expression that is similar in some respects to the rhapsode but not in others. Again, there is probably nothing exactly analogous to it in our society. Rhapsodes conveyed the dramatic narratives through verse, and stirred the audience to a state of emotionality.

Ion says that Homer is his favorite poet, and praises Homer above all the others. Homer was oft acknowledged as the greatest among the Greek poets and dramatists, having given us the most monumental works of Hellenic Greece. Socrates is therefore somewhat radical in that he is more than willing to criticize Homer, both in the dialogue with Ion, as well as in the famous work, *The Republic*. For Socrates, Homer runs astray by depicting the gods flying into fits of rage or jealousy, lamenting the hand dealt to them by fate, or transforming themselves into men and beasts. Socrates believes that the gods should always be depicted in terms which encourage mankind to act virtuously, and he finds in Homer much that is objectionable in this respect.

Ion himself is portrayed as possessing a naïve innocence and sense of mock importance. The "dialogue" goes as most Socratic dialogues go – Socrates questions Ion with the intention of undermining Ion's claims. Most of Ion's answers to Socrates' questions become, after a while, a mere set-up for Socrates to demolish Ion's philosophical outlook. As it is Socrates' student, Plato, who reproduces the dialogue, this should not surprise us.

Socrates charges: "The gift which you possess of speaking excellently about Homer is not an art, but, as I was just saying, an inspiration."

Central to Socrates' criticism of Ion is the argument that Ion doesn't practice an "art" at all. Socrates says that the reciter of dramatic poetry is nothing more than a conduit for *divine inspiration*. The Muses are the source of this divine inspiration, or *possession*, another name by which Socrates calls it. The Muses are intercessors between a whole world of divine forces and the world of mankind. According to Socrates, it is the Muses who are responsible for all poetry.

As Socrates says that poetry and reciting poetry is not an art, we should consider what he does count among the arts. Socrates lists architecture, fishing, sculpting, driving horses, and so on. Architecture or sculpture would obviously be included in the modern understanding of the word art, but fishing and driving horses would typically not be. As such, Socrates is using the term "art" in a different way than we would in modern parlance. Thus, we should keep in mind that when Socrates says that Ion does not practice an art, what Socrates means by "art" is what we would call a *craft*. He means "a technique or series of techniques that can be learned and taught".

There is, it is true, technique involved in all art, in the modern sense of the word. There is a technique to painting, for example, or to playing guitar in a doom metal band. Technique can be judged as better in one individual than another on an objective basis. A technique can be honed through practice, and judged based on the empirical results gleaned from practicing it. The development of technique is therefore a scientific process. The extent to which a discipline involves a technique is the extent to which that discipline can be practiced and studied rationally.

In the modern sense of the word, therefore, a craft exists primarily for pragmatic reasons. What we call crafts are judged primarily by the competency of technique rather than by the measure of creativity – and we don't typically use words like 'spirit possession' in assessing the work of a woodworker or a fisherman. Creativity enters into a craft, but the craftsman must make things that are functional first and a means of self-expression second. The carpenter's building must be structurally sound. The blacksmith's horseshoes have to function as horseshoes. In the practice of a craft, artistry serves science, not the other way around. Furthermore, the craftsman improves by imitation of the techniques of experts, whereas the rhapsode might speak whatever wild inspiration flows from the lips of the Muses. Craft or technique is based on imitation, whereas art is self-expressive.

Art occurs when divine inspiration is served by technique instead of the other way around. Here, I am using the term "art" in the modern sense of the term, and not as Socrates would use it. In True Art, science serves artistry. If art itself is irrational, then the practice of an *art is artistic to the extent that is irrational: an end unto itself.* Technique may comprise part of what it means to be an artist, but the art is first and foremost a form of creative expression. If there is any pragmatic functionality to a work of True Art, it is secondary.

These categories may be somewhat confusing, because even in modern usage, we sometimes use terms like "art" and "craft" relatively interchangeably. Meanwhile, a purely pragmatic craft – like fishing, or driving horses – is exactly what Socrates would call an "art", whereas I would contest that such things are definitively *not* art. When I use the term "art", I am not talking about the techniques, as Socrates does. Why? Because these techniques will vary from discipline to discipline, as Socrates points out. A master of brushwork doesn't necessarily know anything about music theory. A study of technique cannot inform us about the mystery of art itself. It brings us no closer to understanding what unites all the different things that we call by the name, "art". If we wish to understand this unity, we must instead look to the artistic impulse, the feeling of inspiration, "communion with the Muses". By True Art, I therefore refer to exactly this concept of *inspiration* that Socrates speaks of.

Inspiration seizes us, and appears to us in our subjectivity as so compelling, so foreign to pragmatic ego-consciousness, that Socrates here describes it as alien to the human mind. As such, he sometimes identifies creative expression with spirit possession.

Socrates argues: "All good poets, epic as well as lyric, compose their beautiful poems not by art" [by technique] "but because they are inspired and possessed. And as the Corybantian revelers when they dance are not in their right mind, so the lyric poets are not in their right mind when they are composing their beautiful strains: but when falling under the power of music and meter they are inspired and possessed; like Bacchic maidens who draw milk and honey from the rivers when they are under the influence of Dionysus but not when they are in their right mind. And the soul of the lyric poet does the same, as they themselves say; for they tell us that they bring songs from honeyed fountains, culling them out of the gardens and dells of the Muses; they, like the bees, winging their way from flower to flower. And this is true. For the poet is a light and winged and holy thing, and there is no invention in him until he has been inspired and is out of his senses, and the mind is no longer in him: when he has not attained to this state, he is powerless and is unable to utter his oracles."

The best approach to such a passage is not to evaluate the religious claims about the Muses as if it were a claim about an objective phenomenon. Instead, I am interested in why Socrates would associate the poet with the oracular priest, or with revelers and Bacchic maidens. What is it that they have in common? To Socrates, the inspiration for a poem is a purely irrational thing; the dramatic recitation of a poem is, similarly, an irrational thing. Poetry is not, therefore, something that can be taught, or studied. It is, above all, a state of mind. Socrates calls it "not being in your right mind" or "going out of one's mind".

Socrates describes a state of heightened emotion that he likens to insanity, caused by forces which are outside of the human mind. In the context of the mystery cults, driven by Dionysian music, we might call it *ritual madness*. It is caused not by a human will, but by a deity. This divine or ritual madness is where we find the origin of the creative drive. The creative drive is an *experience*, a *state of mind*, a *feeling*; this places it outside the domains of reason or knowledge. It is akin to a religious experience. It is associated with a loss of self-identity, or the perception that the inspiration is coming from outside of oneself.

Socrates makes the analogies that he does because of this loss of self-identity associated with the Bacchic rituals. Through dance and drunkenness, the Greeks who participated in the mystery cults lost their identification with the ego-consciousness. These rituals occurred under the influence of wine and hallucinogenic mushrooms. Many who take large doses of psychedelics report vivid religious experiences, including the experience termed, "ego death".

Even in some sects of Christianity today, such as the Pentecostal Church, there are living examples of ecstatic religious practices. People scream, dance, gyrate, speak in tongues, handle poisonous snakes. The normal feelings and behaviors of the individual are interrupted, and are thought to be seized by divine forces. Religion is the nearest analogy that Socrates has for the creative drive that underlies all art, and it is through religion that he explains the divine inspiration behind art.

In modern terms, we might consider the idea of "a stroke of genius". *Genius* comes to us from a word once used for spirits, and the word genie derives from the same etymological root. Genius is something immaterial, something that seizes us, like a spirit. This is the term that Schopenhauer used to describe the source of all artistic inspiration, and which Nietzsche later adopted himself as a description of the artistic and philosophical process. This is how we understand artistic talent even today, when we call someone a prodigy, or say that someone is naturally gifted. When we speak of artistic genius, we are speaking in terms that presuppose something incomprehensible about those of great artistic talent. Importantly, there is a sense in which a stroke of genius is *not you*. Genius is not learned, nor controlled by the conscious intellect – it comes forth unexpectedly, takes hold of the artist, does its work, and then departs. We allow for this concept in our language, which is to say that it exists within our collective thinking.

Socrates' description of the true nature of the creative arts – as generated by divine madness – are the same grounds for the Socratic attack on art. Socrates does not approve of counting dramatic poetry among the useful crafts, which are by their nature practical, respectable and valuable. He expresses a low opinion of Ion as a person, and asserts how unimpressive Ion is as a mere tool of the gods. Ion has achieved nothing on his own merit.

Socrates is the natural enemy of inspiration, because he himself was famously unartistic. Friedrich Nietzsche writes, in *The Birth of Tragedy*, that this is because Socrates was a "despotic logician". He argues that Socrates could only really comprehend that which was knowable, discussable, provable. As the "mystagogue of science", his outlook was strictly theoretic.

And yet, after Socrates was condemned to death by the people of Athens, he had the feeling of having a "neglected duty" with respect to art.

Nietzsche: "As he tells his friends in prison, there often came to him one and the same dream apparition, which always said the same thing to him: 'Socrates, practice music.' Up to his very last days, he comforts himself with the view that his philosophizing is the highest of the muses, and he finds it hard to believe that a deity should remind him of the 'common, popular music'. Finally, in prison, in order that he may thoroughly unburden his conscience, he does consent to practice this music for which he has but little respect. And in this mood he writes a prelude to Apollo and turns a few Aesopian fables into verse. It was... his Apollinian insight that, like a barbaric king, he did not understand the noble image of a god and was in danger of sinning against a deity – through his lack of understanding. The voice of the Socratic dream vision is the only sign of any misgivings about the limits of logic..."

Nietzsche references Apollo here because Apollo is both the god of dreams, and the god of the plastic arts. In *The Birth of Tragedy*, Nietzsche holds Apollo in contrast to Dionysus, the god of ritual madness, wine, and music. These two apparently opposite deities, Nietzsche argues, equally nourished the artistic spirit of the ancient Greeks.

The Apollinian impulse is how Nietzsche designates the will to represent one's self-image and his image of the world. The Apollinian stands for self-creation, for self-reflection, for the contemplation of one's place in the world through art. Dionysian ritual, meanwhile, was the means by which the Greek's animal impulses could be discharged. Through ritual, wine, dance and music, the suffering individual was annihilated and returned to the primordial unity. Nietzsche argues in his first book that these twin artistic impulses, while seemingly opposed, enhance one another. Their union in Greek art speaks to the complete, healthy spirit of the Greeks.

If the notion of Dionysian rituals seems strange, this sort of thing was not unique to Athens. There were similar rites in the ancient festival of Saccaea. Historians of the middle ages have documented the as-yet-unexplained, "St. Vitus' Dance", a series of incidents in which groups of people, sometimes whole villages, were stricken by the sudden and unexplained need to dance. Some danced for days, or even weeks, wrecking their bodies in the process. A few died from exhaustion. Sometimes bands were assembled to perform music, with the intention of actually assisting in the dancing, under the hypothesis that the urge to dance would 'burn itself out', so to speak. I suppose the thinking was that they just needed to get it out of their system; the music might help speed the process. Sometimes it worked, sometimes it didn't. The result was that these bouts of dancing madness sometimes culminated in wild, village-wide dance parties.

These incidents occurred all over Europe, sometimes decades or centuries apart. They eventually ceased with as little apparent cause as when they inexplicably began. The malady was attributed to St. Vitus, as his curse. That was the best explanation they could muster. The modern world has never seen such a thing. Or have we? (Is this what I've witnessed at metal shows? It is for this feeling that the doom band St. Vitus was named, and the music venue in Brooklyn, New York.)

The loss of self-consciousness is not a good thing in the Socratic view, since self-knowledge is required for virtue. To Socrates, who sought the truth in order to do the good, the dictum "Know Thyself" was paramount. The Socratic school scorned the Dionysian. Socrates' admirer, the playwright Euripedes, tried to remove the Dionysian elements from Greek drama. Nietzsche argues that Euripides artistically represented the view that the individual can be confined "within a limited sphere of solvable problems". This was the dramatic manifestation of Socratic philosophy.

At best, then, dramatic poetry is worthless – and at worst, it is dangerous. Years later when Socrates is dying, he is nevertheless visited by dream visions commanding him to compose poetic verses – *and he does so*. Even Socrates, a candidate for the most unartistic type of man, had an artistic streak that he had to satisfy before death. A god demanded it.

From these passages in *Ion* and in *The Apology*, we can draw a few conclusions about Socrates. First, Socrates had great respect for the technical skill that an artist develops. Second, when Socrates did have an artistic moment, he associated it with Apollo, the god of dreams and reflective self-consciousness; he ties his artistry to the opponent of Dionysus. And third, even the ultimate logician attributes his own artistic expression to divine madness, insofar as it is commanded or inspired by Apollo. The moral of the dream visions of Socrates: perhaps even the most logical man has need of the irrational, if only in small doses, or as a punctuation mark on a long life of reason. There is some aesthetic need even in the most ascetic type of man.

***

It was a gray afternoon when we arrived, though the rain was light by now. The roadways in Genoa didn't make any sense to my eyes, as is often the case in cities that have been continuously inhabited for centuries. Genoa is ancient; as a coastal city, it was once a nexus of trade. It was built upon, over and over again, in fits and starts. In the 1300s, it was one of the first to bear the brunt of the Black Death, when ships arriving from ports in Central Asia brought the plague-bearing fleas to its port. In the late 1800s, Nietzsche lived there, and wrote much of his celebrated work *The Gay Science* while walking its avenues and coastline.

Now, dozens of cruise liners were docked at the marina, painted with garish designs and the likenesses of superheroes. There was one cruise ship painted with the image of Wonder Woman, another with Batman and Superman. Buildings erected hundreds of years before stood among roads and intersections, parking lots, banks, theaters. The city was ringed by hills, and villas of every pastel color peer out over them. The streets were choked with autos, busses, vespas and people. Davide maneuvered effortlessly through the absurd web of city-streets.

Light precipitation continued as Davide pulled onto the shoulder, across the street from the venue. Cars and busses shot past us as we disembarked from the vehicle. We waited for ideally timed moments to haul the gear across the street. The speaker cabinets were much lighter and less of a burden to carry than our U.S. equipment was. Once we were across the street, we carried the equipment between stone columns and under the canopy that extended in front of the block of markets and restaurants, then continued onto an alleyway that slanted upwards, blocked off from any traffic or bicycles by a metal gate placed there for that purpose. After this, it was about thirty yards uphill on the damp cobblestone that paved the narrow alleyway, until the destination, indicated by a little sign jutting out from the left: Lucrezia Social Bar.

From there, we entered the tiny barroom which was on the ground level. It could fit maybe twenty people at the most. One then took an immediate right, down the stairs that snaked into a basement venue beneath the bar. The stage was tiny, set into a little nook, the walls were stone. The cell phone service was non-existent. It was like being in a cave. Arduous as the loading process was, with nine pairs of hands between us we quickly brought everything inside. Unlike the night before, we had several hours to ourselves before the show was set to begin. Maybe I could actually take in something of the city.

Nick and I left in search of a Bancomat, and used his phone to calculate a walking path. It was only five minutes or so on foot. The rain mostly abated by the time we reached the machine and withdrew our money, both interested in the novelty of the foreign notes but hastening to tuck them away somewhere safe. A short distance away there was a little fair or festival going on down by the docks. There were white tents everywhere, and food trailers, music and pop-up restaurants and bars. We walked onto the grounds, and several children intersected our path, running to some sort of carnival game. Families and couples thronged everywhere. The smell of fried seafood was thick in the air.

The boardwalk extended far into the water. The overcast sky had permitted a bit of the sunset to peek through, cascading orange light across the gentle ripples and waves, though the light was now steadily being swallowed up by dusk. From the boardwalk, we had a panoramic view of the city: the Mediterranean, the docks, the historic architecture, the green hilltops with its villas, still wreathed by caresses of mist.

On our return journey, we took notice of one of the 'boats' docked at the marina. It was quite literally a two-story house. It was rectangular and minimal, without any architectural flourishes, and floated atop the water. It was complete with a tiny astroturf lawn and even flowers in the windowsill.

"What's the point of that?" I said, pointing to it. "There's no way it sails."

"Probably not," Nick agreed. "I suppose if you wanted to live in a houseboat..."

"Surely you'd still get seasick on the second floor..." I speculated. "What does something like that even cost?"

"Was that Plato you had out this morning?" He asked, changing the subject.

"Oh, that? I was just skimming, not really reading... looking for something. Jotting down some quotes. I also brought Schopenhauer. Tried to read some of his magnum opus on the drive here."

"How is it?" he asked.

"Erm," I paused, then admitted, "I'm not finding it as enjoyable as I thought I would. A bit dry. I'm having to go slowly. Nothing like his essays and aphorisms. Sadly, it's one of the heaviest books I've brought with me."

"That's a shame," Nick said.

"Did you get any sleep on the way in?" I asked.

"No," Nick replied. "I think I'll try sitting in the front tomorrow. My neck is killing me."

I hesitated before speaking further. There is a power to negativity. While it might feel good to vent, you can kick up the flames of negative thoughts already seething. I'm not convinced that venting is necessarily a good thing.

"This is insane, man."

"What do you mean?"

"A Sprinter van with nine people in it? I don't think I realized how tight it was gonna be when Steve talked about sharing a vehicle."

"Me neither."

"I've been so tired. But I can't sleep in that thing."

"Yeah," he said. "And booking a gig right after we fly in..."

"Insane," I repeated.

"Well, nothing we can do about it now."

"In for the ride."

It's not like I thought we'd be touring in luxury or anything. We'd done a tour with nine people in a single vehicle before. But that was many years ago, back in the U.S., in the Ford passenger van. It was two to each bench seat that tour, which was not exactly comfortable. This, on the other hand, was like recreating the claustrophobic experience of the trans-Atlantic flight, every single day. There'd been a big gap from my preconceptions in comparison to the actuality. Perhaps it was my fault; I hadn't pressed enough, asked enough questions. Whatever. *Just a rough start*, I said to myself. *This is barely the beginning. Things will get better.*

***

We met up with the group again. Steve and I went with the Italians to find food, Penny and Nick stayed at the bar with the gear and merchandise. We found a Napoli-style pizza place a few blocks away. They introduced us to more new things. Andrea suggested that we try Amari, a digestive shot. The flavor was not very nice – like a medicinal syrup. I supposed the point was to help down all the beer and bread. The Italians got a chance to utilize their English, and we got to learn some Italian. Mostly, they introduced us to new curse words. They asked if I knew any.

"Porco dio," I said. I'd learned that one from Messa, when they toured the United States.

"Yeah, porco dio," said Andrea. "Every band that comes through must learn it."

"All the main Italian curse words are about religion and God…" Luca said. "'Fuck God', 'God is a dog', 'God is a pig', that kind of stuff."

When we checked out and paid; Andrea gestured toward the cross and rosary hanging near the entrance.

"Maybe we should not have been saying porco dio and all these words so loud earlier…"

The face of the chef taking our cash was indifferent. If he had taken offense, he didn't show it.

We walked back to the Lucrezia Social Bar as the sky darkened and it started to rain again. Steve and the Italians walked just ahead of me, laughing uproariously at something that I didn't overhear. When they spoke directly to us, they spoke English, but to each other they spoke Italian. Half the time, we Americans were simply deaf to the conversation around us. It was a strange feeling.

Davide split off from us, and walked back to the van to get some sleep. I ordered a whiskey on the rocks, and joined Steve and the Italians out into the alleyway in front of the venue. I asked Luca for a translation of a phrase that I knew I would find useful. He taught me: "posso avere una sigaretta?" – handed me a smoke, and lit it. The rain got in my whiskey and onto my cigarette. We already loved the Italians. Steve was winning them over with his love of Italian horror and comprehensive knowledge of metal lore.

As the night grew damper and darker, the inside of the bar filled. The breath of the occupants fogged the window. The locals seemed undeterred from the nightlife by the rain. Eventually, there were so many people in the cramped alleyway that we'd formed two lines, one on either side of the alleyway. A wino – red-faced, and drinking from a plastic cup – danced comically and sang loudly, gyrating and stumbling.

"This is Italy," Doc said, gesturing to the guy. "You will see this guy at every bar in Italy."

Some of the locals tried to make small talk, but whenever I tried, the language barrier was too insurmountable. All my conversations quickly turned into awkward silences, and I got tired of standing by other people I couldn't understand while nodding as they spoke in Italian. Steve and I mostly just talked with the guys from Hell Obelisco. We talked about past tours.

Davide showed up again after a couple hours. There was a woman with him.

"We're going to see the Duomo," Davide said – meaning, the church in the center of the Piazza. "It's a short walk."

They invited me and I went with them. After a brief trip up the alleyway, and a few turns here and there, we arrived. The black and white stripes created by different colored bricks, laid in a certain pattern was typical for the cathedrals of this type. As we got closer to it, they pointed out the details etched into the stone – the gargoyles and little statues of saints and all the intricacies of their armor, or the texture of a dragon's scales carved centuries ago.

On our way back, we waded through occasional mobs of people gathered in front of other bars, the conversations and shouts echoing through the city streets.

"Where are you from?" I asked.

"Pescara," Davide said. "On the east coast."

"And are you from there as well?" I asked his friend.

"I'm from Genoa," she said, lighting up a cigarette. "Here."

She handed me one of her smokes. I attempted my best, "Grazie."

"We met the last time I came here," Davide said.

"How often do you make it out here?"

"I've toured around, taken lots of bands around, too," he said.

Davide had been in a stoner metal band called Zippo, and was in a new project called Shores of Null. Not only did he work as a driver fairly regularly, he also ran a festival in his hometown of Pescara, and booked bands there for one-off shows. I'd never heard of any of it – his fest, his bands, his label. This is part of the reward of making underground music. You realize, over time, that there are more great bands and records out there than you could ever know or listen to. You find windows into scenes about which most know absolutely nothing. These local scenes represent a whole network of artists and influences, a subcommunity within the subcommunity.

These local scenes exist everywhere, all around the world. They're all loosely connected, and yet the surface world is not aware of it. On the other hand, how fortunate to live in an era where this music can be discovered internationally, where we can record it all and save it all, however obscure it may be destined to become! Modernity is wonderful. In some ways.

***

The stage was cramped and the attendance was poor for a Saturday night. Financially, it would not have been abysmal, if not for the high cost of getting to Europe we had to recoup in order to merely break even. It was a hurdle we were far from clearing. What was worse, we hardly made any sales at the merch table. Merch sales had been poor the previous night as well. I remembered something a fellow musician who had toured Europe had told me before we left. "Italians are poor," he'd said, shrugging as he warned me about touring there. Maybe things would pick up once we left Italy.

At the end of the night, we once again left our equipment at the venue. Our host explained that the apartment where we were staying was accessible only by foot. By the time we'd gathered up all the personal effects from the van, and gathered up ourselves in the alleyway, it was in the dark hours of the early morning. The streets, which had just been alive with music, drunks, and revelers a few hours previously, were now silent, save for the sound of our bags rolling on the bumpy cobblestone streets. We passed a few other parties wandering home, a few beggars and drunks collapsed into a dark corner, but for the most part, we were the only source of noise or sign of life. Once again, we followed people we'd only just met into the darkness, and trusted in the local scene.

The apartment was cluttered, yet accommodating. There was room to spread out, mattresses and couches to sleep on, at least five or six rooms. I think the hostess said something about her roommates being out of town. There were easels and paintings and canvasses lying around, and lots of vintage advertisements and artsy stuff like that on the walls. She mentioned that her boyfriend made his living as a street musician.

Again, I shoved down the anxious thoughts and tried to make my peace with stashing our gear elsewhere, with having to trust that the club owners would wake up at the time they said they would, and open up for us so we could get out of Genoa on time. I selected a couch and laid down. All the liquor and cigarettes, the excitement of the show and the frustration of our impotent sales figures, the jet lag, the neck aches, the insecurity – everything swirled about in my head. I was tired when I needed to be alert. I was agitated when I needed to relax. Eventually you wear yourself out. My mind collapsed from exhaustion, like a bum into a dark cranny.

CHAPTER FIVE
GENOA - LYON

The management at Lucrezia Social Bar opened the bar early the next morning. Another quick, efficient load-out. The Italians were seasoned musicians like ourselves. For whatever the flaws in planning this tour, we were with solid, effective people. Davide fought his way through the morning traffic around the marina, and we ascended a series of crisscrossing roadways woven onto the hills, and betook ourselves from the historic city.

In a couple hours, we were onto a vast, flat plain, speckled with farmhouses and vineyards and wheat fields. It was not too different from the drive from the airport to Bologna, except that now the Italian Alps loomed dramatically in the distance. The road stretched on into infinity as if the mountains were a mere background, stubbornly refusing to get any larger as we approached. It would be hours of driving before their visage would finally swell before us, attesting to their enormity.

I sat in the front seat this time. Doc was on my left, and then Davide in the driver's seat. We chatted for a bit. But they began speaking Italian, and the midday fatigue began to set in. I slumped against the door, cheek pressed on the glass, and watched the windswept prairies.

In due time, we pulled into another Autogrill. We were almost to the foot of the Alps. We spilled out of the van, eager to unbend our limbs and work out the kinks that had already knotted us up from the few hours in the Sprinter. The sky was a storybook blue, in contrast with the mirk of the previous day. The breeze rushed through the valley, loudly shaking the branches of the trees neatly arrayed besides the rest stop and pummeling me with a wave of cold. The air had a pleasant, rustic smell to it.

"We will leave in..." Davide said, checking the time, "Ten minutes. Fifteen minutes at most."

Italian time, (n): the implied extension of almost any duration of time, as given by an Italian. I'm not sure if I ever figured out a hard and fast rule to translate American time into Italian time, as it seems contextual. One could reliably double the stated duration of any stop we made. We filed into the store, bought sandwiches, chips, pasta, l'acqua frizzante, espresso, and the rest, then gathered at the picnic tables to take our lunch outside in the spring breeze. We conversed and carried on. We didn't leave for half an hour.

Nick and I switched places when we all crammed back into the van again. There was limited cellular coverage, at least for us Americans, especially while out on the highways. Most of the time, we had a maximum of 3G. Still hadn't had a chance to call my wife. Even if I had the service, she wouldn't be awake anyway. I had only my books, my notes, and my thoughts – against the backdrop of the European countryside. Eventually, we began pushing uphill and into the Alps. It was a slow, steady climb, and the Sprinter could only push onward so fast. It would be a long time before we would stop again.

***

Socrates' attitude towards music and poetry culminates in a political attack upon the arts. These are among his more notorious views, expressed in Plato's *Republic*, that poetry ought to be censored. This is because poetry, being a form of spirit possession, is dangerous, and cannot be allowed to run out of control.

Socrates' vision of the ideal state would be organized into three classes or stations: the rulers, the soldiers, and the tradespeople & laborers. The lifestyle and attitude of a given class are heavily restricted in this system. The rulers must listen only to music that ennobles, only read poetry that inspires them to virtue. The soldiers must concern themselves only with martial music, or poetry that urges them on to heroics. Unrestricted artistic expression would adversely affect people's emotional states, which would impede the ability of people to fulfill their role in society. Since the perfect society involves everyone perfectly fulfilling his or her role in that society to the maximum degree possible, this decadence is unacceptable. Thus, Socrates argues that the types of artistic expression allowed for a person must be catered to his caste or position. This necessitates the state's censorship of art.

Socrates' asks his interlocutors about certain metaphors or images that might appear in poetry. "And what about horses neighing and bulls bellowing, and rivers splashing and the sea roaring, and thunder rolling, and so on?"

"We have already forbidden madness and the imitation of madmen," one of them answers, having been effectively coerced through the Socratic method into expressing agreement with the old gadfly.

The overall treatment of poetry and music in *The Republic* indicates the Socratic view of artistic expression as profoundly powerful and dangerous. This is because Socrates believes that art possesses a mimetic quality. This means that the emotional states conveyed by art are a form of *mimesis*: through art these emotional states are transmitted, received, and imitated. They are quite literally infectious.

Socrates argues, to return to his dialogue in *Ion*: "There is a divinity moving you, like that contained in the stone which Euripides calls a magnet, but which is commonly known as the stone of Heraclea. This stone not only attracts iron rings, but also imparts to them a similar power of attracting other rings; and sometimes you may see a number of pieces of iron and rings suspended from one another so as to form quite a long chain: and all of them derive their power of suspension from the original stone. In like manner the Muse first of all inspires men herself; and from these inspired persons a chain of other persons is suspended, who take the inspiration."

As Socrates explains, the first link in the chain is the Muse, or the deity. The Muse inspires the poet, the next link, who then composes the poem. The next link after that is the rhapsode, who performs the poem. The audience is the final link in the chain; but, inasmuch as the emotions of people can affect those around them, the members of the audience may even continue to radiate the effects of the Muse through their emotional states.

Though we may question Socrates' understanding of magnetism as a power flowing forth from one source and "linking" various other objects, it is explanatory as to how he sees the power of creative inspiration. Divine madness takes hold of the artist; when the artist performs his art, it takes hold of the audience. The audience's emotional state is altered, and even after they have returned to their equilibrium, the emotional experience remains in their memory and can affect their behavior.

The mimetic view of the power of art is thus incredibly old, but it is not unique to antiquity. This view was also put forward by Leo Tolstoy, in his essay, "What is Art?". Tolstoy is most famous as a novelist, but his essay, "What is Art?" contains a modern version of the idea of art as a form of mimesis, that moves hearts and minds through the transmission of feelings. Interestingly, he and Socrates basically agree on the nature of art, but take completely opposite stances in regard to its value.

Tolstoy: "To evoke in oneself a feeling one has once experienced, and having invoked it in oneself, then, by means of movements, lines, colors, sounds or forms expressed in words, so to transmit that feeling that others may experience the same feeling – this is the activity of art. Art is a human activity, consisting in this, that one man consciously, by means of certain external signs, hands on to others the feelings he has lived through, and that other people are infected by these feelings, and also experience them."

Tolstoy thus also employs the language of art as infectious. But while Socrates would have seen art running out of control as similar to an infectious disease, Tolstoy did not intend the same negative connotations. For Tolstoy, art's infectiousness carries a sense of joy and communion. From the way that Socrates speaks of the poets, it is obvious that he did not see this value in artistic expression.

Socrates' argument applies not merely to poetry, but to artistic expression in general. Socrates explains in an addendum to *The Republic*, "We can take the poet, and set him beside the painter. He resembles him both because his works have a low degree of truth and also because he deals with a low element in the mind."

The low element that exists in both painting and poetry is later described as the power to corrupt even the best of characters. Art can do this because it gratifies and indulges our basest emotions and instincts. In the normal course of life, we keep ourselves from expressing uninhibited indulgence in grief, or excessive sentimentality or voluptuousness. Think of how reluctant most people would be to openly weep at their workplace. Socrates thinks that our sense of shame in such emotional expressions is a good thing; we conceal our grief on behalf of our better nature, as Socrates would have it. Art gives a voice to these emotive expressions that we forcibly restrain.

As for why we forcibly restrain these feelings, it is because they render us unreasonable. Through the emotional resonance of these feelings when amplified through art, we risk annihilating the boundaries between self and other, which are key to Socratic self-reflection. Tolstoy agrees with this assessment, but views this mimesis in a positive light. The communion found in mimetic emotion is valuable for Tolstoy precisely because of the loss of self-conscious composure, which is necessary to break the barriers between souls.

Tolstoy: "A real work of art destroys, in the consciousness of the receiver, the separation between himself and the artist – not that alone, but also between himself and all whose minds receive this work of art. In this freeing of our personality from its separation and isolation, in this uniting of it with others, lies the chief characteristic and the great attractive force of art feelings) of joy and of spiritual union with another (the author) and with others (those who are also infected by it)."

What Socrates identifies as the Muses are, in truth, the creative expression of one's passions. In modern terms, the Muses are our unconscious drives, as experienced in the emotions, our states of mind, the deepest yearnings of our hearts. We can remove the supernatural element, and recognize that the madness stoked by the numerous links in the magnetic chain is *the madness of emotion*. To the extent that emotionality is opposed to logic and self-awareness, the Socratics are opposed to the emotions. Socrates sees art in intractable opposition to reason. Schopenhauer, too, who was heavily influenced by Socrates' student Plato, regarded the passions as united only by the common trait that they are all irrational. Emotion has long been defined by its antithesis to reason.

The Stoics, such as Epictetus, would go on to propound a view of virtue that consisted of self-mastery over one's emotional states. The association with the emotions as with our baser nature would endure in this philosophy of Stoicism which persists even to this day. To Epictetus, the passions are things to be mastered by the rational mind, lest the passions rebel and take hold. He repeatedly warns us to distrust the passions, writing: "It is this that introduces disturbances, tumults, misfortunes, and calamities; and causes sorrow, lamentation and envy; and renders us envious and jealous, and thus incapable of listening to reason."

Early Christians, such as St. Paul, would further moralize this conflict between reason and the passions, and correlate the rational mind with the immortal soul, and the passions with the sinful flesh. Everything bodily, earthly and instinctual came to be denigrated over the course of western civilization's development. Paul writes, in Romans, "For I know that nothing good dwells in me, that is, in my flesh. For I have the desire to do what is right, but not the ability to carry it out." For Paul, the true self is the immortal soul. The soul is correlated with the conscious mind, the locus of self-awareness. The body, the emotions, the animal urges: all of these are redefined as foreign and harmful, and the ego-consciousness as synonymous with the true self.

With these considerations in mind, it is no mystery why Socrates is in favor of censoring or restricting artistic expression: *he thinks that art has real power*. Specifically, it is the power to reshape the emotions of others. This is a contradiction that runs through modern liberal thought in regards to art. We will wax poetic about art's power, but if we were to take this thought seriously, there is a good argument for the position of Socrates – for what is powerful must also be regarded as dangerous. But the idea that art should be censored is anathema to our modern values. How could this be?

If we believe in both Socrates' claim that art is a dangerous force if left unchecked, and also observe the unchecked proliferation of art around us, we find a contradiction. Should we let art run amok? Or do we not truly believe in art's power, as we claim to?

The divine madness can spread mimetically through a society. Therefore, Socrates sees the poet not as an inconsequential wordsmith, but as a type of magician. The poet, the rhapsode, the painter, and the musician have the power to affect the emotional states of others. They can rouse people to an agitated frenzy, or calm them to sleep. They can drive them out of their minds with grief, or make them feel lusty and sensuous. The name for this phenomenon, that Socrates has identified, is something I shall call *emotional resonance*.

Socrates is, first and foremost, an optimist. He believes in the power of human knowledge and ingenuity to improve the human lot. To the extent that the artist learns techniques, advances his own knowledge of his discipline, and advances himself and his craft, Socrates can respect the artist. The extent to which the artist is a locus of emotional resonance is the extent to which such a person is a threat to logical thought. In the Socratic view, emotional resonance does nothing to advance the good of humanity, and may actually harm it. This is another similarity that Socrates sees between artistic types (such as poets) and religious types (such as the oracular priests). They are anti-logical, and therefore backward-facing, opposed to progress.

We in modern times tend to lump the intellectuals and the artists into the same category, whereas the religious type (who is usually conservative by nature) seems a natural enemy of the artist (who is often open-minded to a fault). But in ancient times, the artist and the priest were far from separate. Meanwhile, the philosophers of antiquity recognized that rather than an inherent kinship, there is a deep contradiction between the artistic project and the philosophical project. In some sense, the artist is the antithesis of everything Socrates stands for.

To some more than others, music stimulates the brain in a way that produces physical reactions: the tingling of frisson, a sense of expectation, even the watering of the eyes and other physical symptoms of excessive emotionality. For myself, music has always been a physical experience; I suspect I am among those more affected. But this reaction is by no means universal, and music holds more physical sway over some than others. This is one reason, in a long list of reasons, that there is no universal conception of beauty.

The philosopher within me does not understand the artist. The philosopher demands a definition. Logic is universal, and wants universalization. The arbitrariness of the creative inspiration is no satisfactory answer to the philosopher. Being arbitrary is irrational. We cannot leave the answer at divine madness; madness, after all, can still be explained, for madness has its reasons, even if those reasons are absurd. To say, "art is valuable for its own sake" no longer satisfies – for we have not said what sake that *is*, exactly. *What is it* that making music satisfies? *What is the artistic need?*

***

The Alps reminded me of the Colorado Rockies, where my father's side of the family lived, and where I'd spent much time in my youth. The peaks squeezed against the road on either side; aspens and pines swayed in the wind above us. I had to tilt my head in order to peer up to the very top from inside the vehicle. As we climbed higher and higher, pushing the engine, the silhouettes of these towering giants haloed by clouds rose up, behind each mountain, another after another.

There was a sixty-euro toll, required to pass through Le Tunnel and enter France. It was only day three, and our overall revenue had been lackluster up to that point. A sixty-euro toll on top of this was financially painful. So was the price of fuel on what was the longest drive thus far. But Davide had explained on the way there that there was no better way to enter France from this part of Italy than Le Tunnel. It would only cost more money in gas and a great deal more in time if we tried to avoid it.

Doc handed Davide the money for the toll. He and Steve briefly talked across the length of the van – Steve was sitting in back – about splitting up the respective costs. They'd worked out the details of this before the tour, but Doc was keeping a running tally of what we owed. Hell Obelisco had fronted a good deal of the travel costs already. The barrier was lifted, and the automated voice bid us farewell.

"Arrivederci," she said.

***

The streets in this part of Lyon were at even steeper inclines than in Genoa, not unlike some of the streets in San Francisco. The city felt quiet, which I learned was typical for such a medium-sized European city on a weeknight. We pulled up to the venue, Le Farmer. Davide dropped off Steve and Andrea and circled back around. After following a series of one-way streets that seemed to turn us further and further away from the bar, Davide finally navigated back to the destination. The staff stood out in front of the venue, and directed us to pull into a short alleyway, then directed us into a parking lot around back. It was private, surrounded on all sides by apartments; the bar itself was topped by an apartment, where the bands were hosted. There was graffiti all over the walls, and a smattering of litter on the asphalt. Ah, back in the city.

Our host in Bologna had warned us about the accommodations at Le Farmer, and told us that they were no good. In truth, it was a fine little apartment above the bar. Adequate, but the room couldn't fit both bands. Hell Obelisco agreed to take the accommodation above the venue, whereas we would stay at an Airbnb in the home of one of the bar staff, someone who was out of town at the moment, or something like that. I wasn't sure I fully understood the situation, since it was relayed to me by Steve who was getting it translated from Doc. Whatever, we had accommodations for the night.

My neck and shoulder ached as we hauled gear out of the van again. Once again, just as we pulled up to the venue, I found myself fatigued, after a day of driving and not sleeping.

I fumbled a cardboard box marked, "blueberries". I couldn't catch it before it hit the concrete. It contained some of Doc's stuff. I apologized; he said it was fine, nothing was damaged. We moved the teddy bear Ryoko back up into the little loft above the back of the van where we stashed small items.

"Why is the bear called Ryoko?" I asked Davide.

"It was a gift from a girl. Her name was Ryoko."

We finished loading in. Everyone else went inside, but I stayed in the little parking lot, pacing on the concrete. I'd promised my wife that I would call her, and this was the first real chance I had for a phone call. I was seven hours ahead of Amberly. It would be late morning for her by now.

"How is the tour going?"

"So far? It's been a shitshow."

I told her of the impossibly long first day, how we'd stayed awake for so long. I told her about the van, how tight it was with nine people. She already knew that things weren't perfect. But it was hard to explain how painful the fatigue was.

"I've just been tired all the time," I finally said.

"Still dealing with jet lag?" she asked.

"I guess so. I can't sleep in the van. There's just a dull pain behind my eyes all the time."

"How's the other band?" she asked, changing the subject.

"I like them," I said, "We all like them, a lot. They speak good English, too. And our driver is really good. But sitting shoulder-to-shoulder like this... I don't know. Nine people in one van. I would have loved this back when I was nineteen or twenty. I'm getting too old for this shit."

"Didn't you know this is how it would be?"

"I did..." I admitted. "But... I hear we're going to tour with another band from the label... okay, good. We're going to share the costs of the van and the gas and the lodging, that all sounds reasonable. But I don't know... I guess I didn't really understand what I was getting into..."

"I'm sorry, babe," she sighed. It wasn't what she wanted to hear. You don't drop a grand on plane tickets and go on a tour of Europe only to complain about it.

"I don't think I can keep doing this. This was supposed to be a big breakthrough. Now it just feels like the same thing all over again. I should have known it was going to be like this. I just have that same feeling."

"Did you talk to your bandmates about this?."

"No point in arguing about it now. I'll just bring it up when we get back."

"If you're not going to bring it up until you get home, then do that. But don't perseverate on it while you're over there. Don't let anxiety ruin it."

"You're right."

"Focus on the moment. It's an adventure."

"Yeah. It's an adventure."

"Miss you."

"Miss you, too."

After the call, I didn't want to go inside the bar. I didn't want to socialize. Not with the staff, not with the Italians, and definitely not with my own bandmates. The air felt nice. But mostly the aloneness.

CHAPTER SIX - LYON

I decided to go on a walk. I left my phone to charge at the venue, behind the merch table. Wandering alone without a GPS was quite normal before the days of smartphones, but now that I'd always had one with me, it came with a sense of vulnerability. I remembered my trip, backpacking Europe. I hadn't had a smartphone then. I'd relied on paper maps, the kind the hostel provided at the front desk. Of course, I didn't have a map with me either. I tried to keep a mental note of where I was walking, and notice the landmarks.

The sidewalks wound down the slopes of the city, following the curvature of the hillsides. I passed through a park, which was almost entirely on an incline. I followed the sidewalk as far as it went, then trotted down the concrete stairs. I eventually reached the byzantine alleyways of the city blocks below. Businesses on the ground floor, apartments stacked on the floors above, streets paved with cobblestone, every building showing its age, all indicating that this was the old town. Patisseries, coffee houses. On one of the walls was graffiti reading, "I hate the invader" complete with a spray painted Space Invader next to it.

Eventually, I found the Saône. The river was girdled by bridges that rose high above it. I did not cross, but walked alongside it. I shivered as the breeze kicked up, and studied the rippling flow of the river, while trying to grab hold of my thoughts and feelings. When you're tired all the time, you feel like you're in an altered state of consciousness, and even ordering my thoughts had seemed impossible in the previous days. The sense of frustration brought up memories – past frustrations on past tours. It was strange to have that feeling in this regal European city.

I couldn't help but think of three years before, when I'd almost quit the band. Back then, I took six months off from going on tour, and told bandmates that I had to sort some things out. I'd started having worsening anxiety while on tour, and it was causing an obsessive-compulsive habit from my childhood to flare up again in adulthood – trichotillomania, the urge to pull out one's hair. My lower back was fucked, my neck was fucked, but worst of all, my ears were fucked. Tinnitus, a terrible affliction for one's mental health. It eventually subsided after a couple years, but back then, it would get incredibly loud at times. All of it together was enough to make me question everything about the worthwhileness of the musician's life.

My bandmates were relatively understanding, and thankfully didn't find someone to replace me, but toured as a three-piece. While I didn't know at the time whether I would return, in the long-run it ended up being only a short absence from the group.

Now, as I'd already begun to wonder if this tour would turn out to be a disappointment, I tried to recall why it was that I ultimately decided to rejoin the band. I'd spent months at home, while my bandmates were touring the West Coast. I remembered feeling just as miserable and anxious at home as I felt on the road. I remembered feeling as though my identity was compromised, and I was no longer the artist I once was. I became convinced that no decision I made would bring me contentment. I was bound always to struggle against my own happiness: to yearn for the safety of home while on the road, and yearn for the magic of touring while at home. I remembered wanting it all back, and missing the experience dearly.

I supposed that all of those reasons explained why I went back to it. But I wondered if I'd made a mistake. The same sentence kept echoing in my mind. *What the hell am I doing here?*

I decided to make my way back to Le Farmer. I traveled a few blocks from the river and promptly got lost. I wandered from one alleyway to the next, trying to just keep moving in the general direction of the venue, and trying stoically not to panic. I finally found my way up the exhausting avenues, and thankfully recognized the city park from before. When I reached the top, I was breathing rapidly, the cold air burning in my throat. I'd walked a bit too quickly. I was out of shape. I passed a butcher shop with a neon outline of a cow in the window and some beautiful, very red cuts with little to no marbling, the kind of thing which made me question my lukewarm commitment to vegetarianism. The sun was starting to set, and by the time I'd spotted the venue, my brow was dripping beads of sweat chilled by the night air.

Inside the bar, they'd laid out a cold pasta salad for us, with bowtie noodles, tuna, boiled eggs, celery, and onion. There were baguette slices, and a brie. I tried a bit of the pasta but didn't care for it. I mostly just ate bread and brie. We briefly talked with the local band, but their English was somewhat limited. I wasn't in the mood to have to expend effort just to have a conversation. They seemed like perfectly nice people. I mostly kept to myself, enjoyed the complimentary beer then got ready for soundcheck.

It is fairly uncommon in the States for a small club to have the headlining band load their gear on stage and soundcheck before any of the other bands start, but most clubs in Europe operated this way. Usually, each band does a line check before they play, and that's it. It's only in the medium-sized venues and bigger where they have the headliners come in to check sound before the club even opens its doors.

The soundguy started to piss me off with repeated requests to turn our volume down. We were already playing through half stacks, with no distortion pedals. We were relying on the on-amp gain and volume to create the tone. There was only so much we could turn down before our sound would be lost. The language barrier made this difficult to communicate. The soundguy seemed to have a fuse as short as he was. We reached a compromise eventually, and found a volume amenable to us both. Later, one of the Italians mentioned that the soundguy's girlfriend had just broken up with him that week. Probably why he was in such a sour mood.

I went out front and bummed a smoke from Alex. I tried to make conversation, but my Italian was basically non-existent, as was his English. I thanked him for the cigarette – he understood that. We both exchanged glances and nodded.

A couple walked up. There was a familiar logo on his hoodie, and on her shirt. Finally, it registered: that was a Greenbeard shirt, and a Destroyer of Light hoodie. Greenbeard was another band from Texas; Jeff, our former bassist, now played with them. I didn't recognize the couple; I had to stop them and ask. They instantly recognized me.

"We've seen you play before, man," the man said. Judging by his accent, he was a local.

"Where?"

"The Lost Well."

"What?" I asked, excited. "When?"

"We used to go there, back when we lived in Austin," the lady explained.

"You lived in Austin? What brought you there?" I asked.

"Work," the man said. "A tech company there. We just happened to catch you one night. A year or so ago, we moved back home. When we saw you were coming through here, I knew we had to come."

"That's incredible! I have to get a picture of ya'll."

"Of course!"

I suddenly felt my spirits lifted. Here, on another continent, were a couple sporting the merch of two Austin bands. It was incredible, the bonds one formed without even really knowing about them.

The first band was somewhere between country, psychobilly, and stoner metal. The singer's ragged, deep and throaty vocals clawing their way up above the downhome, Kentucky-fried-pickin' and bluesy chord progressions. They all wore denim overalls and trucker hats. They played on homemade instruments. Some were hand-carved, some had only two or three strings, one such 'guitar' was capped with what looked to be a coffee tin. They ended with a breakneck cover of Ace of Spades by Motorhead, which got a huge response from the small but engaged audience. Amplified and hitting as hard as anyone, they would have fit right in at a bar in Louisiana, or our home state of Texas more so than France. But then again, I'm not very much familiar with rural France; maybe the French have their own kind of hillbilly. They were right at home at a place called Le Farmer, at least.

As the venue started to fill up, the soundguy's girlfriend unexpectedly showed up. Penny pointed her out to me. "That's his ex", he whispered. Honestly, we were a bit worried that this development was about to derail the whole show. The soundguy didn't seem to be in a good place, emotionally, and he looked like he was on the verge of just walking out of the venue in the middle of the gig. She tried to get his attention a couple times. She approached him in the crowd, intercepting him from walking behind the bar. He ignored her, and walked around. As he passed her by again, cables in his hands, she tugged at his sleeve. He grabbed his nose and squeezed it, as if she stank. It was amusing enough to make up for my impatience with him.

Hell Obelisco ratcheted up the volume, and brought their brand of sludgy aggression, followed by our pounding, doomy tones. Each set went a few ticks up on the volume knob. The soundguy told me to turn down after the first song, I pantomimed my compliance, and resolved to turn up after the next number. He'd warned us we would scare away the audience, but this crowd was here for doom. They loved every second of it. The crowd was still only a few dozen people – it was a Sunday, after all – and everyone who was there was there to party.

Why do we like loud volumes? What is the appeal, exactly? There's been a bit of research on the topic. Our brain tends to designate songs that are louder as better. There are a few potential reasons why. The brain can hear more details at a louder volume. At the highest volumes, the sonic experience becomes tactile as well as auditory. And there is of course the novelty of the experience.

For myself, it is not enough for a band to be loud. I like the specific kind of loudness found in doom metal, and other slow or downtuned genres of metal. The tones are low, warm, fuzzy, vibrating. At high volumes, these tones radiate and rumble across the room. You can get way over the acceptable threshold of loudness relative to someone playing with a high-pitched, or trebly guitar tone. It is an enjoyable physical experience; the sound seems to wash over you. The most important aspect of loudness to Destroyer of Light is in the creation of our guitar tone. Without a distortion pedal, I rely solely on the on-amp distortion, created by the gain channel.

The first amp I ever played at a show was a Vox with a power switch, some tone knobs, and a volume knob. If you wanted tone out of it, you had to turn the volume all the way up.

This is why we perform on speaker cabinets without casters. Wheels may make for an easy load in, but they separate the speaker cabinet from the stage. When a stack of nice, powerful speaker cabinets is resonating with a big, wooden stage, the sound is more massive and rich than any PA boost could give you. This is another reason why underground touring is so challenging. The quality of the stage changes every night. The acoustics of the room can be wildly different every night. Every show, you must get the lay of the sonic territory.

After the set, I bummed a cigarette from one of the locals and ducked out to the back parking lot to smoke it by myself. I'm usually spent after a performance, and have no desire to talk to anyone in the first fifteen minutes or so after the show. On my way back into the venue, I ran into Penny. In the darkness of the hallway leading from the parking lot into the bar, he pointed out the back of the door. It was painted up with the image of the Man from Another Place, dancing in the Red Room. It was a famous image from *Twin Peaks*, David Lynch's mystery series from 1990. The Man From Another Place is a mysterious dwarf, a spirit from a mirror dimension who offers clues and hints to Detective Cooper as he tries to solve Laura Palmer's murder. He is also confoundingly odd. He says things which are dream-like and make no sense; he speaks in an odd cadence created by recording his lines in reverse, then reversing them to create forward speech. The little man had been dancing to our show all night, just on the other side of the door.

We left Hell Obelisco behind, as they'd be staying in the accommodation above Le Farmer for the night. Davide would drop us off at the Airbnb, then return to the secure parking lot at the venue, park the van and take a cab back to the apartment. Davide parked the van around the corner from our destination. The apartment that had been offered was in downtown Lyon, only ten minutes from the venue. After all the travel time, the plan would give him just ten minutes of leeway to get back before they locked the gate at midnight.

We grabbed everything important – luggage and day-bags, mainly – and followed Davide down the block. The nights were getting increasingly colder – much colder than it ever got this time of year in Texas. Finally, we came to the address, and stepped into the nook serving as an antechamber for the apartment stairwell.

Davide was the first to step inside. His glance darted immediately to his left, recoiling slightly in surprise. I couldn't see what it was that he saw until I got closer. As we all began crowding in, we were polite, and tried not to gawk at the bum as he slowly got up from sleeping on the stoop. He rubbed his eyes, groggy, and sauntered off into the darkness.

Davide punched in the code the bar staff gave us. The door didn't open. He tried it again. Still nothing. We stood there. Davide dialed the bartender's number, only to get the voicemail yet again. He hadn't answered the text messages either. We each took our turns trying the door, and all failed.

Our ten minutes were almost up. It was getting closer and closer to midnight. It was starting to look like Davide would be locked out of the parking lot. For the most part, all we could do was stand there while he tried to figure the damned contraption out. It's just fine to be placed entirely in the hands of others when everything goes swimmingly. But there is a real sense of helplessness when things go wrong. He was visibly frustrated as the keypad rejected him for the dozenth time.

Finally, the bartender called back. The bar napkin with his instructions hadn't said anything about hitting the pound key before punching in the number, but apparently that was our problem. Davide entered the code and the lock clicked open. We all breathed a collective sigh of relief. We made our way inside. I let my luggage drop to the floor. Davide dropped his things and hurried back down the stairs to make it back to the venue in time.

Penny rifled through the guy's cabinet and started eating his chips.

"You can't just eat his food," I said.

"He said make ourselves at home, didn't he?"

"That doesn't mean you can eat his food."

"It's just a fucking bag of chips."

"What are the rules? Can you just eat any food you find at an Airbnb?"

"Of course you fucking can. I'm hungry, goddamnit."

"I'm too tired to argue about this shit."

I plugged into the charger, chose a bed, and crashed down onto it. For once, I wasn't wide awake when I hit the mattress. I was actually tired when I was supposed to be tired. I was asleep before I knew it.

***

The next morning, I woke up fairly early, and had time for another walk before the day's drive. I found my way back to the Saône. I stood on the bridge above the river and watched it rushing beneath me, and greedily gulped up the morning air.

It never felt like the right time to have an important conversation with Steve or Penny. Sure, we had hours together every day in the van. But any conversation about an important topic feels potentially dangerous, because talking about anything important always comes with the possibility of an argument. The potential of conflict is what keeps introverts and other socially awkward types from broaching difficult subjects. It's incredible to think how scary talking can be, given that it poses no physical danger.

But conflict is required. For any social group to flourish, difficult topics have to be discussed. Communication is the foundation of the social life. It's the nervous system of any group of humans. On our own, our brains are fallible, limited, self-motivated. In groups, we're still subject to these limitations – but the more human brains that interface, the more chances you have of overcoming them. When a group of humans all direct their focus to a shared goal, we become greater than the sum of our parts. The capacity for communication is the main limiter that we find on collective human potential. The problem of how to communicate effectively is therefore the chief existential question for any group. It was only natural that our main challenge would also be communication.

III. Art is Communication

In our inquiry so far, we have reached three important conclusions. First, art is irrational. Second, that artistic expression is a state in which one is seized by the creative power of an emotion as by an external force. Third, that art is a means of transmitting these emotional states.

The artistic drive originates in states of ritual madness, in which this transmission of emotion occurs. The *sina qua non* of art is this quality of emotional resonance. The question that arises next is the most religious of questions: *for what?* Why should these emotional states seize us, and compel us to creative expression? And why should we find it valuable?

Although I went on to read a great many more philosophers than Socrates over the years, I cannot say that any of them gave a description of art that explained more than the Socratic assertion that it was essentially just spirit possession. Even though this explanation must be translated into a modern psychological understanding to have any value – and was meant as an attack by the man who uttered it – I was forced to concede this point to The Gadfly. We may accept this view without necessarily sharing Socrates' negative assessment of art's value, and without accepting the Socratic prescriptions for censorship – as does Tolstoy. Art as spirit possession translates, in modern terms, to the notion that *art is emotion transformed into the mimetic.*

If we strip away the technical details of any given art, as none of them can inform us as to the character of art itself, and consider art with this understanding – that it is a means of transferring emotion – then a compelling conclusion about art's value emerges into the foreground. *Art is a form of communication.* When we make art, or enjoy art – we are communicating. This is what unites the Rembrandt painting and the Cannibal Corpse performance. In addition to language, and the other ways in which it is possible for humans to communicate, we also communicate through art.

Any evidence for such a description of art would require an understanding of the emergence of communication in the human species. Usually, those interested in the emergence of communication among human beings have turned to language as the obvious subject of study. The philosophers of language propelled the school of analytic philosophy into fame and broke open a whole new era of philosophical inquiry. We have since come to a new understanding of how language shapes our attitudes, our ethics, and our very thought patterns.

Suppose, however, that artistic expression is a parallel form of communication, which developed alongside language. These two forms of communication have become interwoven over the ages – since language is contained in art, or even comprises the whole of certain forms of art, as is the case in poetry, literary fiction, or screenwriting. The spoken, sung and written word fills our artistic representations and activities. And yet, the domains of art and language are clearly distinguishable. Straightforward linguistic communication is not classified as art in the common usage of the term. Furthermore, there are forms of art that don't use words, or even recognizable imagery or symbols: we might consider abstract painting, and instrumental music.

The difficulty in arguing that what we mean by the term "art" indicates something necessarily communicative is that this understanding of art is not itself part of the common use of the term. Suffice to say, we do not universally speak of art as a form of communication in the same way that we understand language as a form of communication. This is because the most popular artforms also serve as forms of popular entertainment, or as hobbies, and we are not usually inclined to think of these things too deeply. And then there are of course the artists we've already spoken of, who claim to do art for themselves alone, and to care nothing for its reception among others. This is not to say that there is nothing in the common understanding of art that captures what I consider to be its core aspect. "Self-expression" is the nearest phrase in the popular consciousness that approximates an understanding of art as communicative.

As such, we must abandon our easy assumptions and instead look to the evidence in anthropology. There was a time, long ago, when art was the primary form of communication. We will have to depart from the ten thousand years of human civilization with which we're more or less familiar. We must go back – long before Socrates – into man's prehistory. To the extent that we know anything about their means of communication, human societies during the period of mankind's prehistory primarily expressed themselves through myth and ritual.

Religious expression predominates all of the earliest forms of human expression. The earliest stories we have are mythological in nature. Prior to any oral traditions of storytelling, the first means of conveying mythological narratives was to dramatize them by means of ritual. Mankind has engaged in ritual since time immemorial. In considering both language and art as parallel forms of communication, my hypothesis is that art and language emerged from the same source. That source could be called religion, but this refers to something more primal, more fundamental, than the religions of today: the *religious experience*, rather than religion itself (the modern use of the word has many unwanted connotations). This is what I will generally refer to as myth or the mythological experience.

There has always been an element of art in the expression of religion: whether in the rendering of idols, the painting of frescoes, the aesthetics of the religious garb and ritual trappings, or the art of storytelling. The only difference between the irrational, frivolous, weird, wonderful absurdity of artistic expression and the same qualities that we find in religious expression are that the latter has attributed to it all sorts of metaphysical significance. The supernatural claims that accompany religious visions are what the scientific mindset finds contentious. If we set the metaphysical claims aside, as they are not important for our purposes here, and regard religious expression as simply a production of the human mind, which reflects only its inner contents, religious expression and artistic expression are almost indistinguishable. Or, if we assume as a matter of course, as the ancients did, that in any artistic expression there is a Muse speaking through the artist, then we find art and religion to reflect exactly the same inner state: divine possession.

My first inkling of this common origin for art and religion arose when I encountered a clear-cut, real-world example of language and ritual drama emerging from the same source. This particular bit of research is what I consider to be the most unusual etymological finding ever encountered.

Frits Staal was a professor of philosophy and Asian studies who specialized in Vedic hymns. Staal investigated a particular set of Vedic hymns sung by an obscure, rural people in India. He was particularly interested in the Agnicayana Ritual. Taking place over the course of twelve days, this ritual involved the creation of an altar and a wooden bird. At the end of the twelve days, the bird was placed on the altar and both were ritually burned. In these rituals, each action has a tone to accompany it: the physical motions and actions of the priests and practitioners are tied, in effect, to the vocalizations. It is a harmony, or synchrony, between the auditory and the physical.

While some of these hymns were already written down, linguists found that many of them were largely unintelligible. Staal set out to decipher them, knowing that their syntax patterns did not match any known language. He began with the hymn known as the *Jaiminiya Gramegayagana*, one of those which had never been translated. Working on a hunch, he eventually compared the syntactical structure to local birdsong. Two local birds – Blyth's reed warbler, and the common whitethroat – were found to be the source of the structure. The hymns were an imitation of the birds' calls.

This type of imitation has been discovered in more recent examples of art. Igor Stravinsky, for instance, while living in northwestern Ukraine, seems to have imitated in his syncopation and timing the calls of the European pied flycatcher, according to some who have analyzed his compositions from that time period.

The absurdity of it! The reason the birds would develop the impulse to sing in the first place had to do with procreation. The birds sing to attract one another – to attract a potential mate. But the song also attracted Stravinsky.

Staal's conclusion was that animals and humans have the same "deep generative grammar." In other words, animals such as birds possess the same mental hardware for developing linguistic communication as *homo sapiens*. While none of the other species can match the linguistic complexity of humans, the grammatical foundations are the same. It is the randomness of genetic mutation and geographic selection pressures that has led to the development of all the linguistic variety we see today.

Human language as a whole developed independently of birdsong, of course. Stravinsky obviously could speak Russian before he produced any compositions imitating the birds. And yet, the Vedic priests who chanted the hymns of the Agnicayana were speaking some of the oldest words ever memorized and passed down by humanity. Passed down through oral tradition, these verses were originally just meaningless sounds – and how could they be otherwise, being derived from birdsong? Whether these songs have meaning to the birds or not, the human priests listening to the birdsong could not know of it.

This was exactly what fascinated me. The words in these chants came ready-made from the birds, with their own tones, and syllables – and if we believe Staal, grammar. But before the symbolic meaning of language was incorporated into human utterances, the raw sound was all there was. These dumb utterances must have preceded the meaning assigned to them. The meaning was only infused into the sounds later, through the power of ritual symbolism.

This would imply that the melody, the rhythm, the tempo, the syncopation, the harmony: all of these aspects that comprise what we now call "music" had a power all their own. There was a beauty, or an attraction, that was independent of the intelligible meaning: the meaning in rational and thus linguistic terms, which was nonexistent in this case. The Vedic priests, or whoever their predecessors may have been, found the birdsong beautiful enough to imitate: it emotionally resonated with them.

Suppose that the imitation of animal sounds predated linguistic communication of any type at all? The first birds who sang could not have any knowledge or understanding of what they were doing. They were not consciously attempting to attract a mate. The mates came nonetheless, impressed with the songs; certain birdsongs gained utility and were passed along. Certain relationships between the tones became recognized as beautiful – and thus as more advantageous. Like all things in evolution, the impulse emerges as an end unto itself. The question is whether it can endure. The only thing that can determine its survival is whether there is advantage given by following the impulse.

Suppose, then, that emotional resonance preceded language itself. What does this mean, in light of the conclusion that art contains the power of emotional resonance? This is not a chicken or the egg question – there is a clear predecessor. Humans had to make sounds before sounds could be assigned a symbolic meaning. *The arbitrary selection of tones and syllables came before linguistic meaning* – what are the implications of this idea?

If these tonal utterances were utterly stupid when they first emerged, the question arises as to why it would be the case that we found these utterances compelling. The first time a human being intoned a series of notes with his mouth, creating a rhythm and a melody, why would the other humans join him in this practice? Why would they not find his vocalizations repulsive, and cast him out? Instead, these random mouth noises became songs, and rituals, and finally... language itself stumbled out of the drunken haze of infancy and man first started to *communicate*.

Suppose we trace back further than this. What predated even hymns, songs, or imitations of the animal world? What is the most natural thing in the world for a baby to do, the moment it is born? It cries. It screams. Even as an adult, in moments of intense pain, we cry out. This reaction is physical. You stub your toe, you cry out. It is also psychological. You lose a loved one, you sob and ruminate. It is an irrational impulse that seizes us: to let out a scream, or a cry.

We make a stupid vocalization – I call it stupid not to be insulting, but because a cry is not imbued with intellectual or linguistic meaning. *But it is not emotionally meaningless.* The cry of a baby is meaningful to the baby's mother. It may be the most meaningful thing to her. The cries of babes are meaningful to most people, in fact. A cry carries an emotional meaning alone. It is the arbitrary, auditory expression of an emotional state, and this state resonates with other human beings and impels them to a similar state of distress. The inevitable conclusion is clear. The cry of pain might be the most fundamental form of artistic expression. The original form. The first form of communication between human beings.

This is because a cry of pain is an *involuntary* expression. There is a pre-rational human urge to express our pain to the world. Originally this was very much a physiological pain, and a physiological impulse to expression. The emotions, more than being "just" or "mere" feelings, would seem to be the first motivator we ever possessed to use auditory means of communication. Staal's work suggested to me that the auditory world, prior to the existence of a written or perhaps even spoken language, is emotionally rich nonetheless.

Perhaps it is utterances like the cry of pain that served as part of the crudest pallet of primordial expression. The other shades and hues might include howls of aggression, moans of pleasure, or that most human of all vocalizations: laughter. This pre-linguistic auditory state is probably impossible for us to imagine, but it seems to me a necessary stage in human development. These vocalizations would provide the raw material for the construction of languages.

Rational-cognitive communication, which we achieve through language, would therefore be built upon the foundations of *irrational-emotional communication*, achieved through vocalization. Just as our capacity for higher reasoning did not evolve to replace our lizard brain, but was simply layered on top of it, our linguistic communication did not replace our ability to communicate emotion, via tones, facial expressions, body language. Our linguistic faculties constructed a logical, symbolic structure on top of this fundamental system.

The philosopher Marshall McLuhan, in his anthropological study of the earliest human communities, came to fascinating conclusions. In McLuhan's view, the purely auditory world of pre-literate man was "implicit, simultaneous and discontinuous, and also far richer than those of literate man."

McLuhan writes: "The man of the tribal world led a complex, kaleidoscopic life precisely because the ear, unlike the eye, cannot be focused and is synaesthetic rather than analytical and linear. Speech is an utterance, or more precisely, an outering, of all our senses at once; the auditory field is simultaneous, the visual successive."

When McLuhan describes the life of pre-literate mankind, his description fits perfectly with the notion of the solely auditory mode of communication as more artistic. McLuhan attributes magical thinking and religiosity to the pre-literate way of life; with all we have considered so far, this should be unsurprising.

"By their dependence on the spoken word for information," McLuhan continues, "people were drawn together into a tribal mesh; and since the spoken word is more emotionally laden than the written – conveying by intonation such rich emotions as anger, joy, sorrow, fear– tribal man was more spontaneous and passionately volatile. Audile-tactile tribal man partook of the collective unconscious, lived in a magical integral world patterned by myth and ritual, its values divine and unchallenged, whereas literate or visual man creates an environment that is strongly fragmented, individualistic, explicit, logical, specialized and detached."

Thus, a major inflection point, in McLuhan's view, between tribal and societal man, is the advent of written language. With information encoded into successive, visual symbols, linguistic communication became possible. This type of communication is no longer merely the subjective experience, but also a record. Figures and scenes could become immortalized.

But the written word cannot convey emotion in the same way. The accounts of facts can be imprinted onto a written record, but the emotional resonance of those facts is not quite as obvious, nor as powerful. Emotional resonance is obviously still possible to convey in writing, and the old age of poetry proves that this was the case in antiquity. But within the medium of writing, a deadening of the emotional communication occurs, and a purely linguistic conveyance of meaning becomes possible. Because of the separation brought about by language – the information separated from the experience – the rich emotionality of human communication is diminished. With the discovery of the written word, the divergence of linguistic communication from artistic communication becomes possible. Both forms of communication, linguistic and artistic, emerge from the mythic experience, and dwell together within a purely "audile-tactile" world in which ritual and the spoken word convey meaning. The linguistic and artistic split as soon as mankind begins to write.

***

We loaded up and left. Davide navigated through downtown. We passed a luxury hotel in the town square on our way out of the heart of Lyon. Stately trees were planted in neat rows on either side of the sidewalks running alongside the river. Lots of people with scarves and cigarettes.

We started talking politics. I was far more interested in politics in those days, and it was primary season for the Democrats. American politics had begun to seem more and more unhinged, and it sparked off a conversation about politics in Italy. Eventually, we somehow got onto stories about military service. Most of the Italians had served a short stint in the Italian military. Andrea recounted his first day on base.

"I told them I was a musician," Andrea said, "so they assigned me to be a cook. Another guy says, 'Hey, I'm a mechanic'. They tell him now he is in the marching band."

After fighting through the Monday morning traffic we got out onto the highway, and stopped briefly at a gas station, what looked to be a French equivalent of an Autogrill. They had coffee, sandwiches, and baked goods. It was two euro for an espresso, instead of one euro, which is the customary price in Italy, and the Italians muttered about how this was thievery and that the coffee was terrible. Frankly, I couldn't tell the difference.

We drove on. I couldn't sleep. I looked out the window. Hills, sloping along gentle contours, dotted with little copses of trees and spilling out into plots of farmland and grazing cattle. We passed the occasional factory or a stripmall, but mostly it was just rolling nature. I imagined as I looked out over the countryside that we were passing through past ages of history. How much of my perspective was my Americanism, and the inherent romanticism for the fabled "old countries"? No, it doesn't matter. One has to be a little childish to make general observations at all. A sense of naïve enchantment is necessary to truly lose yourself in an adventure, as my wife's advice had compelled me to do. Maybe it was just the jet lag, but I felt periodically as though I were on the edge of dreaming and waking. The road noise was deafeningly loud, and there were hours more of it to come.

CHAPTER SEVEN - TOULOUSE

About five hours into the drive, we stopped. Only four more to go. We pulled into a little travel plaza just off the road, no particular town in sight. It was busy that afternoon. Families on road trips, whole busses full of people disembarked in the parking lot.

"We are stopping for ten minutes only," Davide announced.

There were several fast-food restaurants, even a buffet, but none of it seemed worth the price at that moment. I grabbed a bag of paprika chips and water. I stepped outside and took a seat on the edge of a waist-high stone wall that ringed the garden outside. It was a pleasant, violent breeze, pulling the trees into waves that hissed and exhaled, their leaves shimmering uncontrollably. Nick soon joined me there and we took to people-watching.

There was a middle-aged couple pushing an elderly woman in a wheelchair, equipped with an oxygen tank and mask that was wheeled off with her. Between the man's pointer and middle finger was a cigarette, its ashen tip impossibly long and still hanging on, trailing tufts of smoke. We both couldn't help but laugh at the darkly ironic image.

"It seems like a lot more people smoke in this country." I said.

"You think so?" Nick replied.

"Just based on how many smokers I've seen."

"That's what I'd thought too," Nick said. "There's a podcast I listen to, for non-French speakers to learn the language. They talk about current events and articles. An episode the other day, the host mentioned the view that Americans have that French people smoke more. But statistically, Americans smoke more cigarettes per capita. They were discussing why it was that people view the French that way... they seemed to think it was just a stereotype."

"I've seen a lot of French people smoking," I said. "Way more than in America."

"Yeah?"

I realized I was being a contrarian.

"Yeah. But who knows."

Nick shrugged. "Who knows."

We were quiet for a while. I glanced back at our group, and watched from afar as Steve and Penny laughed and joked with the Italians, walking in a herd from the front doors of the travel shop. As it had been ten minutes, I assumed we were about to depart, but they stopped and lingered for a while longer.

IV. Communication is Metaphor

These two primary forms of human communication – logical (linguistic, philosophical, technical) and emotional (artistic, religious) – are related, and share a common origin. They developed alongside one another, in interdependence upon one another. This common origin is the use of metaphor. Metaphor is the link between language and art, and their common ancestor of myth. *Metaphor sits at the foundation of all human attempts at communication.*

These forms of communication diverged only after mankind was able to distinguish rational-discursive information from emotional resonance. The rational-discursive world evolved from the foundations of the emotionally-resonant world, but by the time of Socrates the artist and the philosopher had become two very different types of people. To understand why the artist and the philosopher parted ways, it is necessary that we first understand this common origin of both emotive and rational-discursive communication: metaphor.

To clarify the term metaphor: I mean to indicate the process by which one invests a representation with a symbolic meaning. It is in the process of metaphorical thinking that we find the origin of emotionally-resonant artistic communication, and only later, as a further development, rational-discursive thinking. The earliest form of metaphorical thinking in human civilization appears in the form of myth. The inception of myth, in practical terms, indicates what it means to begin to think metaphorically. Why would human beings ever develop the ability to think metaphorically? What were the environmental conditions that would necessitate such a way of thinking?

These questions motivated the research of Hermann Usener. Usener was a German scholar of comparative religion and philology. His method was based on examining the ethnographic data and philological research. He taught a number of students who went on to become influential in the fields of philology, philosophy and the study of the classics – including a young Friedrich Nietzsche. Notably, he criticized Nietzsche for the unscholarly quality of *The Birth of Tragedy*, as the work contained no citations or footnotes and was written in an effusive, poetic style. He was by no means alone in this, as Usener's opinion was shared by most of the other philologists.

For Usener, the prerequisite for human beings to be able to think metaphorically is the ability to reason from the specific case to the general rule, and in turn from the general to the specific. This involves perceiving some quality in something that is shared by other things of the same type. The value of metaphor is therefore the ability for *abstraction*: to 'abstract' a property from a given object, and recognize this property as common to several objects.

To make this idea clearer, we might consider the example of a poet, writing about human mortality. Perhaps the poet compares people to leaves on a branch in autumn, dangling by their stems, waiting to fall at any moment or be carried away by the wind. In this case, the poet has identified that the leaves in autumn and human beings both share a quality: what we might call fragility, or impermanence. The poet identifies that the human being *shares* this quality in common with the leaf, and, upon recognizing this shared aspect, we gain the ability to speak in abstract, general terms. This ability, to reason from the specific cases to a general idea – in this case, a *quality*, a description or definition that is applicable to multiple phenomena – is key to metaphorical thinking. However, the phenomenon of metaphorical thinking puzzled Usener, as he studied the origins of human language.

Usener: "The chasm between specific perception and general concepts is far greater than our academic notions, and a language which does our thinking for us, lead us to suppose. It is so great that I cannot imagine how it could have been bridged... It is language that causes the multitude of causal, individual expressions to yield up *one* which extends its denotation over more and more special cases, until it comes to denote them all, and assumes the power of expressing a class concept."

Through Usener's work in comparative religion, however, he eventually came to an understanding of the origins of metaphorical thinking. This origin was in mythmaking, which is perhaps an unexpected place to look from the perspective of the modern mind. Usener's research indicated that language – the foundation for all of our intellectual knowledge – did not arise separately from our irrational, religious impulses. Rather, the two are uncomfortably intertwined. Usener charted the social evolution of mythmaking, which explains how metaphorical thinking could have gradually arisen as our mythological ideas developed.

Usener designates the first and oldest gods that human beings ever worshiped as *momentary gods*. The examples Usener gives are water found by a thirsty person, a termite mound that hides and saves someone, or any novel experience that inspires a man with sudden terror or wonderment. These extreme experiences are focused into an image or icon associated with the event and transformed directly into gods. These very examples of momentary gods come from the Eve tribe, and their concept of the *Tro*, a nature spirit that can manifest in water, in a tree, or in anything in nature.

Jakob Spieth, an anthropologist who studied the Eve tribe, wrote, "To the mind of the Eve, the moment in which an object or any striking attributes of it enter into any noticeable relation, pleasant or unpleasant, with the life and spirit of man, that moment a *Tro* is born in his consciousness."

Usener saw this most basic mythological impulse to momentary worship as enduring in Europe as late as the time of Hellenic Greece. For the Greek, any state of mind or lofty sentiment which dominates the sole focus of the individual was deified. The examples given in the case of Greek deities are Reason, Wealth, Chance, Climax, Wine, Feasting, etc. "In absolute immediacy," Usener writes, "the individual phenomenon is deified, without the intervention of even the most rudimentary class concept." The individual human being perceives something external, with power greater than himself, and calls it a god.

The next type of deity that a society comes to worship is the category designated as *functional gods*. This requires a further broadening of the idea and a further reification. The functional gods (or special gods) are a further step in the social development of mythmaking. These gods always appear in the anthropological record *after* the momentary deities.

The Romans are the perfect example of this principle, with a god for every domain of human activity, every occupation. The difference in the Roman gods from the nature spirits of the Eve tribe is that these gods have attained permanence and generality. Usener: "The patron god of harrowing... Occator, rules not only this year's harrowing, or the cultivation of a particular field, but is the god of harrowing in general, who is annually invoked by the whole community..."

It is only after the momentary gods of fleeting experience have been generalized into special gods that they can then proceed to the final stage of deification. This is a stage with which we're all familiar: *personal gods*. The personal god emerges when the god's name comes to denote a proper name.

Interestingly, Usener believes this happens as the word loses its connection to the activity or state that the god originally signified. The proper name of the deity can begin to designate a person only after it stops designating the activity or the state that the word originally referred to; another name is given to the activity or state for which the god's name once stood, and now the deity becomes an individual. The imagination invests the god with a personality. In the human imagination the god can live and suffer, just as human beings do.

This development of myth therefore proceeds: from the immediate perception and correspondent emotional state; to the representation of this momentary experience; then, to the representation of general categories based on repeated momentary experience; and finally, to anthropomorphism.

By the time mankind was able to anthropomorphize the world, man was fully in possession of metaphorical thinking. Anthropomorphism is the ability to distill the traits or qualities of humankind in order to use those traits or qualities to describe the non-human parts of nature. The subjective is hardened and crystallized into the objective. Then, through objective representation, we can create the image of a phenomenon in the form of another subject. The means by which this objectification occurs are, *first, by image-making*; and *second, by the act of naming*.

Usener emphatically denied that the conscious mind used its intellectual volition to contrive the various names which primordial man assigned to things and concepts. "People do not invent some arbitrary sound-complex," he wrote, "in order to introduce it as the sign of a certain object, as one might do with a token. The spiritual excitement caused by some object which presents itself in the outer world furnishes both the occasion and the means of its denomination. Sense impressions are what the self receives from its encounter with the not-self, and the liveliest of these naturally strive for vocal expression..."

***

"Keegan."

"Yeah?"

"Walnuts?" Andrea asked me.

"Hmm?" I asked, looking up from my scribbling. "Oh."

I reached forward and held out my hand underneath the package, labeled Noci. He tapped the package a few times until a small handful came out. The Italians usually bought healthy snacks like nuts or fruits, and overall, their eating habits seemed far healthier than ours. For my part, I'd been eating plenty of chips and sandwiches. High caloric American junk food had seemingly made its inroads here in Europe. That was international capitalism for you.

The countryside around the highways hadn't been ruined yet. On American roadways, every rest area looks more or less the same, because it is always the same handful of brands. Brands of gas stations, eateries, coffee houses, diners. We all know them. There is a sense of familiarity when you pull into a Flying J with a Burger King and a Starbucks connected to it, and a Denny's right next door. You probably just visualized all those brand logos.

The familiarity is nice, but it breeds contempt, as always. Eventually, the visual landscape becomes predictable. Boring. There was less of that homogeneity over here. They still had their brands, but they were different brands that I didn't recognize. Their logos had novelty. Plus, there just didn't seem to be as much of it overall. The Europeans already had a visual palette for their societies; there was less space for the capitalistic tendrils to push their way into.

Around that time, we received bad news. Doc got a message from Valerio, the booking agent for our record label. The show on the following Monday had been cancelled. It was supposed to be the final date playing together with Hell Obelisco. There was a string of cursing from the middle row of seats as he told them what had happened. It was mostly in Italian but some fucks were in there too. Steve and Andrea began conferring about it.

"We could do a post on Facebook," Steve suggested.

They began taking a photo to use for the algorithm's sake, of Andrea looking as if he was begging – which we were. Honesty was the best policy.

"What happened?" I asked Steve, prying for information.

"I don't know," he said, shaking his head and looking a little bewildered. He jabbed his thumbs at his phone, typing rapidly. "Guess the promoter couldn't get anything together."

"*Mother. Fuckers.*" Penny said.

"Well, we'll see," Steve said. "It's short notice but maybe someone can help us out. You never know."

"You never know," I muttered. This just couldn't happen. We had precious few dates while we were here, but I wasn't optimistic that another show could be put together in a week. Not based on how the shows had been planned so far. I stared out the window at the passing towns, little rooftop seas. My reflection, with my notebook on my lap, sat there, looking back at me; a vague ghost superimposed on the moving picture.

***

These primal vocalizations, brought on by spiritual excitement, are the first truly *artistic* expression. Usener far predates me in arguing that there was a pre-linguistic period of auditory communication. But following Usener, if we consider myth as a predecessor to what we call art in the modern sense of the term, then emotional expression in a ritual setting is the first formally artistic endeavor.

To once again consider the psychological meaning of these developments in human intellect, we find that *the momentary gods mark the first time that man had cause to form concepts.* Out of the originally emotive and irrational expressions, man developed the process of designating these concepts. Intense emotional experiences, life-or-death struggles, 'miraculous occurrences', and the like provided the raw material for this process. In a moment where a man fears to lose his life, he feels panic; he then casts an idol in the form of the panic he experienced; the panic is then objectified – literally made into an object. But it is still a specific moment of panic, and therefore a specific local god. Myth, language, and art are all unified at this point in man's infancy. Every subtle distinction was hard-won.

The functional god comes only after this objectification of the momentary into images, and, later, names. This is where we find the next major inflection point in human existence. A symbol comes to stand for an activity, experience, or state of mind. This objectification develops by the diminishing of the emotional resonance of the initial experience. By expressing the experience as a symbol, the emotionality is discharged. The point in the process at which the concept exists devoid of the original emotional charge is the point at which concepts become *functional*, or, to speak more plainly, *useful*.

Despite Usener's criticisms of Nietzsche's scholarship, Nietzsche made a similar argument as Usener about the origins of language in his essay, *On*

Truth and the Lie in the Non-Moral Sense. Usener was certainly unaware of the essay, since it went unpublished during Nietzsche's life.

In this essay, Nietzsche examined the cultural or moral truths which societies held to be objective and universal. As one of the first true relativists, Nietzsche was suspicious of these claims. He suspected that most of that which we took for granted about man's innate nature was the result of cultural upbringing. He believed that the "congenital defect of all philosophers" was the inclination for taking the examples of people we found near to us, who grew up in the same culture at the same time period, and using them as an example of universal truths about mankind.

Nietzsche thought that the relatively short period of civilization has had very little effect on the nature of mankind, in comparison to the hundreds of thousands of years that human beings spent as hunter-gatherers, and the millions of years of prehistory before that. If we are to speak of human nature, it was formed during this pre-history by the forces of evolution. It was *this* human nature, forged in prehistory, that Europe's Christian values system refused to acknowledge. This led, of course, to mind-body dualism.

On Truth and the Lie in the Non-Moral Sense begins with the observation that knowledge was something "invented" by "clever animals" on a lonely star somewhere out in the cosmos. This framing of things, from a naturalistic perspective, emphasizes the fact that knowledge is something that evolved out of a dumb world. This opposes the Christian perspective that knowledge – in the form of a personal God with an all-knowing consciousness – preceded all existence.

Nietzsche sought to understand why language and communication would have developed. Particularly, he was interested in how human beings ever came to value the truth and gain a taste for the scientific spirit and the pursuit of knowledge. In the Christian worldview, truth is something that exists independently of mankind, and there is an absolute standard of truth in the form of God. Without the possibility of truth independent of human perception, in a world with no absolute perceiver, why would humans come to value the truth?

Nietzsche concluded that what has counted for truth among human beings is determined by the strength and survivability of a given belief. It is the advantage a belief gives that makes it survive, not some correspondence to an objective reality. There is simply no natural process to select for such a thing as truthfulness: the only selection process is based on survivability. History is written by the winners – we all know the adage. To the extent that human beings have employed lying, it was developed by those who were weaker: for the weaker animal always has to use deception to defeat the stronger.

"What then is truth?" he writes, "A movable host of metaphors, metonymies, and; anthropomorphisms: in short, a sum of human relations which have been poetically and rhetorically intensified, transferred, and embellished, and which, after long usage, seem to a people to be fixed, canonical, and binding. Truths are illusions which we have forgotten are illusions – they are metaphors that have become worn out and have been drained of sensuous force, coins which have lost their embossing and are now considered as metal and no longer as coins."

While we need not take up Nietzsche's challenge of truth as such, we may notice that he sees our language as a set of metaphors that have discharged all their emotional power. The many names in our language for all the things and experiences in the world have long since lost their connection to myth and have come to designate only the concept: the general category.

The idea of magic words – a mere set of syllables that invokes fear and danger in its utterance, a very common idea among ancient mankind – is now foreign to the modern consciousness. Such beliefs were commonplace during man's prehistory, when words were still charged with emotional power. This is why so many religions begin their creation myth with a sacred word, or the utterance of a creator God. *In the beginning was The Word...*

***

Slumber overtook me. I'd thought it impossible to sleep in the Sprinter van, yet, with my face smashed against the window, I slipped into unconsciousness. I didn't rouse until the van slowed. We hit traffic as we entered the city. I was groggy. My neck didn't feel any better after the afternoon shut-eye. I didn't get a good glimpse of Toulouse. I don't recall seeing the skyline. I don't know if the city has one.

It was a neighborhood bar, somewhere out of the downtown hullabaloo, which had been par for the course so far on this tour. The bar was set into a long commercial building, its parking lot facing a row of trees behind which were the suburbs. Basically, a strip mall – though I'm not sure of the European term. Usually not a good sign for a show (though there are exceptions to the rule).

There was a restaurant and bar, and next to it was the venue. Behind the venue, in the same building, were rehearsal rooms and a recording studio. There was a gym just next door and a bicycle shop or something on its other flank. It seemed like a newer construction, a very clean and sterile place. Pleasant enough, but very "yuppie". At least they had a ramp with a gradual slope that made loading in the gear much smoother.

We soundchecked. Obviously, we played at full volume. Management emerged from elsewhere in the building, waving their hands and shaking their heads and telling us to turn down. I sighed deeply, the guitar hanging on its strap as I rubbed my face. A repeat of the past few nights.

Again, the tug of war between us and the staff. I resisted the urge to start explaining to them what doom metal is. I tried the tack of explaining that we create our tone through amplification, once again. It was futile. They spoke very little English; the language barrier made it impossible.

We tried to compromise. It was a Monday night, after all. We turned down and down, trying to inch the knobs into lower volume as slowly and gradually as we could. Over and over again, the soundguy shook his head and said it was still too loud. After a half hour or so, we reached a volume on which there was mutual agreement. The soundguy assured us, as soundguys usually do, that he would make it sound plentifully loud, and control our volume through the PA speakers. Then the comedy began.

He asked us to play all together. We started into the first half of one of our songs. There was a low rumbling; it built and swelled into a loud whine. At first, the soundguy thought it was the bass, and Nick turned down and down and down. The soundguy changed out the microphone for another one. We went through the song again. Still, the same problem. He went to me and Steve again, asking us to turn down.

Penny finally realized the problem during the last playthrough. He waited until no one else was playing. With one thunderous 'thump' of the kick drum pedal, there was a swell of low feedback from the monitors. The soundguy swapped out whatever microphone he was using for the bass drum. We tried checking the drums again. Same problem. The feedback continued. The soundcheck took over an hour as he struggled to fix it.

It seemed like the soundguy hated our guts by the end of it. The feeling was mutual on my part, since the problem hadn't been our loud amps. Penny's kick pedal is not amplified, but fueled only by his own muscles. It was the soundguy's own lack of experience. It was a perfct example of why we oftentimes preferred to not even have our cabinets miked. It was a small room. The PA system is only necessary for drums and vocals, damnit! We had enough amplification without relying on the PA. But, the soundguy always wants to have the illusion of control.

Hell Obelisco's turn for soundcheck. I found my way to the green room, apologized to them for taking so long. They laughed it off. I collapsed onto the leather couch. It was the first proper green room of the tour so far. I lied there and texted with Amberly to tell her good morning, then shut my eyes for a few moments. The lighting was a bit too bright, too florescent, which ruined the vibe. I was used to dimmed lighting in a venue setting. Even though this bar had a real green room, it didn't quite seem like a real venue.

After the Italians finished their soundcheck, everyone else found their way into the green room, and sat, slumped or lied down. The bartender, a young woman, brought us pitchers full of beer and plenty of pint glasses, a plate of charcuterie, complete with room temperature salame, some of which was covered in beautiful white mold, a plate of cheese, with bries, a few soft, aromatic cheeses, including one with a wine-soaked rind and another with a rind of ash, then fruits, berries and a baguette. The kitchen took care of us, at least. Communicating with the bartender was its own small challenge. Now that we were in France, the Hell Obelisco guys were also foreigners. Nick would have been able to speak with her, but he was off jogging. But by the time everyone had a beer in hand, suddenly things felt right with the world, and a moment of ease washed over me.

I excitedly showed Nick the cheeses as soon as he wandered in from his jog. The selection was for a much broader palette than the typical American's, and the quality was better simply because of the laws and traditions regulating cheese making here. It is not difficult to make a band feel like royalty.

I took my beer and had a seat on the patio. Once again, I did no exploring. After the longest drive so far and the most frustrating soundcheck, the hospitality did wonders for my state of mind. Still, I didn't have a good overall feeling about the show. The energy level was low, and there were no paying customers yet in attendance. While the halfway decent Sunday show the night before had helped make up for the poor weekend in Italy, it looked like Monday night was going to underwhelm. It was a nice enough place. Quiet. But quiet is the last place you want to be for a doom metal show.

***

Other philosophers took up Usener's work, and considered its implications for explaining language. The philosopher of language Ernst Cassirer, continuing in that tradition, argued that the unity of the verbal and mythical worlds can be found in metaphor. He drew heavily on Usener's research. In Cassirer's view, the inflection point at which man creates the mythical image was only the beginning.

"The same tendency which the image of the god performs," Cassirer writes, "the same tendency to permanent existence, may be ascribed to the uttered sounds of language. The word, like a god or daemon, confronts man not as a creation of his own, but as something existent and significant in its own right, as an objective reality. As soon as the spark has jumped across, as soon as the tension and emotion of the moment has found its discharge in the word or the mythical image, a sort of turning point has occurred in human mentality: the inner excitement which was a mere subjective state has vanished, and has been resolved into the objective form of myth or of speech. And now an ever-progressive objectification can begin."

Cassirer titled his book *Myth and Language*, and considers these two as the fundamental forms of communication. This is slightly different from my schema of categorization. But if we add the caveat that art had not yet branched out from myth during the time of human history that Cassirer is writing about, then the two of us are saying roughly the same thing. Before language, art was not yet distinguished from myth, because language is the very thing that creates the opportunity for such conceptual distinctions. While Cassirer's project in this book was not about determining where art came from, but determining where language came from, he finds in the course of this study that the common origin of both is in myth. The impulse to mythmaking is the most inchoate form of art.

"Language and myth," he writes, "stand in an original and indissoluble correlation with one another, from which they both emerge but gradually as independent elements. They are two diverse shoots from the same parent stem, the same impulse of symbolic formulation, springing from the same basic mental activity, a concentration and heightening of simple sensory experience. In the vocables of speech and in primitive mythic figurations, the same inner process finds its consummation: they are both resolutions of an inner tension, the representation of subjective impulses and excitations in definite objective forms and figures."

To Cassirer, the project of mythmaking and the project of language-making are much the same: language is simply a further development built on the foundation of myth. Elaborating on the work of Usener, he draws a parallel between the social evolution of gods – from the mere momentary god to the personal god – and the development of language. The analogy Cassirer sees in the development of metaphor is the act of *condensing and expanding*. The metaphor condenses an experience, which is part of a dynamic, subjective reality, into something objective: an image, or a word.

Through this discharge of the subjective into the objective, that which was formerly a fleeting experience has its essence distilled from it. We take a thing's essence to be its commonality with other experiences distilled out of it. That is to say: we consider the essence of the concept, "tree", to designate some general quality or category, and not any individual kind of tree.

The emotionality and the subjectivity of the experience, on the other hand, cannot be preserved. When one creates an idol to commemorate a life-or-death panic he felt, the idol cannot convey this feeling to subsequent generations. Only the image remains. This process eventually leads to the creation of an abstract, discursive world of concepts of generalities. This is the domain of the philosopher, the domain of the logician. Like Nietzsche, Cassirer holds that our capacity for logical thought is something that emerged from the irrational.

Cassirer: "Now it is here, in this intuitive creative form of myth, and not in the formation of our discursive theoretical concepts, that we must look for the key which may unlock for us the secrets of the original conceptions of language."

Language and mythological thinking both operate through metaphor, but Cassirer concludes that these two tendencies of thought represent two opposing directions from that origin. In the case of language, there is a concentric expansion of ever-widening spheres of perception: one discovers that the individual is the member of a general category, and that this category is itself a member of other categories, and so on. In the case of mythological thinking, however, the tendency is to compress the mental perspective rather than expand it. In linguistic-discursive thinking, we recognize the individual animal as distinct from its species; in mythological or magical thinking, the species and individual are indistinguishable.

Cassirer: "Whoever has brought any part of a whole into his power has thereby acquired power, in the magical sense, over the whole itself... to hold magical dominion over another person's body one need only attain possession of his pared nails or cut-off hair... even his shadow, his reflection, or his footprints serve the same purpose... If a rain-making ceremony consists of sprinkling water on the ground to attract rain, or rain-stopping magic is made by pouring water on red hot stones where it is consumed amid hissing noise, both ceremonies owe their true magical sense to the act that the rain is not just represented, but is felt to be really present in each drop of water."

There is a value in expanding our conscious perceptions through language and its tables of categories – it allows us more precise perception and thus manipulation of the external world. But this world of categories that we create brings with it a correspondent need to contract the conscious perception. The spiritual practices of so many religions involve an intense, undivided focus: in the form of a meditation, a mantra, the counting of rosary beads, the repetition of a deity's name, and so on. We may notice similarities in these forms of mythological or ritual thinking to the divine madness of Socrates: the point is to "go out of one's mind." The means of doing so take many forms. According to Cassirer, when anthropologists discover word magic in a society, it is always accompanied by picture magic. The image and the word both serve the aesthetic function as a sort of magic circle to contain or express a formulation of the divine.

In my own experience of touring for the better part of a decade, and having played countless gigs in countless cities, I agree wholeheartedly that the true artistic experience compresses one's attention solely into the sensory reality of the present moment. This is another dimension of art that is just as characteristically religious as it is artistic.

Cassirer writes that language and art are therefore the two children of myth, which will now further develop after having been "emancipated" from mythological thought. Perhaps because aesthetics was beyond the scope of Cassirer's book, Cassirer does not have much more to say about art than this. But the insights he provides into the origins of human communication are invaluable. Thus, we are closer to understanding the link between art and religion: art is tasked with carrying on the emotive communication that formerly existed in myth making. Language deals with communication of concepts, art deals with communication of emotions.

One may raise the issue that there are plenty of religious people around; is it really permissible to say that religion has declined and art shall take its place?

The mythological state of mind is lacking in our modern religions. Even though plenty of religions endure today, their orthodoxies – of institutions, hierarchies, symbols, names and formulations – are facing crisis precisely because of the discharge of the emotional resonance that Cassirer describes.

The ritual symbolism behind the Eucharist, for example, does not hold the same emotional sway over the Christian that it once did to the medieval worshiper. The Christian in the Middle Ages lived in a world of angels and devils and saw every event and happenstance as ordained by providence and a test of his immortal soul. The communion ritual does not have the energy it once did: to captivate the imagination and compress the Catholic's focus into the single point of emotional and spiritual intensity. The symbols of communion have discharged their divine spark and are now the rote communication of an abstract meaning.

Maybe this is not universally true of the religious types – at least not yet. But the trend is clear, judging by the fact that "non-religious" is the fastest growing religion. Even in the time when religion still dominated the Western mind, there was secular art. Art therefore branched off from religion long before religions declined, and it remains the child of religion, for it takes after the original nature of mythmaking. Accordingly, the philosophers, like Socrates, distrust the poets and artists. It is for this reason that the artistic experience has so often been associated with the religious experience, even though the religious types and artistic types seem diametrically opposed in modern life. The artistic impulse is the mythmaking impulse: the need to express the intensity of subjective experience, to discharge it into sound or image. Sound seems to have come first as an artistic medium; image came second. The act of naming came last of all: bringing with it metaphorical thinking and the whole process of rigidification of experience into object. *All of these means of expression arose originally for the purposes of emotive expression.* Discursive communication was only a later development on the foundations of emotional communication: it provides the possibility for the conceptual to separate from the emotional.

We have a provisional answer to the question of where the artistic impulse comes from. It is an instinctive form of expression that is so old, so powerful, so inculcated into the human animal that it *is* like hunger, like thirst, like sexuality. It is the desire to express oneself and one's emotions. Art, in the form of myth, is the oldest and most primordial form of human communication. While we think of language as the most direct form of communication, it has never been as effective as even our own body language, facial expressions, and tone of voice. The raw linguistic content, in many cases, can tell us very little of what someone is feeling. Though we have words for our feelings, and may attempt to express them through the use of language, this may only call to mind the abstract *idea* of the feeling. With the emotional resonance of language debased, we find we need new means of emotional expression.

This suggests to me that the emotional resonance of art, which Socrates thought was so dangerous, is a basic human need. Basic human needs can be dangerous. Just as some people may have a higher sex drive than others or a different metabolism than others, there are various degrees to which the artistic drive may exert force on an individual. Furthermore, art is not the only means of emotional expression, as we've suggested. One may convey at least something of the emotions through language, through intimacy, and, yes, some still find it through religious worship and ritual.

That emotive expression eventually had the consequence of giving rise to the dispassionate world of logic is something demanded by these conclusions, yet still anathema to our cultural ideas.

Nietzsche wrote, in *Beyond Good & Evil*: "How can a thing develop out of its antithesis? For example, the reasonable from the non-reasonable, the animate from the inanimate, the logical from the illogical, altruism from egoism, disinterestedness from greed, truth from error? The metaphysical philosophy formerly steered itself clear of this difficulty to such extent as to repudiate the evolution of one thing from another and to assign a miraculous origin to what it deemed highest and best... The historical philosophy, on the other hand, which can no longer be viewed apart from physical science, the youngest of all philosophical methods, discovered experimentally... *that there is no antithesis*."

The logician has come to see reason as a power that moves and directs the world, rather than a mere description of the world. From the artist's perspective, the logician is simply working within his own system of metaphors, metonymies and anthropomorphisms: and admittedly a highly complex and useful one. The logician may imagine that his dispassionate consideration of the world is fundamentally different from the magical and metaphorical thinking of irrational religious man. This is true to a degree. But his own logical systems rest on the same irrational foundations. It is not a perception of an objective reality that gives the impression of logic as describing fixed and universal laws. We do not possess sense organs capable of discerning such an 'objective reality'. This impression only comes to us through the illusions of language, which, as Usener says, "does our thinking for us".

***

The sun went down as I drank on the patio. Davide went off to the van for some shut-eye. Tomorrow would be the longest drive so far, he said. I began to wonder about the route we were on. Why exactly were these drives taking so long? What kind of tour route was this, anyhow?

I pulled up a map on my phone. I punched in the starting place, Lyon, and the destination, Toulouse. Then, Toulouse to Strasbourg – our destination for tomorrow.

My suspicions were confirmed. The route was completely illogical. If we'd taken the day off on Monday, which is normally the closing day for most bars and venues anyway, we could have skipped this show and just driven straight to Strasbourg. Strasbourg was a mere four hours away from Lyon. Instead, we'd spent the day going six hours in the opposite direction of Strasbourg, and we now had a ten-hour drive to get there tomorrow. Given the speeds the van was capable of, and the amount of stops we'd need to make, we'd be lucky to make it in twelve.

The illogic of the situation, the lack of common sense, the lack of communication. I should have looked at the tour routing, but the dates had constantly gotten scheduled and rescheduled. But *someone* should have caught this! With whom does final responsibility lie? This was the kind of thing that had turned me off from touring in the past, and I raged internally yet again, but said nothing.

I found myself sitting with Penny and Nick at the merch table, right across from Hell Obelisco's. I drank a second beer, and a third. We watched the bar patrons dwindle, and no one was showing up to pay the cover charge.

The bar staff were polite enough but seemed indifferent to the show. We already knew how the soundguy felt about us.

In all, only two fans showed up to watch us perform. They said they'd found out about the show online. They watched both bands' sets in their entirety. They were blown away by the performance and seemed thrilled that our tour had come through their town. They cheered and provided at least some evidence of life during both of our shows. After the show, they complained about their local scene, angrily wondered aloud why more people hadn't shown up. There's supposedly this big internet fandom for metal, but when a live act comes into town, the scene is often nowhere to be found. Everyone talks shit about their own scene, and thinks the problem is a local predominance of lame people. But the truth is that the majority of people are lame, and the scene sucks everywhere. That's life.

It must also be said that the final responsibility is always on you, as the performer. If you can draw a crowd, then you'll draw a crowd. And yet, promotion can make all the difference, because if people don't even know that you're playing, it's impossible to draw them out. The two people who came bought a few things from our respective merch tables. At least we could say that everyone who attended bought something. At a show with two people, making twenty-five euros is a consolation of sorts.

The show ended before midnight. We loaded out. During the process, the stuffed bear tumbled from the top of the van. I caught it before it hit the pavement. As I tried to stuff it back inside, I fumbled Doc's box labeled blueberries, yet again.

"You really want to kill this box don't you?" he said, jokingly. I laughed. I was honestly a little embarrassed.

It was a hotel for lodging that evening, though the rooms were tiny. We'd have to split into multiple groups for the night – three to a room. Nick went with two of the Italians; Penny, Steve & I piled into another room; the remaining three Italians would occupy a third. There were two beds, both twin size, with barely enough space to walk around them, and a little closet of a bathroom. The next day we would drive from the western part of the country all the way to the border with Germany. We set our alarms for 5:30 the next morning.

The sweat had mostly dried. I changed my clothes, and took a whore's bath, as we say in America. A splash of warm water on the face and armpits. I put on deodorant. In the time it took me to ready myself for bed, they'd already turned off the lights and drenched the room in pitch darkness. I stumbled over my shoes, cursed loudly, then climbed into bed next to Steve. He snores like no one else, which could make it difficult to fall asleep, but I can sleep through almost anything once I'm out. I had to reach unconsciousness quickly or risk never getting there.

***

It can't be time to get up, I thought. *I just fell asleep.*

The alarms were going off. The sound felt like an icepick into the skull, right between my eyes. I grabbed my phone and confirmed the awful truth: 5:30 AM. It felt like it had been mere minutes since lying down, as if no time had passed at all.

The lamp went on. My eyes were on fire. My muscles and brain ached with a vengeance. I dragged my body out from under the covers and into my jeans. I assembled my baggage. I consciously forced myself to walk outside, bag strapped to me. The Italians were already awake. Nick told me as we congregated in the parking lot that they'd woken up thirty minutes before we did. They were up before we were almost every day. How did that fit into the idea of Italian time?

In the blackness before the dawn, we loaded the van with our luggage. It wasn't as intense as loading or unloading gear, but finding a spot for nine different bags in the completely stuffed vehicle was not always easy. Sometimes things tumbled out of the back whilst we shoved and pressed and wedged bags in any space available.

Davide started the engine. I laid my cheek against the cool glass again, hoping to find sleep again. Traffic lights reflected and scattered their red and green lights along the morning dew stuck to the windows. We set off to cross the country of France.

CHAPTER EIGHT
STRASBOURG

Steve had smuggled out one of the bries from the night before. He held it between two paper plates. Any free food on tour is valuable, after all. We all imagined we'd save it and eat it sometime that day. Alas, there'd been no refrigerator in the hotel room. A ripened cheese left out at room temperature begins to 'run away', as they say. It loses its structural integrity and the buttercream softens and becomes more liquid.

After a few hours, we made a rest stop in the early dawnlight. Steve peaked between the plates. It was a runny mess. We filed out of the van, and we gathered up any remaining trash from the previous day's drive. The cheese went into the trash with everything else. Farewell, sweet brie.

The rest stop was atop a hill, the highway on either side, overlooking a windswept plain. Wide open space. Stone picnic tables stood in the middle of the tall, green grass. It was all farmland, as far as the eye could see. You could see the little brown herds of dairy cows grazing – over there, they were dispersed across the hillsides, over on the other side they were clustered together, sleeping and loitering. The silhouettes of farmhouses were visible just on the ridgelines at the horizon.

The Italians and I sauntered over to the lone building where the shops and restrooms were. Before stepping through the automatic doors, I turned and surveyed the scenery once again. I watched as Nick emerged from the van after all of us, his hair disheveled. It was quite unlike him. He preferred to present himself to the world in a respectable manner. On tour, you see your bandmates at their least polished. He walked only for a few moments, then dropped himself onto the middle of the grass, like a cat in a sunbeam.

V. Art's Social Function

We have established that art and language are parallel forms of communication, and share a common ancestor in myth. Though they developed on separate courses, it is worth examining how it was that language developed, and why such a thing was possible in human beings. It does not follow that every development in language will be mirrored in the development of art. However, a study of how communication through language developed can shed light on how artistic communication developed.

By every indication, language developed communally. Language is an emergent property of multiple human brains capable of cognition. The term *emergent property* means something that only occurs as a result of a combination of factors, and which is therefore greater than the mere sum of its parts.

America is an individualist culture: it is difficult for Americans to conceive of concepts premised on social interdependence. It may even be the case that modern people in general are less likely to understand the development of human thought in collective terms, driven as we are by economic forces. But it is especially true in America, where the social organization around the nuclear family has destroyed our extended kin-group ties, that we regard our minds as our own. We tend to think of our morals, our values, our goals in life, our place in society – and yes, our thoughts and our emotions – as determined by ourselves, our own willpower and gumption. The contents of the modern mind are thought to belong uniquely to an individualized, personal, *private* experience.

Perhaps the most famous philosopher to cast a doubt on this intuition was the philosopher of language, Ludwig Wittgenstein. In his work *Philosophical Investigations*, he challenged the idea of a "private language." For a straightforward explanation of what Wittgenstein criticized in the idea of a "private language," we might quote the man himself: "The meaning of a word is its use in the language."

Meaning is not determined by an individual's arbitrary designation, but by collective use. Use creates meaning. We may think that, for example, when one experiences "pain" what he experiences is something solely his own. But on the contrary, he has no way of knowing that what he experiences as "pain" is exactly what someone else experiences when they feel pain. We have only the observable behavior of others as an indication of what they are feeling. While the word "pain" may have originated to designate a subjective experience, the meaning of the word is eventually debased of its subjective content. Through repeated usage, the word "pain" comes to mean, "what other people mean when they indicate pain." The very functionality of the word is based on its mutual intelligibility, which means that it cannot refer to a subjective experience, as this is the least mutually intelligible thing in the world.

To argue this point, Wittgenstein imagines someone who experiences a sensation for which they're not aware of any word, and designates that sensation by the symbol, "S". The person writes "S" in a journal every time they experience the sensation. They do this once on the first day, a second time the next day. But on the third day, they experience a sensation, and can't remember if this sensation is really the same as the "S" sensation of the first or the second day. Wittgenstein thereby suggests that language does not have the power to symbolize our individual subjective experiences, because we don't have the memory for such a thing. The subjective experience is fleeting: it slips through our fingers. By ossifying such an experience into a word concept, we necessarily leave behind the emotional ephemera.

The philosopher David Foster Wallace offered an explanation of Wittgenstein's argument, which is just as good as anything I can manage, so I will simply quote Mr. Wallace:

"In the case of Private Language, the delusion is usually based on the belief that a word such as pain has the meaning it does because it is somehow 'connected' to a feeling in my knee. But as Mr. L. Wittgenstein's Philosophical Investigations proved in the 1950s, words actually have the meanings they do because of certain rules and verification tests that are imposed on us from outside our own subjectivities, viz., by the community in which we have to get along and communicate with other people. Wittgenstein's argument, which is admittedly very complex and gnomic and opaque, basically centers on the fact that a word like 'pain' means what it does for me because of the way the community I'm part of has tacitly agreed to use 'pain'."

When drained of their subjective content, the metaphors signified by words eventually come to represent not specific experiences but general cases. The information conveyed by words, especially the written word, comes to communicate conceptual meaning. The nature of this conceptual meaning is inextricably communal. As Wittgenstein and other philosophers of language have argued, conceptual meaning can only emerge within a community and shaped by the language that shapes the thought of the community. The community, in turn, shapes the language.

The implications of language as necessarily communal and non-private are profound. I'm not sure if we've seriously grappled with those consequences. Individualism is such a powerful cultural prejudice that it may be almost impossible for us.

Wallace: "If words' meanings depend on transpersonal rules, and these rules on community consensus, language is not only conceptually non-Private but also irreducibly public, political, and ideological. This means that questions about our national consensus on grammar and usage are actually bound up with every last social issue that millennial America's about — class, race, gender, morality, tolerance, pluralism, cohesion, equality, fairness, money: You name it."

When Wallace made the claims above, they may have seemed more shocking than they do today. In the last number of years, we've fought a number of culture wars in which the use of language has been at the heart of the conflict. If the conceptual meanings of our word-symbols delimit the boundaries of our thought, then transforming the agreed-upon meanings can transform the shape of our thought. Conceptual thought is not possible outside language, *because conceptual thought is not a tool of the individual, but a tool of the community.*

While there have always been many hypotheses for why human thought is necessarily communal, perhaps the most compelling explanation rooted in anthropological evidence was put forward by the psychologist William von Hippel in his book, *The Social Leap*. Cooperation and socializing were the very evolutionary forces which drove the human intellect to advance. Mankind's social life is the reason for its intelligence.

Von Hippel: "Once we left the trees, our very existence depended on our ability to work together... our psychology was shaped by this need more than any other... Smaller, slower, and weaker than many of the grassland predators, [early humans] would have been doomed had they not happened upon a social solution to their problems. This solution was so effective that it put us on an entirely new evolutionary pathway. Our ancestors grew ever more clever precisely because they could leverage their newfound cooperative abilities to develop better ways to protect themselves and make a living."

This social solution von Hippel references began with the innovation of throwing projectiles as a means of killing prey and warding off predators. As arboreal mammals, proto-humans had strong shoulder rotation muscles to aid in tree climbing. They were largely defenseless once conditions drove their migration onto the open grassland – at least in comparison to fanged and clawed predators like lions. But their shoulder muscles allowed them to lob projectiles both powerfully and far.

When we staggered onto the savannah, we were hardly distinguishable from chimps. A single proto-human was not a threat to most savannah predators, even when equipped with the ability to throw projectiles. Our incredible visual cortex had not yet been fully developed. Projectile-throwing proved ineffective as a solitary action for hunting or defense. But it was extremely effective when employed as a group activity.

Von Hippel: "Individuals in groups who learned to work cooperatively... were at an enormous advantage... Stone throwing not only massively enhanced the benefits of cooperation but also created new means to enforce it.... Ostracism and rejection have remained important tools for enforcing cooperation through to the present."

The *social leap*, as von Hippel designates it, therefore designates the introduction of selection pressures that drove the intellect forward. Those new selection pressures were driven by the need for cooperation, whereas before competition had reigned supreme. Eventually, man's way of life developed into a social life which became the whole ecosystem of the intellect.

As von Hippel points out, there are plenty of large primates who are more competitive than cooperative. Chimpanzees, for example, are hindered in developing more cooperative communities due to their proclivities for infanticide and sexual aggression. Our social existence is the 'special power' that has driven our intellect to such extremes. Because the social existence is the need that the intellect serves, the intellect does not exist independently of our social life.

Von Hippel: "If you drop one of us naked and alone into the wilderness, you've just fed the creatures of the local forest. But if you drop one hundred of us naked into the wilderness, you've introduced a new top predator to this unfortunate stretch of woods."

Cooperation was the source of our power and, indeed, our very dominance over the natural world, to the point where we began to shape our environment to suit our needs. Accordingly, those who threatened to undermine the power of cooperation were socially shunned.

"Living the good life is largely a matter of meeting our evolutionary imperatives," von Hippel writes; as for what "the good life" is, von Hippel suggests we look to the social life. He attributes much of our modern existential chagrin to humans pursuing lifestyles and activities that don't adequately satisfy their social needs. Von Hippel eventually concludes that our social life is responsible for our very conception of happiness.

This would suggest that the community has not only shaped our conceptual world, but our emotional world. Instincts, physiological needs and possibly even primitive emotions may predate the social existence that drove human intellect to advance as it did. Through the forces of evolution, human emotions have been subject to the same social pressures. We feel the way we feel, in large part, due to social conditions around us, our place in the social hierarchy, and so on.

Once again, Friedrich Nietzsche anticipated the work of both Wittgenstein and von Hippel in his philosophical writings. To Nietzsche, social pressures on human inner states are the basis of morality. Nietzsche doesn't take a positive view of the community's morality – it is what he calls "herd morality." He believes that all moral sentimentality can ultimately find its origin in the community acting on the psyche over long generations. When we feel pangs of conscience after doing something that our society considers immoral, we take this as evidence that the deed must have been immoral in and of itself. "Morality is the herd-instinct in the individual," he writes.

But Nietzsche asserts that feelings of displeasure after "immoral" deeds are not universal. In other societies and ages, different moralities guided the human conscience. The Victorian Englishman feels guilt at his sexual fantasies that many who live today are completely free of; the samurai feels shame that a Westerner cannot understand, which can only be remedied through seppuku; the Muslim feels, in his very core, that he has transgressed if he takes a drink of alcohol, whereas the non-Muslim might imbibe with no such accompanying feeling. Perhaps most uncomfortably, societies such as those of the Spartans engaged in practices such as infanticide, as a means of eugenics, and saw this not as evil, but essential to the community.

Nietzsche: "Wherever we meet with a morality, we find a valuation and order of rank of the human impulses and activities. These valuations and orders of rank are always the expression of the needs of a community or herd: that which is in the first place to its advantage – and in the second place and third place – is also the authoritative standard for the worth of every individual. By morality the individual is taught to become a function of the herd, and to ascribe to himself value only as a function. As the conditions for the maintenance of one community have been very different from those of another community, there have been very different moralities..."

Nietzsche anticipates Wittgenstein's arguments against private languages. Nietzsche goes as far to argue that *the development of consciousness itself is as a means for communication*. In his book, *The Gay Science*, Nietzsche writes that "the subtlety and strength of consciousness always were proportionate to man's (or animal's) capacity for communication, and... this capacity in turn [is] proportionate to the need for communication." Nietzsche then takes this even further, arguing that "consciousness is really only a net of communication between human beings: it is only as such that it had to develop; a solitary human being who lived like a beast of prey would not have needed it."

Language is not the mere tool of an individual consciousness, to be used for its own ends. Rather: *communication is the whole point of consciousness*. Communication is an ends served by the means of consciousness, and not the other way around. The conceptual reality in which man lives is a shared reality created by the language he speaks. Nietzsche: "Consciousness does not really belong to individual existence but rather to man's social or herd nature."

This hypothesis has interesting implications when we think about pangs of conscience. Conscience is often called upon to justify what we intuitively feel to be true. In conscience, the moralist thinks he has proof of the objective reality of morals.

The example at hand from literature is Raskolnikov in Dostoyevsky's Crime and Punishment. Raskolnikov believes himself to be beyond good and evil, yet still feels pangs of conscience after committing a murder. Nietzsche's considerations would suggest, however, that the conscience is merely the voice of culture, ever-whispering in our ear. Our displeasure in the wake of an immoral deed is intimately tied to our perception of how we will be perceived by others. We evaluate the morality of a deed in respect to whether the public knowledge of it would enhance our reputation or degrade it. We cannot think of our self-image separately from how other people would regard us. In our conception of our own moral character, we find the voice of our society.

That the message of Crime and Punishment emotionally resonates is not evidence of some eternal truth about Dostoyevsky's morality – it can only be evidence about *ourselves*, and the fact that we have internalized the same moral ideas as Dostoyevsky. Morality is not a series of abstract principles. Our morality represents how we *feel* about others and about ourselves, just as much as what we think of them. Not only is our conceptual world communal, but so is our emotional world. Our feelings of self-worth, happiness, satisfaction, disappointment, anger, irritation, guilt, shame, worthwhileness, and so on – these all make up the emotional world, whose boundaries are defined by the social reality. Dostoyevsky, like many artists, gives voice to those moral feelings which grew within the soil of our shared culture – in this case, Christianity.

If emotive expression predated linguistic expression, the powerful communal forces must have exercised even greater power on man's emotional world (of art, music, poetry and drama) than on man's strictly conceptual world. The creation of gods was communicative from the start: a collective concern. The social pressures worked on religion and art for long ages before language was even born. The conclusions are clear: No private language; but also, no private art. No private conceptual world; no private emotional world.

***

I was in and out of sleep that morning. I was so physically exhausted that sleep became momentarily more powerful than my ruminating mind. But I couldn't ever doze off for too long. We stopped again. It was a grocery store, part of a big strip mall complex. I'm not sure what town or village we were outside of, exactly. I piled out of the van with everyone else, rubbing and stretching my neck. The wind was still blowing strong, as it had been the past few days. Davide said we absolutely had to make it back to the van in fifteen minutes in order to keep our schedule. It was around one in the afternoon.

I spent more money than I should have, and probably didn't make it back to the van for twenty-five minutes or so, but I wasn't the last one back. I'd mostly thrown my vegetarian diet out the window at this point and bought a sandwich with ham on it and some snacks. I'd offered to share food with the Italians since I figured reciprocation of sharing was important, but usually they turned down what I had. This time, I'd bought some Nutella mini pastries. Everyone had one.

***

Let's return to Socrates once again, and his debate with the rhapsode, Ion. Socrates says that with a magnetic power, the Muse speaks through the poet, and the poet goes out of his mind. The poet, stricken with an intense emotional experience, passes this divine madness onto others through the dramatic expression of his art. Emotions seize people. Emotions move mimetically through a community. The Muse is a desire: and this desire wishes to inflame other hearts. Emotions *want* resonance.

Not only does this fit with our picture of human cognition and emotion as communal, but it would be surprising if a man as brilliant as Socrates were to characterize art differently. If emotionality is not private, then emotions would have to be transmissible to other people. Leaving aside epistemological questions about the consciousness of other beings, for evolutionary purposes we made a great logical leap and came to believe as a matter of course that there was a similar subjective experience to our own occurring in the minds of others. We accept, for evolutionary reasons, that we can, in fact, transfer our experiences.

The understanding that there are other subjective experiences is called *theory of mind*. The development of theory of mind was advantageous to man's social way of life. Coming to a cooperative understanding in the context of theory of mind is what von Hippel calls, colloquially, "getting on the same page": the collective centering of attention on the same focus. The social leap was the technology that allowed us to dominate the world, but it required first that mankind get on the same page. In order for this to be possible, mankind needed to be capable of shared attention.

Von Hippel: "Humans have evolved white sclera which clearly advertise the direction of our attention... The fact that we advertise the direction of our gaze in this manner provides clear evidence that we gain more from others knowing what has grabbed our attention than we gain from keeping it a secret."

An answer is immediately forthcoming as to what grabbed the attention of the first humans: *momentary gods*. The momentary god is the very definition of that which captures our attention. According to Usener's research, the first deities were created on the basis of encountering something novel, surprising or powerful. The images that mankind formed on the basis of these intense experiences are the first attempt at metaphor and thus at communication, while still pre-linguistic. The primary activity of the human mind remained firmly in the category of mythmaking.

The selection pressures on the first humans were extreme. These earliest instances of imagistic and vocalized communication could only have endured if they provided mankind with some kind of advantage. Because of the importance of cooperation to man's survival, any innovation would be checked against the social forces, and either incorporated into man's social life or excised from it. This means that such images, ritualized vocalizations, and reverence for momentary deities, were all advantageous to man's social life. From von Hippel's explanation, it would seem that anything that can captivate our shared attention was useful to developing our powers of cooperation. Therefore, the momentary gods, *defined as that which captivates and captures our attention*, were advantageous. These were the first metaphors, the first symbols. We find the same sentiment in the work of psychologist Jonathan Haidt, who has asserted that human cultures formed by circling around sacred values – often literally, as Muslims today circle the Kabbah.

These first symbols survived to the extent that they could capture the shared attention of the most humans. Thus, over many iterations, human religiosity would have been honed onto those metaphors and images which man found to be most moving, most profound, most emotionally resonant. That which captures our attention we wish to bring into the attention of others. The significance of the emotional experience takes hold, and we always want to share it. This is the reason why art radiates emotional states through the community, as Socrates alleges.

The most intense experience compresses our attention completely into itself as the sole reality. In this state, we go "out of our minds." There is, paradoxically, a loss of subjectivity, a loss of the subjective itself by compressing oneself fully into a subjective experience. What is actually happening is the destruction of the individual subjectivity in its joining with a communal subjectivity. It is the Dionysian ritual that brings on ego death, as Nietzsche described in *Birth of Tragedy*. He wondered if a shared mass hallucination were a possible explanation for the origins of tragedy. Nietzsche invites us to suppose that entire peoples could be placed in conditions that would produce identical hallucinations. This is the upper limit of the power of art.

Far from being a danger to society, as Socrates alleges, if our analysis so far is correct, this process is in fact the *beginning* of society: it is the birth of all culture. But of course, an advocate for civilization such as Socrates would find himself opposed to artistic expression. The dynamic nature of new mythmaking always poses a threat to the old myths, which grow weaker over time in the course of their rigidification. Thus, the eternal struggle between the subjectivity of religious experience, and the dogma of religious institutions.

***

If I sat with my neck hanging forward, it left me liable to be shaken violently awake by random bumps or turns. I knew it wasn't advisable to lean all the way forward and rest my head on the seat in front of me. This is a terrible position, supposing there were to be an accident. The window remained the best option. The main drawback was lower back pain, from sitting at a weird angle. I was sacrificing my back's comfort for the sake of my neck. And then there was the soreness in my knee. My right knee would start to ache after hours of being in the same position.

"Goddamnit, I wish I could stretch my legs…"

"You know you can stand up in here, right?"

"What?" I asked. The thought hadn't occurred to me.

"Yeah," Penny said, matter-of-factly. "Try it."

Slowly, I raised myself to my feet. Relief. What the Sprinter van lacked in interior space, it made up for in height. Even someone of my height – 6'3" – could stand up fully while we were in transit. I could even stretch out my arms and rotate my neck a bit. It was a revelation. I felt stupid. It seemed so obvious in retrospect. I suppose I never considered it for the simple reason that such a thing would have been impossible in our Ford 15-seater back in the States. Funny how easy it is to miss the most obvious things.

The day's drive was still a test of patience. The afternoon was a never-ending series of naps, attempts at reading, attempts at writing, a few scattered conversations, stopping and disembarking and piling back in and going. The enchanted French countryside was the most entertaining companion. It was an extended daydream. Hills and valleys filled the backwoods of my psyche. It was like looking at a painting, a 21st century idyll. Is there such a thing as contentment, laced with angst?

***

It was twilight as we entered Strasbourg. I wasn't fully conscious until we reached the city's downtown. The trip took about thirteen hours, when all was said and done. Even after the abysmally early start, we still managed to arrive late.

It was Tuesday night. My expectations were immeasurably low. Encouragingly, the promoter of this show was out front to meet us as we pulled up to the venue. For those who do not know what a promoter does: in the underground scene, the booking agent contacts the promoter, who works with the club to set up the gig. Sometimes they work for the club exclusively, but most are free agents. They're responsible for getting the bands the best deal they can possibly get them. The quality between promoters can vary greatly. A promoter does not always care about the show enough to attend. The level of involvement of the promoter usually indicates how much he cared about promoting the show in the first place. And thus, it's a good sign when the promoter is there to greet you. He was a tall, handsome man with long blonde hair tied back in a ponytail, and a thick beard. He had a backpack on – he wore it for the entire show. He smiled and directed us as to where we should park.

The venue was in another historic-looking district. I suppose this is the way most places in Europe appear to Americans. The architecture was not grandiose or ornate by any means. The surrounding blocks consisted mostly of apartments, shops and a couple bars. But it looked old, like these buildings had been standing since the time of the war. Only a guess. The neighborhood reminded me of the apartments near where I'd stayed in Amsterdam, those ten years or so previously. White, olive green and sky-blue paint. Flowers in the windowsills. Old-style street lamps, burning a warm, golden light.

We loaded gear down a spiral staircase leading into yet another basement venue. Loading gear up and down stairs is difficult enough, but a spiral staircase is particularly annoying. This venue was even smaller than the place in Genoa. Downstairs, they played black and white movies on a projector, footage from the fifties or maybe earlier. The film showed lesbians in lingerie spanking each another. The shots looped between a selection of spankings with bare hands, with hairbrushes, with paddles, etc. There was a bar down downstairs as well as upstairs, but it wasn't in use. We stashed as much gear as we could behind it, shoving speakers beneath the wall of liquor bottles.

Nick changed into his running clothes and jogged off. I envied his energy. I wondered why it was that one feels tired after a day of sitting and doing nothing. Perhaps it was just inertia. I took a different strategy for dealing with my drowsiness than Nick, and ordered a beer.

The bar was adorned with all sorts of photographs, all in black & white, all of sultriness and sex acts and bondage. A great deal of it was gay intercourse, though all kinds of intercourse was depicted. Submission and dominance, sodomy, dick-sucking, spanking, ladyboys and the like. On further inspection it looked like these pictures were taken in the very same bar. The lowkey atmosphere of the place contrasted strangely with the raunchiness of the photos.

I stepped out front for a cigarette, where Davide and Doc were dealing with the hotel reservations for the night. Davide was calling to confirm and make sure everything was taken care of. Valerio, the label's booking agent, was the one who'd made the reservation. This was the guy who had booked the insane route from Lyon to Toulouse to Strasbourg. I was thankful someone was double-checking his work.

The promoter stepped outside for a smoke also. Davide spotted him, and asked him to help with making the phone call, since it would be better to have a French-speaker talk to staff. After a short conversation, where the promoter translated what the clerk was telling him for us, we learned that the booking was only for eight, instead of nine.

"Valerio…" Doc groaned, shaking his head.

Between the three of them, they sorted it out. We got an additional room, for a total of nine beds. I was glad to have Davide and Doc working on the problem, but was growing more and more distrustful of the record label.

Back inside, Steve called me over to the merch table.

"The promoter says he'll smoke you out," he said.

I got up as quickly as I'd sat down, and went to find Nick and the others. Nick, Andrea, Luca and I then followed the promoter to a stoop next to the bar. As we smoked, Nick began asking the promoter a question in French. The promoter answered him. Soon, they were chatting away.

"I studied French when I was in college," Luca told me, as we listened to the conversation. "He speaks better French than I do."

"I hadn't realized he spoke it so well," I said.

A middle-aged woman approached us. She was walking her bike alongside her, with groceries stuffed into reusable bags, hanging from the handlebars. She yelled at us in French. Her meaning was clear, even if her words were not, probably equating to something like, "Read the damn sign!"

She pointed at a sign that, as I turned to look at it, clearly said not to sit on the stoop and block the entrance, even to someone who didn't speak the language. We stepped aside, all apologizing, in French of varying degrees of competency. I blurted out, "Sorry, dumb Americans."

The promoter immediately rejected my reflexive, dishonest response – to include all of the others in the same category as myself, as a way of absolving them. He came clean, shaking his head, saying, "Non," a couple times. He spoke to the woman in French, and said that he should have known better. I was suddenly a bit ashamed of myself. I'd been willing to lie on behalf of everyone else, and cloak them under my own plausible deniability. No good Frenchman wants to be identified as an American under any circumstances.

As the group broke off, I found myself apologizing to the promoter. He said not to think of it. I asked him whether Nick's French was any good.

"Yes..." he said, nodding. "He's *very* good."

Three bands performed that night. The volume gradually escalated with each show. The first band, the local act, was a psychedelic rock band. It seemed like they were mostly just jamming. I enjoyed it, for what it was. That tiny basement began to pack in as the night progressed. The best thing about playing in small rooms is that they're easy to fill. The show felt more like a party than a gig out at a venue. They said we could project anything we wanted in their video library while we played. It was almost all older films, in black and white, probably because they were in public domain. I had them put on an old Dracula film while we performed.

At the beginning of the night, my expectations had fallen so far that they might as well have been in the gutter. After a warm reception from a halfway decent crowd, a halfway decent night in merch sales, and a halfway decent reception from the bar staff, I once again felt a glimmer of hope for this tour. It's hard to describe just how low the lows can be when on tour. The night before had put me in a very low place. The slightest encouragement was helpful now.

As we packed up the merch and gear, Davide told us the van had a flat tire. We must have punctured it somewhere on the long drive. I counted us lucky: it could have just as easily blown out on the way there. Davide thankfully had a spare. Penny and a few of the Italians went over in case he needed help. Knowing that I wouldn't be of any help, I remained at one of the tables outside the bar. I smoked another borrowed cigarette and studied the little square. It was late at night, and deathly quiet in the city, except for us musicians, the sounds of metal clanking and echoing against the buildings while they changed the tire.

I rubbed my head to stave off my simmering headache and watched them put on the spare. After the punishing drive, I'd been looking forward to an early bedtime that night. It was another hour or so later that Davide pulled the van to the front of the venue for load-out.

***

In the hotel shower, the ruminating thoughts returned to the fore of my mind. I didn't hate the tour. I tried to keep reminding myself what a privilege it was to be there. By feeling gratitude, I'd been able to center myself in the present. There'd already been some great moments. And yet, every day so far had begun and ended terribly, with a terrible drive wedged in the middle.

It was, again, a problem of communication. Booking was achieved through communication. The tour that the label booked was godawful, and Valerio had failed to communicate with the venues as to what kinds of bands he was booking. Multiple shows had fallen through.

The problem whenever you voice these issues is that people take it as an accusation. Things can become personal really quickly, especially when someone's life passion is involved. Steve, as the one who had suggested taking the record deal with Argonauta, probably wouldn't want to hear my complaints about it, especially after I'd agreed to it. He had sometimes had a tendency to take things personally.

For Steve, *this was all just rock n' roll*. It was that old ethos. There was something admirably Stoic about Steve's approach. For him, the sense of gratitude always outweighed the discomfort. He'd sleep on a bong-water-stained couch, he'd play in the dirtiest dive, he'd play gigs for two drink tickets and a handshake. All in the name of rock n' roll. He was right, in his way. It never hurts to remember how lucky you are, to appreciate the journey, to immerse yourself in the adventure. I understood the appeal of that outlook on life. But it didn't satisfy me. I was overwhelmed in a vague feeling of pointlessness, like coming to the realization that the light I was grasping for at the end of the darkness wasn't really there.

You can't just air grievances, express your dissatisfaction. Groups need a clear and shared picture of both the problems and the solution in order to function. Sometimes you need something concrete to anchor the discussion. We'd agreed to a one-record deal. We had no obligation to them in the future. I didn't want to work with this label ever again. That would make for a good start.

But there was something deeper, some holy mystery to why art drove us to such crazy things – something beyond me and beyond this band and beyond all the specifics of my own situation, which I could not grasp in the darkness, which was unsurprising as I'd grasped for it in abject futility all day. I climbed up to my bunk above my sleeping bandmates. I texted goodnight to my wife, and she texted goodnight to me, and I did my best to feel grateful.

CHAPTER NINE
STRASBOURG - DRESDEN

We had a typical continental breakfast at the hotel. It was a cool morning, and a clear sky. Steve, Andrea, Doc, and I shared a table, ate, and watched the news. The news was bad, as it usually is. We loaded up our luggage and departed. The Rhine divided Strasbourg from Germany. We crossed over the bridge and entered yet another country. Immediately on the opposite side, we stopped for gas and a bathroom break. The foreign food and water had finally taken their toll on my guts. My stomach ached, but I couldn't make myself shit. Eventually, I had to stop trying, as we had a long way to go from there.

There are no tolls to drive on the autobahn itself; instead, the tolls are for the restrooms on the autobahn. You pay a couple coins to a machine to use the restroom, then it gives you a voucher for that amount to use at the shop. Of course, if you claim your fifty cents by purchasing something, you end up spending a lot more than you would have otherwise. There is an upside to this: the restrooms are generally cleaner.

We all bought German beer. It was probably a bit early to start drinking, but it wasn't as if I had anything to do that day, except to be a passenger. Maybe it would make me feel better. The German purity laws for brewing beer are a wonderful thing: the beer really does taste cleaner in Germany, as beer should taste. The lackadaisical attitude towards patrons cracking open a tall bottle of beer in the convenient store was somewhat perplexing, if one thinks of the stereotypes about the Germans. They're supposed to be an orderly people, and I'm certain that they are. But this didn't seem to fit.

Of course, as an American, I grew up in a country with irrational attitudes towards alcohol, perhaps caused by the period of Prohibition and its after-effects. Not to mention our history of religious lunacy. The Germans, for their part, have never been accused of divorcing alcoholism from their religion. For them, quite the opposite is the case. The German monks had to be limited on how many pints of beer they were allowed to drink per day. The Pope himself intervened when it became commonplace to see monks staggering around the monastery during the times of fasting, where the heavy beer offered enough sustenance to make an attractive substitute for water. Or so I had heard.

It was a day of driving, drinking, laughing, conversing, and stopping to piss. The eternal fog of fatigue was finally beginning to dissipate.

VI. Control of Art

Sensation is the bleeding edge of our rational conception of the world. Sense impressions are our only direct perception of reality, however frustrating or limiting we may find such a prospect. The conceptual representation must only follow after the experience of the senses. Likewise, artistic expression is at the forefront of philosophical thought. This holds true in the world-historical sense that we've explored, in which artistic expression preceded linguistic expression; I would argue that it also holds true insofar as artistic expression precedes conceptual expression. Mythological expression is the ignition of concept formation.

Because art stands in this relation to discursive thought in both origin and function – as its precursor – the artistic-creative state itself may seem to be free from any rules. If language is the result of emotive expressions that have become objectified and drained of passion and excitation, then artistic expression may be seen as simply a chaotic roil from which concepts emerge. As such, human societies since time immemorial have attempted to impose rules on art.

The way in which art interjects into our emotional world might be totally different from the way language conveys thought. In language, there is the possibility of expressing that which is incoherent or meaningless. This indicates, almost by definition, a failed attempt at the use of language, since no one will understand the expression. In art, however, symbols and images can be combined in unexpected and seemingly novel ways. Tones, rhythms, consonance and dissonance would seem to have endless possible combinations. It is not required that art convey a definite, logical message, and a work of art can convey a profound emotional meaning without being consciously understood by the audience.

Due to this lack of logical meaning, there is a modern tendency to designate art as open to never-ending interpretation. But if art is a means of genuine communication, that would mean that art carries a meaning, even if not a logical meaning. This would mean that the artist's intent is important, that the correct interpretation of the piece by the audience is important. This would consequently mean that if the audience takes away a completely different interpretation from the one the artist intended, the piece is, in some sense, a failure. Considered in all its implications, this line of reasoning indicates to us that the popular idea of art as completely open to endless interpretation falls apart.

We must remember that the modern artist is unusual. Art in our own time is mostly unbounded by cultural constraints on what kind of expression is permissible. In the days before our open societies, each culture had an agreed-upon lexicon of symbols, and its sanctioned forms of expression. It is an invention of modernity that an artist might work with unconventional symbols, pulling them freely out of his psyche in order to express something personal and individual to himself. This is a relatively new experiment on which we have embarked. The trade-off of the open society is that we allow the artistic forces to run wild among the populace, allowing all sorts of misshapen, warped, postmodern, or abstract forms of expression. Our open societies are therefore what we might call, "Socrates' nightmare". We allow art that is disturbing, ugly, even traumatizing to some people.

If there was any experimentation, it was tightly controlled. This made miscommunication less likely, as the meaning of a given symbol was mutually agreed-upon. In order to enforce this common aesthetic, art had to be regulated and censored. If we take a broad view of what artistic expression constitutes, then we must conclude that for the majority of human civilization, certain forms of art have been made effectively illegal or at least taboo. This is only natural, given art's emergence from the womb of myth and religion. As a rule, we treat new aesthetics like new religions: with hostility.

In Ancient China, there were laws concerning the depictions of dragons in art. The common folk could illustrate dragons with three claws, the nobles could depict them with up to four, and only the emperor could illustrate a five-clawed dragon. This came with similar prescriptions involving the color of the dragons. In Egypt, the pharaohs achieved immortality through art, insofar as their depictions were intended as a form of picture magic in order to secure their destiny in the afterlife. These images were then sealed off from the public, for their defacement would mean very serious consequences for the pharaoh in his afterlife. In the Old Testament, God gives his name as YHWH. The name appears to us in an encoded form in the text, as to prevent the linguistic utterance of the name of God. YHWH forbids the Hebrews from making graven images of deities – an intersection of artistic and religious law.

If we have been paying attention to Usener, this makes the Hebrews an example of a people with a socially advanced view of deity. It is understandable that Moses (and YHWH) would prescribe against aesthetic expressions that would drag the Hebrews backward towards the days of idolatry. The prohibition on portraying personal gods seems to be a feature of late-stage human religiosity. Most are familiar with the absolute ban on depicting Mohammed, especially in Sunni Islam. This is enforced to varying degrees in different Islamic sects. The Jehovah's Witnesses in modern-day America secure exemptions for their children, to keep them from having to say the Pledge of Allegiance in schools. To swear loyalty to an object – in this case, a flag – is unacceptable to them. The ritual swearing of loyalty, the placement of the hand over the heart, the speaking of the oath in unison: this is all *ritual*. A mytho-artistic form of expression. These ritualized aesthetics are not permitted in the Jehovah's Witness way of life: for where the rest of us see a mere habit or convention, the Jehovah's Witness sees the artistic expression of one's devotion to an idol.

These attitudes were not limited to the days of primitive man or to strictly religious considerations. The three-part harmony, or *tertian harmony*, forms a major or minor chord and was central to the structure of western music for hundreds of years. The three-part harmony hearkened to the Holy Trinity: three tones in perfect relation to one another, with no ugly dissonance. The excessive use of the 7th chord by jazz musicians was discouraged, according to the tastes of the musical establishment around the turn of the century. In a 7th chord, a fourth note is introduced to the three-part harmony, creating dissonance that transforms the chord from a mere major or minor intonation. The syncopation of jazz music, which broke up the rhythm in an unorthodox way, also challenged the musical norms of the era in which it emerged.

Similarly, in Islam, the attitudes towards music have evolved. In Sufism, music was honed into a "science of ecstasy," and viewed as a legitimate means of achieving communion with God. In the most hardline sects of Sunni Islam, the only music permitted is a male voice singing the call to prayer. The types of instruments allowed are meticulously regulated – not unlike in Plato's Republic – and musical expression is tightly controlled such that it is only used as a means of worshiping God. The fundamentalists of Islam see the Qawwal devotional music of the Sufis as nothing short of heretical.

Human societies have developed the techniques and aesthetic boundaries of the various artforms over long generations, just as we have cultivated all the various human languages (and the specialized languages and lexicons *within* those languages). The linguistic framework for communication serves the same function as an aesthetic framework: it creates the possibility of greater clarity. Languages developed in order to minimize the number of miscommunications. This is the advantage to a system.

But we may remember from the research of Cassirer that where linguistic communication is concerned with expanding human perception into that which is general and abstract, artistic and religious forms of communication *condense rather than expand*. To achieve greater clarity in an aesthetic system is to condense the aesthetic down to the fewest means of expression possible: to only the central, powerful symbols with a definite meaning. Whereas linguistic clarity can be achieved by greater complexity (although, this is certainly not always the case), aesthetic clarity is achieved by greater simplicity. This is why the Islamic fundamentalists want as few forms of musical expression, until, in the most extreme forms, finally we settle on only one: the lone male voice chanting or singing the call to prayer. The entire musical aesthetic of Islam contained in the single, static, predictable form of expression.

The clarity of the emotional and spiritual states expressed in, for example, the Sistine Chapel, is the result of an aesthetic system that was developed and honed within Roman Catholicism, culminating in the Renaissance. Thus, while we might object today to such social attitudes as restrictions on musical composition, we nevertheless recognize that it is through such boundaries that the nature of the project becomes directed and focused, and successive generations of work can build upon one another.

Control of art therefore begins with categorization: by identifying the type of emotional resonance caused by different types of art, different representations or metaphors. A canonical aesthetic is a later development in society: I believe that such a thing will only arise once language, a division of labor, and theology have all come into existence. In other words, in a society that has a conception of morality and hierarchy. Human cultures categorize the various means of expression common to their respective societies. Within these categorizations, certain features of artistic expression are recognized and placed in relationship to one another. This is what is occurring when certain colors are assigned to different castes of society, as we discussed earlier, or when certain musical tones are correlated to emotional states.

In Han China, for example, the five tones of the zither could be correlated with the five elements, five colors, five flavors, and five emotional states. In Damascus during the Golden Age of Islam, the four strings of the lute (*al'oud*) were correlated by the Damascan Aristotelians with the four elements, with the phases of the moon, and with different emotional states.

The thin string was like fire, like the heat of passion; the thick string was like earth, heavy and somber. In Plato's Republic, Socrates and Glaucon discuss the various effects that different musical modes have on people, and which emotional states they conjure. The Ionian and forms of the Lydian mode are described as "languid" – suitable for listening during relaxation or drinking. The Extreme and Mixed Lydian are associated with dirges and lamentations. Meanwhile, the Dorian and Phrygian modes are suggested to be appropriate for stirring courage or conveying stateliness and dignity. It is only the last two modes, for example, that Socrates would allow for the soldiers in his ideal republic.

This again raises the issue of artistic censorship. Socrates, in his vision for the perfect state, outlines the only art that shall be allowed: art that is beautiful and produced by the finest technique, and thus which speaks to the ingenuity and virtue of man. His requirements follow naturally from the idea that artistic expression transmits emotional states. Our aesthetic outlook is shaped by where we find joy, what we aspire to, what we find beautiful. The art that people absorb must therefore only radiate emotions that are appropriate to the person, or else they'll be subjected to confusing and potentially dangerous feelings. In the case of dirge and laments, for example, Socrates thinks *no one* should listen to them. In the Socratic view, music that makes you feel melancholic or despondent isn't good for anyone. To Socrates, every member of society must endlessly strive for goodness. This does not mean goodness in a benign sense, but to actively shape one's mind with knowledge and discipline. Nothing short of this is acceptable for the ideal society. Art must be strictly managed, in order to push human development in that direction. Socrates reveals to us why an aesthetic system is formed and how it stands in relation to human ethical questions.

Socrates: "Good literature... and good music, beauty of form and good rhythm all depend on goodness of character... Are not these things which our young men must pursue, if they are to perform their function in life properly? The graphic arts are full of the same qualities as the related crafts, weaving and embroidery, architecture and the manufacture of all kinds...

For in all of them we find beauty and ugliness. And ugliness of form and bad rhythm and disharmony are akin to poor-quality expression and character, and their opposites are akin to and represent good character and discipline."

We moderns react to Socrates with offense. We feel a sense of alterity with respect to such antiquated moralities wherever we encounter them. We must again keep in mind that, in the grand scheme of things, we are the exception, and that Socrates is the rule. Art has always been a social concern, and socially regulated, for it is nothing less than the power to transfer emotional states. Socrates would agree with the axiom put forward by Wittgenstein in his Tractatus: "Every aesthetic is an ethic."

***

It was bleak and rainy by late morning, and the drive was long enough that we still found ourselves falling into afternoon naps as we proceeded. Outside, the white mists clung tenaciously to the black, pine forest canopies. We pulled into a rest stop and stepped out into the subtle downpour. No diner, shop, or services. Just the bathrooms in a little building, just off the highway, overlooking the black-green clusters of trees. One of the guys in the front seats really had to piss, and there was a bunch of shuffling around as people climbed out. I took advantage of the opportunity to rid myself of the afternoon's beer. I had to rouse Penny and Steve and climb over them. Nick got out too.

Nick and I stood in the light drizzle for a few moments while we waited for the restroom.

"Make any more progress with Schopenhauer?" he asked.

"It's a struggle. I don't know if I'm going to finish it."

"That's a shame," Nick said.

"Maybe I'll keep trying," I said. "A bleak, dreary German. While driving through bleak, dreary Germany…"

We shipped out promptly – no Italian time that day. The traffic was slow, and we had many hours to go. But at least the schedule today seemed doable. Perhaps we would actually arrive on time today.

***

The word *censor* itself reveals much. It has a Latin root, and dates from the period of the Roman Republic, where it denoted a magisterial office. The office of Censor did not bear the negative connotation that the word "censor" would carry today. The Censor was associated with the goodness of the community, and was so named because the main duty of the office was to conduct the census. While the census was among the most sacred of their duties, their other jobs included administration of some public finances, as well as the job of enforcing public morality. It is their role as state-sanctioned moralists that gave the word censorship its connotation that echoes down to us through the ages.

The public enforcement of morality by the Censor could mean anything from pressuring bachelors who were of marriage age to get married, admonishing fathers who mistreated their families, or even discouraging luxurious spending. The Censor was tasked with making sure that the rich merchants, for example, did not spend beyond their station in society, and register offenses against those who spent too lavishly.

The term "censorship" still indicates the attempt to impose one's morality on others' forms of expression. This is exactly what the Censor did in the Roman Republic, although, unlike today, the community wholeheartedly supported them in this. The Censor was a valued and respected official who took care of enforcing social mores. The ancients did not generally hold the same ideas as we do about individual sovereignty. The personal choice of the individual citizen was considered to affect the morality of the entire community. If one silk merchant starts displaying gratuitous wealth, he may encourage his fellow businessmen to engage in the same kind of behavior. In time, a whole community could become obsessed with vanity and displays of wealth. This will have a ripple effect, and the people will become avaricious and dishonest.

The social psychologists might agree with the Romans' assessment of the situation, if not their solutions. A trait that sets human beings apart from other primates, as von Hippel indicates, is our hyper-imitative tendency. It is fashionable to consider our moral values to be discovered on one's own, through reason and self-reflection. In reality, what people value is *what other people value*. We determine what has worth, in practical and economic terms as well as moral, by the social consensus. It is through the example of others that people decide what to pursue in life.

It is from this perspective that the office of Censor arises. The ancient Roman sees every person as an individual third, a member of a family second, and as a citizen first. To be a citizen means to be a constituent part of the community. Every act of one part can influence the whole, ever so slightly.

We are allergic to calls for censorship in America because of the pluralistic foundation of our society. There is no state-sanctioned morality and no national religion; there is no place for Censors pushing the society in one moral direction or another. Our society is not designed to have a cohesive, moral code that all the citizens agree with. We tend to take it for granted that freedom of expression is its own good, an end unto itself. In the ancient world, however, the value of the expression itself is often seen as secondary to the emotional and moral effect of the expression.

Censorship in the modern sense is less indicative of simple moralism, and more so of banning artistic expression, or the silencing of journalists. The Roman Censor did not really engage in censorship in this sense of the word. The Roman Censor was more akin to a literal morality police, in charge of regulating behavior rather than art. There was one important exception, however: actors were penalized by the Censors if they remained too long in such a "disreputable" trade. Drama was enjoyed by the masses, but the actors and dramatists were distrusted and kept in a state of low social status.

The Censors therefore antagonized those who created the most popular form of art among the Roman plebeians. Drama is very effective for political and social commentary. When something is genuinely funny, laughter is automatic and spontaneous. If a leader is made to look absurd in a way that is comical to the audience, the audience will laugh, even if involuntarily.

When a whole crowd of people laughs, the individuals in that crowd are primed by their social instinct to change their perception of the object of their laughter. In an empire with an all-powerful and divine state, the dramatist is naturally made into a figure of ill repute.

The Catholic Church became the moral authority of Europe after the fall of Rome. There was never an equivalent office to the Censor in post-Roman Europe, but the closest thing was the priest. The artistic intolerance of the Church was nothing new, but simply a continuation of the existing tradition. The Sistine Chapel, which we considered before, is now universally celebrated among Catholics. But during Michelangelo's life, he earned the ire of many prominent members of the Church for one of the frescoes of the Sistine: The Last Judgment.

The complaint was the "excessive" amount of nudity. Not the least of Michelangelo's critics was the Pope himself. The poet Pietro Aretino wrote to Michelangelo, "Is it possible that you, so divine that you do not deign to consort with men, have done such a thing in the highest temple of God? Above the first altar of Jesus? Not even in the brothel are there such scenes as yours..." Even this treasure of Christian art was not narrow enough in its aesthetic to satisfy the moralists of the day.

The censorship of the Catholic Church was far-reaching. Galileo's work was suppressed. Theophile de Viau was imprisoned and burned in effigy, his poems destroyed. Descartes' philosophy was placed on Church's official Index of Prohibited Books – the main implement of intellectual censorship in Catholic Europe. This was not limited to burning texts: plenty of people were put to the flame as well: Giordano Bruno, Dr. Servetus, the victims of Sir Thomas Moore who were burned for reading the Bible in English. Countless others.

I should clarify at this point that, if we are to mention again that most moderns would have looked on in horror at all this – I am of the same temperament. All the same, it is essential to make an earnest attempt at occupying the perspective of the censorious people of ages past. We must endeavor to understand how they saw art, and to understand why they would have wanted to suppress or control artistic expression. We are all familiar with the notion of a "dangerous idea". We should consider that artistic censorship is concerned with not just dangerous ideas – for ideas are among the least dangerous forces influenced by art – but dangerous feelings, dangerous perceptions, dangerous morals, dangerous stories, dangerous metaphors. The kind of thing that can reshape your understanding of reality.

Today's artist, liberated from the control of art, must still perform this task of culling – this is the work of editing, revising, rehearsal, sketchwork, a million ripped out pages and crossed-out phrases, and other artistic abortions. We censor our own expressions, as artists. To the modern artist, it is not for the sake of the Church that he scraps a song, or starts again from scratch on his painting. He is charged with forging his own moral and aesthetic standards.

But this raises a new series of questions. If art is a collective concern, a communal project, a product of the human social life – then where does the atomization of our aesthetic systems lead? If the artists are not all working towards the same project – or perhaps not towards any goal at all, will this undermine our collective artistic development? Can our modes of expression still find emotional resonance even when there is no shared symbolism, no shared system of values, no shared goal? Are there forms of artistic communication so strong that they cut across all such boundaries, aesthetic, cultural, or religious? To speak to every heart?

***

We pushed two plastic, circular tables close together and all nine of us sat together. We sat close to the window – the whole wall was a windowpane, actually. I broke with my vegetarian leanings again and had a currywurst and some potatoes, carrots, and a beer. Outside, there was the grassy patio area, autos and trucks occasionally zooming past on the highway, and the walls of pine forest that were thrust up on all sides of the signs of civilization... the road, the parking lot, the roadside restaurant. We were surrounded by trees.

After this brief reprieve from the packed highways, we hit traffic once again. The day before, we'd initially been excited to get onto roads that weren't managed as tollways, because of the heavy financial burden they'd caused us so far. As the day progressed, we came to miss the fast, efficient tollways of Italy. Long lines of semis, all forced into the right lane, seemingly moved not at all as the autos crept by them at stop-and-go speeds. Nothing could be as bad as the thirteen hours in the van we'd done yesterday. Or so I told myself.

We began to pick up speed, crossing into rural country again. I watched the little cabins and cottages on the hillsides pass us by, hemmed in by thickets, chimneys puffing away – or rather, I watched as we passed them by. Another traffic jam. Hours added onto the journey. We weren't even going our top speed of 80 km/hr. Before long, it was overcast again, and we drove into more rain.

My phone rang, rousing me out of sleep. It was Amberly. Back in Austin, it was around eight AM or so.

"I'm noticing some weird charges on your card," she said. "Did you use an ATM on seventh street any time recently?"

"Seventh street?" I asked. "No."

She went on to list a few more places – some convenient stores, and a bar.

"No, I didn't do any of those."

"Are you sure?"

"When are they from?"

"The first one was on the 11th," she said.

"I was in Italy on the 11th."

She called the bank, then called me about ten minutes later.

"They said the only way they can do anything is if you cancel the card," she said. "You have to file a claim, and that means they have to cancel it. I don't know what to do... maybe we can have them send the new one to an address where you'll be?"

"No..." I said. "No, I don't think that's a good idea. It would have to get there no sooner and no later than the exact day we'd be at the address... We could get cleaned out if someone has our account info and we don't cancel it. That's how they work, the small charges are only a test."

"Okay. The bank said you have to be the one to do it. I tried to file the claim, so they should have some record of it... but you have to call them. I'll send you the number... This is such bullshit..."

We decided she'd wire money to Steve, who would in turn pull out money from the ATM and give me the cash. I'd lose a certain amount to Venmo, and to the exchange rate, and to the ATM fees... but at least I'd have money.

I stared out the window at the fields of windmills, their blades turning steadily in the distance. I hated this feeling. I didn't want to be dependent on someone else. I didn't want to have to ask Steve for money every time I needed it. And what if something went wrong? The mind of the anxious person thinks that every time something can go wrong, it will go wrong. I'm always aware of the utter unfairness and indifference of nature. What was it like for the people of old, Christian Europe, living in the magical reality of Christian metaphysics? What was it like to walk the earth thinking that your fate is in the hands of something indescribably powerful and loving? It must have been far less stressful.

CHAPTER TEN
DRESDEN

Traffic in the right lane was frozen in place, but a gap somehow opened up between all the semis, and Davide managed to sneak in. Penny climbed to his feet and popped open the door, wet wipes in hand, and stepped out into the downpour. He climbed up onto the guardrail and began the attempt at taking a shit. This is one of the realities of touring, or any lifestyle in which you travel every single day: you have to deal with nature's call, whether you're ready or not.

We spent at least five minutes at a dead stop. Traffic didn't move at all for the whole effort. Maybe we inched forward one or two times. Penny walked back over to the van, which was more or less where it was when he'd left it. Davide maneuvered out of the impossibly slow right lane, and we began crawling along again.

My hand scribbled, in between swigs of Kolsch. Andrea was saying something, leaning over the seat to speak to me. I looked up from my notes. There was an open, plastic package in his hands. I thanked him, and took a handful of almonds.

VII. Chemistry of Concepts and Feelings

Nietzsche was a critic of Socrates. He dared to pose the question of whether Socrates was guilty of the charge levied by the Athenians. Perhaps he did corrupt the youth after all. Socrates' student, Plato, whom Nietzsche called one of the jewels of antiquity, went on to propound a philosophy which designated the world of sense experience as unreal – holding only the world of abstract, general concepts to be real: the world of The Forms. How could Plato have made such a terrible mistake if not corrupted by Socrates? If Socrates truly was guilty of the crime, Nietzsche wondered if this actually justified his punishment. As such, he wrote, in *Beyond Good and Evil*, "Did he deserve his hemlock?" It's hard to imagine a more scathing remark than that.

Nietzsche expressed great admiration for Socrates in spite of his criticism of him. Even on the issue of art, where he probably had the most severe criticism to dish out, he found agreement with Socrates – in one respect. Both men had a certain degree of distrust towards poets and artists. Socrates repudiated the divine madness of artistic inspiration as irrational. But Nietzsche thought the Dionysian impulse was healthy and natural. He grew to become enamored with the figure of Dionysus, and thought that the wild, pagan strength of the ancients was lacking from modern culture. Thus, Nietzsche's problem with artists was far from the concern that they undermined the detached logic of the Socratics.

Nietzsche criticizes the artist for a different reason, but one in which he finds agreement with Socrates' categorization of the artist as the same kind of person as the oracular priest. Artists are backward-facing: to Nietzsche, they belong with the priests and the religious types. Even though the artistic need for emotional expression is real and natural, we've already examined how art is used to transmit religious ideas. This makes the artist a bridge between modernity and the ancient world: of gods, spirits and religious excitement. If it is from human imagination and creativity that all mythology springs, as Nietzsche argues, then art must be regarded as a dangerous force. Nietzsche and Socrates assert this link between art and religion.

"Art raises its head where religions decline," Nietzsche writes in *Human, All Too Human*. "It takes over a number of feelings and moods produced by religion, clasps them to its heart, and then becomes itself deeper, more soulful, so that it is able to communicate exaltation and enthusiasm."

Those with a magical or supernatural view of the world may have interpreted their dreams, fantasies, and emotional states as messages from higher powers in ages past. In modernity, we recognize that these experiences have a physiological origin. But to the naïve artists and oracular priests, these physiological experiences were elevated to metaphysical importance.

These tendencies in thought have not fully died. We all know someone who has taken an interest in astrology, or fortune-telling. The urge to interpret our own reality in a creative, wondrous, or endearing manner can easily override our desire to approach the world logically. The emotional power of art lends itself to this irrationality. The fact that we think of emotions as naturally occurring, rather than as spirit possession, does nothing to interrupt the experience of emotional resonance. Nietzsche: "However much one thinks he has lost the habit of religion, he has not lost it to the degree that he would not enjoy encountering religious feelings and moods without any conceptual content as, for example, in music."

So far, I have implicitly treated artistic expression as though it requires *authenticity*: meaning that artistic expression is presumed by definition to mean a genuine expression. To Nietzsche, on the other hand, the degree to which something is expressed artistically is the degree to which it is falsified. This does not mean that all art is a "lie," per se. Nietzsche's allegation is that art always manifests itself in *incompleteness*.

The philosopher is interested in using reason to get to the truth, and the artists have their truths. But the artist's truths are not reasonable. Art exists beyond the rational-discursive. Art aims at a morality, or the transmission of a feeling: this follows from a value judgment, something which cannot be rationally derived. Art's function is to condense our attention into the sole area of its own aims – and to ignore everything else. Every artistic decision – to place this figure in the foreground and that one in the background, to use light colors or dark colors, to focus on this detail or exclude it – is an alteration to objective reality. Concerning poetry, for example, Nietzsche writes: "Meter lays a gauze over reality; it occasions some artificiality of speech and impurity of thinking; through the shadow that it throws over thought, it sometimes conceals, sometimes emphasizes."

By interpreting, by giving half-truths, the artist thereby lies to us. "When it comes to recognizing truths," he argues, "the artist has a weaker morality than the thinker; on no account does he want his brilliant, profound interpretations of life to be taken from him..." Nietzsche argued that even the most whole-hearted attempts at honestly representing the world, Greek tragedy for instance, have still been deceptions. Throughout *Human, All Too Human*, he attacks the view that dramatic characters ever depict a real personality. In order to create a character for the theater, film, or television, we have to exaggerate character traits. We have to conceal all of those disparate elements of real human personalities that don't fit or don't make sense, or which would confuse the audience. Real people are not consistent, easily comprehensible expressions of one or two strong traits – but this is how we portray them as characters. The difference between a fictional character and a real person is, to Nietzsche, as stark as the difference between a two-dimensional image of a person and a real, flesh-and-blood human being.

This may seem like it is a predominantly negative view of the artist. But Nietzsche resisted moralism. He saw great potential in the artist's ability for emotional resonance. The artist doesn't have to remain backward-facing. In the course of history, the artist departed from the moral values propounded by religion in order to determine for themselves what was aesthetically valuable. Nietzsche argues that the artist must simply go further, and stop dipping his toes into superstition and romanticism. Nietzsche had a great love for the arts, in fact, and especially music. He wrote musical compositions himself; in one of his letters, he writes that he considers his philosophy the most musical that had ever been produced (though also admitted that he'd never been a very successful musician). He quotes Goethe, who had remarked that dramatic poetry was really the only thing that justified life, and that without it, life would be "of no use at all."

Nietzsche praised both the artist and the philosopher in his essays the *Untimely Meditations*, suggesting that "nature made her one leap in creating them." Though he was more of the philosophical type than the artistic type, he intended to infuse his philosophical work with artistry. For better or for worse, he argued that man was an indelibly irrational and passionate animal.

It was exactly man's passionate and creative side that philosophy often failed to account for in tackling the deep questions of mankind.

In Nietzsche's view, Socrates, Plato, and their successors – the Platonists, the later Stoics, and especially the Christians – all wanted mankind to be something other than it is. These figures preached a morality that was "anti-nature," because it condemned man's animal origins and praised only his intellect. The bedrock philosophies of Western society wanted to make mankind into a rational animal. They wished to separate mind from body, and reason from the passions.

Meanwhile, religion remained as the great, emotional safety-valve for the western heart. The value of art to society was formerly tied therefore to the value of religion. The religious project for man, the artistic project for man, and the philosophical project for man have their similarity in this respect – the redirection of passions, and thus the elevation of the mind, or the spirit, above the impulses.

One reason aesthetics finds itself such a lonely and disagreeable branch of philosophy, therefore, is the decline of religion, and the transition to secularism we are now undergoing in the West. Religion was the framework for expressing this divine madness and for interpreting and understanding these experiences. Religion once managed what we now call the artistic half of the human psyche. When we consider the value or purpose of art in a post-religion mindset, we find ourselves, like Socrates and Nietzsche, setting philosophy and art in opposition.

The censorship of art and self-expression is par for the course in authoritarian regimes; this is widely known and indisputable. Furthermore, we can see that the same regimes unfailingly end up devoting their efforts to disseminating their own aesthetic, in the form of propaganda. There is a political motive behind propaganda, yes. But there is an aesthetic agenda as well in every propagandistic endeavor.

Both the fascist and communist revolutions of the early 20th century were undertaken by men who were largely secular or outright atheistic in their mindset (even if, in the case of fascism, they publicly supported religion and national traditions). With these sweeping transformations of social and political life, an aesthetic transformation always followed. Brutalism, the rejection of ostentation, the heroic revolutionary aesthetic portrayals of communist leaders, and so on. The amount of Buddhist religious art that was destroyed in the Maoist revolution is beyond comprehension. Meanwhile, Mao's wife, Jiang Qing, famously rewrote the traditional operas of China into revolutionary plays – understanding, quite in contradiction to dialectical materialism, that the artistic substratum of the culture had to be changed in order to alter the material reality of the society.

Nietzsche recognized this truth: every political power implicitly recognizes the immense power of art. Revolutionaries and reactionaries alike therefore play out an aesthetic war: a battle of sentiment which is parallel to the often-invoked "battle of ideas." A propaganda film is not intended to sway audiences on a cognitive level with dispassionate, detached logic. Rather, all propaganda is the weaponization of the artistic power of emotional resonance. Goebbels, propaganda minister of the Nazis, famously stated that he never wished to produce films with the party-line in the forefront – the goal was to create compelling stories with the propaganda embedded in the background. The audience absorbs the propaganda without even realizing that this is what they're watching, which makes them passive receptors rather than conscious critics. This is emotional resonance as consciously harnessed by the cynical intellect, and the example again reinforces the view of art's irrational character. Edward Bernays, in the wake of Freud's insights about the subconscious feelings as more influential on our behavior than our conscious rationalizations, harnessed this power for the sake of advertising. To this day, the technique of the advertiser is not to convince the consumer that it is reasonable to buy their product. Instead, like Bernays, they use images, signifiers, and symbolism, leading the consumer to form an emotional association with the product.

It is this element, of the conscious manipulation of emotional resonance by the intellect, that leads us to designate a work of art propaganda, or to call it dishonest, an imitation, or inauthentic. Calculated thinking is poisonous to art. When the thinking subject consciously decides to manipulate their artistic impulses, in order to express creative impulses that they do not actually feel compelled to express, but which they express for instrumental or manipulative purposes, what do we have? Do we still have "art"?

This is my disagreement with Nietzsche: that we are now unable to make such a distinction. If we accept the Nietzschean view, we should not expect art to be authentic in the first place. Art is deception. From this perspective, it is tempting to say that all art is propaganda. It would only be a matter of degrees.

Nietzsche's solution is the unification of science and art. He wrote of a "science *of* art," wherein one's creative drives could be harnessed in order to channel the old religious feelings and moods into more productive directions. The priests of world religions once served this function, but their aesthetic systems were based on values that we now realize were errors. To the priest, all value was to be found in a world beyond. First and foremost, Nietzsche hoped for an art that affirms this world, this life, and nature in both its cruelty and beauty.

What we need now, Nietzsche says, is something that has only recently become possible: "a *chemistry* of moral, religious, aesthetic ideas and feelings, a chemistry of all those impulses that we ourselves experience in the great and small interactions of culture and society, indeed even in solitude."

The artist is a sort of proto-chemist of feelings – an alchemist, if you will. The philosopher is much the same. One has remained in his domain of feelings, and the other has entered the domain of concepts. But this new chemistry of concepts and feelings would encompass both. The name Nietzsche finally settled on for this project was *the gay science*: the title of one of his books. Nietzsche got this name from *gaya scienza*, the term used to designate the occupation of the Provençal troubadours. These were true Renaissance men, traveling knight-poets who spoke many languages and wandered through many lands.

Philosophers before Nietzsche, as we have described, usually denigrated the emotional domain of the human psyche. This is the long mark of Socrates on philosophy. Emotive expression, after all, can lead to the manifestation of culturally prohibited feelings and desires, such as the expression of raw lust or violent anger. Emotions must always remain sublimated, pinned beneath man's reason: the passions had to be excised for the sake of the community and its moral code.

This is the reason for which aesthetic restrictions existed, and why artistic expression had been bound to religious expression in ages past. The power over a community must control its emotive world: and to control the emotive world of the community, some expressions must be forbidden. Nietzsche recognized that the priest has always been useful in fulfilling this function. In the same essay in which he praises artists and philosophers as the highest type of individual, he admits that "the saint" was another such extraordinary figure. In spite of Nietzsche's diagnosis of the Christian mindset of Europe as fundamentally sick, and the values of the priest as nihilistic, the self-mastery of the saint was nevertheless a useful example for imparting the teaching of self-control to the people. This was necessary for the project of civilization.

Mankind's desire to become emancipated was often driven, in the deepest recesses of the unconscious mind, by some bestial instinct or passion's desire to break free from cultural or civil constraints and indulge itself. Nietzsche was something of a conservative on the topic of art. He worried about the breakdown of the classical education, of discipline in the academy, of the restraint and observance of stylistic or aesthetic norms. Art would then degenerate from the elevated form it had reached in the course of civilization.

In a passage called "The desensualization of higher art," Nietzsche writes, "Because the artistic development of modern music has forced the intellect to undergo an extraordinary training, our ears have become increasingly intellectual.... All our senses have in fact become somewhat dulled because we always enquire after the reason, what 'it means' and no longer what 'it is'.... What is the consequence of all this? The more the eye and ear are capable of thought, the more they reach the boundary line where they become asensual. Joy is transferred to the brain; the sense organs themselves become dull and weak. More and more, the symbolic replaces that which exists – and so, as surely as on any other path, we arrive along this one at barbarism."

This passage describes what Nietzsche called a "twofold trend in musical development." He considers one group, whom we might call the upper class, with "higher, more delicate pretensions, ever more attuned to 'what [art] means.'" He contrasts the upper class with "the vast majority, which each year is becoming ever more incapable of understanding meaning" and therefore, "learning to reach with increasing pleasure for that which is intrinsically ugly and repulsive, that is, the basely sensual."

The "end of art" is that it is eventually split in twain by the centrifugal forces Nietzsche identifies. On the one hand it deals in deception, irrationality and the passions. But because art is powerful, we became practiced in using its power. Consequently, we have used art to tame these elements of the human psyche, make them symbolic, and force passions to obey laws. Art can even deprive these forces of the metaphysical power they once possessed.

The average person will naturally be attracted to the sensuous experience, that makes the focus of one's immediate attention seem like a thing of the highest significance. The people at large enjoy being struck with encounters of momentary gods. The emotional high of the experience is what most find enjoyable in art: this is to say, *the entertainment value*. The sensation; the novelty.

The "higher culture", on the other hand, will naturally be attracted to the intellectual side of art. The intellect has increasingly become intertwined with art as we have developed our artistic techniques. Intellect plays more of a role in making art when we incorporate narrative, symbolism and subtext, and create forms of art that lend themselves to intellectual play. Both developments trouble Nietzsche, because he believes that they are two different roads to barbarism. But that needn't concern us here.

What is of interest is how our broader inquiry therefore relates to Nietzsche's study of Dionysus and Apollo. To the extent that the total emotional captivation that occurs during the 'momentary god experience' annihilates the subject's attention for every other phenomenon (other than the immediate sensory and emotional experience), the base, sensory enjoyment of art correlates with the principle of dissolution. We may recognize this type of dissolutionist art as Dionysian, and find that the general populace tends to use art for this purpose. Apollo, and the *principium individuationis*, can be correlated with higher art. The Dionysian, meanwhile, existed in those rites and festivals in which all gathered as one: hierarchies are forgotten, and all are simply Greeks. The Dionysian exists in the rustic worship of the god Pan. Nietzsche argued that the pinnacle of Greek art was reached when both these forces were intertwined: the sunlike eye of Apollo, which draws boundaries and holds things at a distance, and the wild, emotional reveries of Dionysus, which makes all one and breaks all concepts into dust. Around the time when Socrates came along, the two began to split. What followed was Alexandrian Greece, in which art became intellectual and self-referential. The period was concerned more with categorizing and responding to what came before, rather than creativity.

In Nietzsche's day, he railed against the opera for its overly intellectual character. In our own time, we can see purely technical or intellectual artistry on Broadway, in the artform of dance, in the films of our greatest directors. Though the expression of feeling is still the fundamental aspect of all that which is *artistic* in film, the medium is overwhelmingly intellectual in many respects, and invites us to self-reflect, to ponder deep issues, to consider our own relationship to concepts and feelings portrayed in the work. Conversely, we might consider most forms of modern pop music – designed to entice people to lose themselves in sensuality and dance. In modern art we once again see our pathological relationship between head and heart.

***

It was hours later that we reached Dresden. We were late yet again. The sun was just starting to set. The town itself seemed remarkably dour. Everything was gray that evening. I'm not certain if it was the weather or the people. We pulled into a gravel parking lot beside the covered patio. It was a DIY spot called Chemiefabrick. It stood in the shadow of a dreary-looking Catholic church, tucked away in some quiet corner of Dresden. The venue didn't look like much from the outside. It appeared as what I would typically think of as a wooden shack.

Now that I had cell service, I called the bank. The rate was a dollar a minute. After they took my call, they put me on hold almost immediately.

After a few agonizing minutes passed, as I paced back and forth in the cold mist of the patio area, I was finally put on the line with a call center worker. She spoke like someone following a script.

"We need to verify your identity," she eventually said. "Can you list some charges from the past few days?"

"Legitimate charges?"

"Yes."

"Umm..." suddenly my mind was blank. "The grocery store the day before we left... the charges at Autogrill, outside Milan, in Italy...."

"Mmm, nope. Not seeing those."

I suppose that not all of the recent charges had come through. For every charge that she accepted as a legitimate charge, there were two that she did not. She started giving me hints. It felt awkward. Eventually, I hit on enough charges for her liking, and the woman was satisfied.

"Mmm-hmm," she murmured. "That should do it. Can I put you on hold for just a little while longer?"

"I'm calling internationally," I said. "I'm paying a dollar a minute, here..."

"I'll try to keep it as brief as possible."

I paced around the firepit. It was nothing but wet ashes. The tiniest flecks of rain misted down onto me. It was finally cold enough to warrant grabbing the hoodie. I walked across the parking lot to retrieve it from the van, gravel crunching under foot. Time passes slowly when you are paying for every second of it. Fuck, it was locked already. I'd have to hunt down Davide for the keys.

Finally, she got back to me.

"So, we're going to cancel your card. But we're sending a new one immediately. I understand you're traveling?"

"Yeah, but..." I paused, struggling to find the words. "I'm in a different place every day. I'm in Germany, but I'll be in Denmark tomorrow." She didn't respond. "So, it's too much trouble to send it."

"You don't want a new card?"

"Just send it to my home address."

She still didn't seem to understand the situation, but said, "Alright."

The inside of Chemiefabrick told a different story from its outer façade. It was much larger from the inside than it had first appeared. There was one side with a bar, some nooks with booths, and the restrooms. On the other side was the stage. It looked like you could fit hundreds in the room. I doubted that would be the case on a Wednesday night. The sight of the venue from the outside and the general mood of Dresden had discouraged me. But the sound system looked impressive. It was the first real sound system of the tour, in fact; the first real stage of the tour.

We were late to the show yet again, and the other band was already soundchecking as I walked in. It was another touring band out of America, called High Reeper. They were a fairly popular stoner metal band from Philadelphia. We'd played in their city five or six times, but never yet shared a stage with them. Funny that we were finally crossing paths in Dresden of all places.

As they soundchecked, I noticed the wall of Orange half stacks behind them. There was no sense in us loading all of our amps and speakers inside when we'd be taking the stage after them. But mostly, I just wanted to play on Orange amps. I hurried over to Steve, who was leaning against the bar, watching them.

"You think we could use their backline tonight?"

"I already talked to 'em," Steve said, grinning. "Since we're late anyway, everyone is cool with us sharing a backline. Will make things run smoother."

Steve seemed to hit it off with every musician or band that he met. The night was looking up. When the boys from High Reeper spotted Davide, they immediately recognized him. One of them called to him by name as they climbed down from the stage, a smile coming across his face. "What are you doing here?"

"I'm driving these guys," he said, gesturing to us.

"It's been a month already?"

High Reeper had played in Pescara at the start of their tour. Everyone knew Davide, it seemed.

We all got a free meal from the vegan kitchen next door. The restaurant, as well as the venue, was community-run and subsidized by the local government. Steve and I went over to get some subsidized grub. Zach, the vocalist from High Reeper joined us. We found a high table where we could eat and stand at the same time, and put back a few German beers while waiting on our noodles. Mine came with pesto, they both chose the vegan goulash. To my surprise, I thought I'd maybe chosen wrongly once the food came: the goulash looked delicious.

Both our bands had spent a good amount of time on the road, though they had years of experience in Europe. We talked about Philly, and about Austin. It's especially fun to talk to other people who know what it's like to tour, or to share stories about home with a stranger in a foreign land who happens to have been there. I don't really remember anything specific about the conversation, just the feeling of warmth and friendship, the familiarity of a fellow traveler. Meeting another cultist, journeying on their own Quixotic adventure, the recognition that we all followed the same crazy way of life.

***

Nietzsche's view of the "splitting of art" brings to mind an unexpected connection: Robert Pirsig, and his metaphysics of Quality. He puts forward his concept of Quality in his book, *Zen and the Art of Motorcycle Maintenance*. For our purposes, however, we find an investigation of moral values contained in the sequel, *Lila*, which will be of great usefulness in our own inquiry.

Pirsig gives a basis of human morality in which the concept of Quality is the source of all moral value. To Pirsig, all things that are truly valuable to human beings compel some sort of action – either to preserve them, or to acquire them. This is an expression of value prior to and independent of our conscious ideas about it. What is meant by "Quality", however, varies depending on the subject and the level of resolution at which the subject is operating. To speak in more concrete terms, Pirsig describes how the evolutionary morality, driven by survival of the fittest, is what has produced all of the biological quality that exists. But the evolutionary morality is not suited for producing social quality – which is why our social mores do not imitate the law of the jungle, and why Social Darwinist, self-liquidating societies are the exception and not the rule.

What makes one level of quality higher than another is its ability to improve on the lower rungs of the ladder. Thus, above biological quality is social quality, and above social quality is intellectual quality. This is because intellectual quality allows us to correct for the errors and missteps of traditional ideas and moral prejudices.

Pirsig: "If an established social structure is not seriously threatened by a criminal... there is no moral justification for killing him. What makes killing him immoral is not just a biological organism. He is not even just a defective unit of society. Whenever you kill a human being you are killing a source of thought, too. A human being is a collection of ideas, and these ideas take moral precedence over a society. Ideas are patterns of value. They are at a higher level of evolution than social patterns of value. Just as it is more moral for a doctor to kill a germ than a patient, so it is more moral for an idea to kill a society than it is for a society to kill an idea."

Nietzsche wouldn't have had much patience for Pirsig's moral notions, but where these two align is in their diagnosis of the course of human expression. Pirsig's assessment of the Hippie Movement of the American sixties is not the usual account – that these were wild, carefree teenagers rebelling against the stuck-up, traditional morality. Rather, Pirsig argues that the intellectuals of the early 20th century had already overcome the Victorian morality of yesteryear. The 20th century types who preceded the Hippie Movement were not Victorian traditionalists: they were analytical, pragmatic, and pluralistic in their outlook. They were a generation absorbed with messianic notions of technocratic planning, and Wilsonian optimism. *This* was the generation the Hippies rejected: *not* the Victorians, who were the grandparents and great-grandparents of the Hippie generation, and whose morality had long since been overthrown by the time the Hippies got there.

It is as if we're stuck imagining that the culture we're rebelling against is always the Victorian culture, because it represented itself as the ur-culture of the English-speaking world. The Victorian culture was a social morality *par excellence*, which openly and proudly suppressed biological quality:

sexual feeling or uncontrolled emotion. All must be buried beneath decency and etiquette. Further, the Victorians resisted the intellectual criticism of their moral beliefs. Pirsig asserts that, because intellectual quality is of a higher moral value than social quality, it was bound to eventually overcome the Victorian ethos. But then came the violence of the early 20th century, caused by the industrialized, bureaucratic atrocities and the harnessing of scientific advancement for the purposes of war, mass murder and authoritarianism. These brutal realities set the successive generations against the paradigm of intellectual morality as the highest good.

The analytical approach to life is what the Hippie Movement rejected. They rejected the pragmatists, the rationalists, the scientists and the industrialists: those who made the automobile freely available, with all its technological efficiency and pollution to boot; who, with their social theories tinkered with society and caused revolutions; who cured diseases but who also built the atomic bomb. The hippies were not intellectual critics of a restrictive, social morality. Rather, they rebelled against the idea of mankind as a purely rational animal, as a deterministic machine with a series of physiological needs that could be mechanistically fulfilled. They rejected the idea of a "happiness pill", or that we could ever discover a universal way of life that would make everyone content, if we'd all just conform to it.

Pirsig's conclusion is that the Hippie Movement rejected both intellectual quality and social quality as the highest good – but they couldn't perceive any higher kind of quality than the intellectual. And so, they turned to the only kind of quality they understood, and deified the biological as the ultimate form of value. Their solution, like the artistic and intellectual movement known as romanticism, was to return to a simpler time. Their conception of nature was an idyll where people could fuck without shame, go unclothed and dirty without a second thought, live in the wild and abstain from the system. They were exactly as anti-intellectual as they were anti-moralistic.

In Pirsig's view, this was a misstep. His solution is a conception of *Dynamic Quality* as the highest type of moral value. To explain this concept requires his entire book, but I shall attempt a summary here. Dynamic Quality is the cutting edge of human perception and experience. It is the indubitable reality of the present moment in which all potential for change exists, in which the limitless future is constantly solidifying into past. It is prior to any division into subjective and objective, internal and external. Dynamic Quality is immediate experience, the present moment, wherein change is possible.

Pirsig thinks the recognition of the evolving nature of moral values will free mankind from the static patterns that have thus far been the source of most of his conflicts. With the new understanding of all morality as provisional, we can conceive now of how each expression of quality was a grasping for this Dynamic Quality. The static, hardened moral values of bygone ages often linger in the psyche of a given culture, the lava of Dynamic Quality hardened into an icon. When circumstances change and the most valuable thing would be to change along with those circumstances, the static patterns become a hindrance. Dynamic Quality is thus, in Pirsig's philosophy, a principle of becoming and being, of overcoming and overthrowing – of creative destruction.

Whether either Nietzsche or Pirsig's ideas about the moral and aesthetic path forward are feasible for mankind and whether we even have any choice in the matter is anyone's guess. Wittgenstein sometimes crudely remarked, "Don't try to shit higher than your ass," meaning simply that many philosophers often have an unrealistic idea of their influence, or what they can accomplish through philosophizing.

Our own inquiry was never going to outline a programme for "fixing art", or for correcting our aesthetic course. Perhaps through exploring how a few minds have assessed how art has progressed, and where it is going, we can come to understand more about the *nature* of artistic expression, which is our real purpose.

***

When we'd started eating, we were the only ones outside. By the time we were finished there were no free tables. They crowded around the patio, beers in hand, lining up for their vegan goulash. They were all punks and metalheads, the same type of crowd as Freakout in Bologna – only crustier, rougher.

They assembled to watch Hell Obelisco. I watched the crowd from behind the stage. Their facial expressions didn't seem to change much throughout the performance. Whether they were enjoying themselves or not was impossible to tell. These were the first adult generation after East Germany and the communist reign – people my age, born the year the wall came down.

***

As it happened, Dresden was the first successful show of the tour. There was a big crowd by the time we went out to perform. They mostly just stood there, stone-faced, but the applause in between songs was encouraging. Dresden was our first really energetic performance of this tour. We'd started to loosen up a bit, and acclimate to the road. There was the energy of the crowd, the hum of the Orange amps. We went crazy up there.

It was about halfway through the set. Things were going great. We were rocking the fuck out at the end of Prisoner of Eternity… I was headbanging like there was no tomorrow. We were a runaway freight train, pounding sheer, raw power – pain stabbed like a lightning bolt down the right side of the neck. Radiating down the shoulder. Only a few more measures to go. I kept playing. It stung. Pain seared through muscles. The song finally reached the abrupt end. The crowd applauded and cheered.

I stood there and panted, the stabbing pain rippling. I knew I wouldn't be able to keep thrashing at the same intensity. I'd pushed too far. There was still half a set to tackle. I took a deep breath. Steve didn't give us too much of a pause in between songs. Almost as soon as the last one ended, he kicked in with the next riff.

I made it through the performance. I didn't want to compromise the physicality of the performance, but I had to pull back. The headbang became more of a full-body motion, to the extent I moved at all, and I made it work. By the end of the set, it was agony. I got another beer, and collapsed in the green room, holding the wet, frosty bottle against the side of my neck, in between swigs.

My delay pedal sounded like shit. It was barely cutting through. It was almost as if it was sucking the volume out of the guitar when I clicked it on. But it couldn't be out of batteries... not already. I'd just put one in, less than a week before, that first night in Bologna. *I should have just bought a European power supply*, I thought, *like Steve did*.

One of the locals found me in the green room, and said Steve had told him I was looking for some smoke. With my neck in pain, there was nothing more welcome than being gifted marijuana at this point.

He and I chatted as he rolled up a joint. I asked him about Dresden, about the history. I told him how dour everyone seemed to me. He simply nodded. He explained that the people are not as expressive of their emotions here.

One of the guys who worked Chemiefabrick told me that his dad was put in jail for having a Mohawk. That kind of thing was against the law under the East German rule. I wondered how many people in America would adopt the punk aesthetic if there were actual legal consequences for doing so.

High Reeper departed, and eventually, everyone else had gone home aside from a few of the staff. One of them, a drunk, long blonde-haired fellow with a beard and a denim jacket, held his phone up with the flashlight on, to help us see while we loaded out. He dropped it. It clattered onto the gravel parking lot. He swore, and dove to grab it.

"I hope it is broken," his friend said, completely straight-faced.

He finally managed to pick it up, then fumbled the phone yet again. The other two guys started kicking at it and trying to step on it as he scrambled to pick it up. This all probably sounds mean-spirited. At the time, we all laughed and laughed.

The good people at Chemiefabrick secured a hostel for us for the night, a short drive away. I'd stayed in hostels during my trip backpacking through Europe, ten years prior. I didn't miss that aspect of the experience, and especially was not looking forward to it now while dealing with all the other hassles of touring. The biggest turn off about a hostel is, of course, sharing your space with strangers. In this respect, the arrangements Chemiefabrick made for us were perfect: it was a room with nine beds. We had the entire place to ourselves.

I was high, for the first time in a week. I stumbled up the steps into the room. They put up a lot of bands here, so they said. The walls had a plain wooden finish, and were scrawled on by countless markers, adorned with countless band stickers. Stickers on top of stickers. They left vegan food in the fridge for us, and said we had to be out of there by noon.

It had been a real show. Like our drive for that day had been for something. We'd made friends. We'd made a good impression on the locals. Above all, we played well. Really well, actually. My neck hurt, and it wasn't helping the prospect of sleeping. The night was still bittersweet, but at least there'd been something sweet.

CHAPTER ELEVEN
DRESDEN - HAMBURG

At first, I couldn't get my body to move. I tried my best not to wake Penny, who was sleeping on the bunk beneath me. I couldn't help all the groaning and grunting as I forced myself into an upright position, then made the arduous trip down the ladder. The floor was cold on my bare feet. I found myself wincing with certain movements and turns of my neck. I'd forgotten about the injury in the course of slumber and remembered immediately upon waking. I rubbed at the muscles in vain futility as I walked.

My neck muscles felt like they'd hardened into concrete. Nothing sounded better at the moment than the first use of the shower. It would be my first shower in at least three days. I hoped the water would get really hot and steamy. Sometimes you stay at a place where the shower has no pressure, or the hot water runs out immediately. As the first person to use it that morning, I enjoyed plenty of hot water.

I dried off and got dressed. I felt infinitely better than before – which is to say, I still felt like death, but death warmed over. I raided the fridge for a couple pieces of vegan cheese, and ate it with some fruit and a rice cake. Steve was the other early riser that morning. He emerged into the commons area a bit after I did, the bleak white morning light beaming over the dining table where I sat as the door swung open. He blinked a couple times, his eye sockets darker than normal.

"Is there coffee?"

"Don't see any."

"Want to go get some?"

We wandered for a bit on the streets of Dresden. It was still overcast and misty. People were going about their day by this time of morning, the compact autos rolled past us on the narrow, little streets. The first of the season's construction work was plodding away on every other side street we passed, and the clitter clatter and banging and power tool sounds filled the morning air.

As irritated as I had been with the tour so far, the show in Dresden was revitalizing. A surprise success on a Wednesday! Perhaps the Italians were correct, and the tour would improve now that we'd left Italy. France had been a bit disappointing, but if the weekend shows were even close to this one… I found myself once again swept up in the spirit of adventure. The jet lag was finally starting to wear off. We'd finally made some money. My neck hurt badly, but what could you do about that?

Walking side-by-side with Steve down the streets of Dresden would have been the perfect time to bring up my issues with communication. But things were feeling different now – and besides, what was the point of complaining? No, we were hitting our stride.

"We should do this again," I said.

"Oh, we'll come back," Steve said, nodding. "We're just getting our feet wet."

"Well, we've definitely learned a few things already. For when next time rolls around."

"Not only that, but Charlie, from Choke, wants us to come with them for a week in Japan," Steve said.

He held the door open and we stepped into a café. It was a single room with four tables or so, with coffee and a case full of delectable-looking baked goods.

"When? Next year?" I asked.

Steve nodded. "Some time next year."

I didn't bother to make the attempt to order in German. I gave my best, "Danke" when she handed me the espresso.

We sat down and discussed the possibilities.

"It would be for a week or so, everything taken care of, except for airfare."

"So… their label would arrange all of the details? Transportation, booking, all that?"

"Yeah."

"I haven't been too happy with Argonauta."

Steve didn't say anything. I had a feeling he didn't want to get negative about the record label. We sat in silence for a long second.

"Going from Lyon, to Toulouse, to Strasbourg," I continued, "That was stupid."

"Those *were* some long drives…"

"I don't think Valerio knows what he's doing."

"Well, look, we don't have to book through him in the future if you don't want to."

"And nine of us? In one Sprinter van?"

"Hey man, before we went on this tour, I asked all of you if you were okay with sharing a vehicle with another band, and everyone said yes. We're doing this to cut costs. You know how much we've already spent on gas? Right now, we're splitting gas, we're splitting Davide's payout, splitting the gear rental…"

"Why couldn't we get Orange? They couldn't get Orange amps? High Reeper's label can get them Orange amps."

"We could have spent more money to pay for a better backline. But this is our first time over here and we're trying to save on costs so we can actually make some money."

"Right…" I said. He *was* right. But it was frustrating. "Well then maybe we should have just gone for it. Should've paid extra for Orange amps. Paid extra for the vehicle."

"You guys said you were cool with it," he said, flatly. "Renting Orange would have costed us more money. Were you going to put up that money?"

"Maybe I would have, I don't know. Definitely to have our own vehicle."

"Well, live and learn," Steve said. "In the future, we'll make sure to always have our own vehicle."

"Right. Hopefully next time…" I said "things will be different."

That was all I could manage.

"That's why we're here man," Steve said. "To get our feet wet, to learn the ropes. The next tour of Europe is going to be way better."

"Good to meet those Chemiefabrick guys." I said, changing the subject.

"Yeah, good contacts for next time."

"Dude, when he dropped his fuckin' phone, that was hilarious!"

"Dude, I know," Steve said, chuckling. He imitated the German accent. "'I hope it is broken!'"

Our breath wisped into the late morning air as we walked. In some places, you could see where the older buildings had been burned during the infamous firebombing. There was blackened stone near the foundations of the old stone edifices. Yet, here they stood, defiantly tilting against impermanence.

When we got back to the hostel, our bandmates and the Italians were stirring. The fruit, vegan cheese and rice cakes they'd left us were mostly gone. We still had a little bit of time before we had to depart, and everyone started to take turns showering. I bummed a cigarette from Doc and went out front. He joined me. We talked for a bit. We talked about our wives. He showed me pictures of his wedding, and then, coincidentally, his wife called, and we broke off the conversation. He paced up and down the street as he talked with her.

I puffed on the cigarette, people-watching as I did so. Everywhere you go, you see people intensely focused on everyday affairs that are as important to them as all of your trifling day-to-day business is to you. I smiled at an older gentleman as he ambled past, walking his dog. He gave me the slightest of smiles back. From the way he looked at me, I think he knew I was a foreigner, but I don't know how he knew it, or how I knew he knew it.

***

We hit the road, bound for Hamburg. At our third restroom stop for the day, Steve and I read two reviews for the new album that had just gone up. Two in one day was a good amount of press. One was a pretty good review. The other practically lavished us in praise. The words of some reviewer on a stoner metal blog wasn't ever the kind of thing that set the world on fire. But it felt good to read nice things about our music.

Half-drunk and high on the praise of strangers, we stumbled merrily back into the van after thirty minutes or so. As we approached the van, Andrea and Alex were bantering in Italian. Andrea switched to English as we walked up.

"Ah, Steve, what was again the name of your cover band?" he asked.

Steve had been talking about his side-project to Andrea earlier. A group he played in with some other local musicians, on holidays, and special occasions. They'd gotten paid more for some of their shows in Austin than Destroyer of Light made on the road.

"Bois, Bois, Bois," Steve said, grinning. "Motley Crüe cover band."

Alex burst into laughter, cackling.

"Have you heard the song?" Andrea asked.

"The song?" Steve asked.

"The pop song."

We headed down the highway, and Andrea played the song from his phone. It was a hit single from an Italian pop singer named Sabrina in 1987. It charted pretty well all over Europe, but not in the United States. Booming bass and a dance beat. Something could be common knowledge to millions of people and be relatively unknown on the other side of the Atlantic. Funny how the name of Steve's cover band – meant as a play on the song, "Girls, Girls, Girls" – triggered a completely different association.

Our new album was released on an Italian label, and they'd invested in European PR. We got more reviews from Europe than we'd ever gotten before. It was exciting to me to read a review in German, in Spanish, in French, in German (again) in Swedish, in Italian. It was like we'd achieved worldwide prominence!

Overall, they were positive. I had to translate most of them, although a few were in English. A couple times, I punched the review into the Google translate, and read something that was wholly negative. A Swedish critic said that we "want to bite, but don't have teeth." That one really stung. Some would say to focus on the positive reviews, but it is not in my nature, and I would question the wisdom of this in the first place. The positive reviews make me feel warm inside for a few moments, but the negative stuff sticks with me. It makes me wish the person was there so I could argue with them. It especially bothered me whenever someone gave us a bad review that was itself badly written, since there is nothing more infuriating than being condescended to by someone stupider than you are. I sometimes used to joke that I was going to set up a website to review music reviewers: I'd write reviews assessing and criticizing the literary competency of their music reviews. I never got around to it.

The best review we got for Mors Aeterna was by someone who had given a lukewarm review of a previous record. Steve showed it to me on his phone. I saw the name of the critic, and braced myself. It turned out that he really enjoyed Mors Aeterna. He even wrote that he'd changed his mind about us. It was not completely unqualified praise, and even though he was just another reviewer among countless others, his review was more meaningful to me than any of the other positive reviews we ever received.

With a translation of a review, the phrasing is usually clumsy and you have to infer the general meaning of the translated sentence. This means that the writer's tone is almost always lost in translation. The writer's witticisms, the connotations conveyed through their diction, or a thousand other literary choices that the writer might make – all of this gets chewed up by the translation program. We get a distorted message.

Here is one mixed review we received, from "Metal 1" Ezine. It is translated from German. I can't read German, but here is the original paragraph in case anyone is interested:

"Auf dem Papier liest sich „Mors Aeterna" wie eine feine Sache: Ein zur Musik passendes Konzept, ein ansehnliches Coverbild und die Unterstützung eines Labels, welches die Band offensichtlich bereits von sich überzeugen konnte – das müsste doch eigentlich halbwegs anständig klingen. Tatsächlich sind auf dem Album zwischen den eher mittelmäßigen Kompositionen durchaus auch einige vielversprechende Ansätze auszumachen. Bezüglich der Umsetzung hätten sich DESTROYER OF LIGHT jedoch weitaus mehr Mühe geben können. Zu abrupt ausklingende Tracks („Eternal Death") und spieltechnische Patzer, wie man sie auf „Mors

Aeterna" zu hören bekommt, sollten einer Band mit mehrjähriger Erfahrung einfach nicht mehr passieren."

Here is the English translation that Google produced:

"On paper, 'Mors Aeterna' reads like a fine thing: a concept that fits the music, a handsome cover image and the support of a label that the band has obviously already been able to convince – that should actually sound reasonably decent. In fact, there are some promising approaches between the rather mediocre compositions on the album. However, DESTROYER OF LIGHT could have gone much harder with the implementation. Too abruptly fading tracks ('Eternal Death') and technical mistakes as you can hear on 'Mors Aeterna' should simply not happen to a band with many years of experience."

Harsh, I know. But it's a bit hard to get a feel for the writer's tone through the translation program. The voice is passive, almost dispassionate. Maybe that's just a function of the German mindset – or maybe it isn't. I have no way of knowing. Maybe in the original language it does not come off so harshly. Or maybe it is even more vitriolic.

For the sake of balance, we'll look at a more positive review. This one is from "Musikreviews.de":

"Dies macht *Mors Aeterna* zu einem überdurchschnittlich dichten und stimmungsvollen Werk. Der hohe Gehalt an Melodien garantiert einerseits unangestrengtes Hören, doch da die Gruppe nicht aufs plumpe Mitsingen ihrer Fans abonniert ist, wird man die Platte nicht schnell satt. Es ist sogar so, dass man sich bei wiederholter Einfuhr an mehreren Details erfreuen kann, die von sorgfältigen Komponisten hinter der Musik zeugen. *DESTROYER OF LIGHT* haben genaue Vorstellungen davon, was sie tun wollen, und versuchen anders als mittlerweile unzählige Newcomer nicht lediglich, um Zugehörigkeit in einer Szene zu buhlen, indem sie lieblos deren kleinsten gemeinsame Nenner abhandeln."

And the Google translation:

"This makes *Mors Aeterna* an exceptionally dense and atmospheric work. The high content of melodies on the one hand guarantees effortless listening, but since the group is not subscribed to the clumsy singing along of their fans, the record is not filled quickly. In fact, with repeated imports, you can enjoy several details that testify to the composers behind the music. *DESTROYER OF LIGHT* have a clear idea of what they want to do and unlike countless newcomers meanwhile, they are not simply trying to court membership by lovingly dealing with their lowest common denominator."

The meaning is clear even if the phraseology of the A.I.'s translation is clumsy. But again, I have no idea of the tone of the original review. I don't even know if either of these reviews represents competent German writing or not. All I have is a facsimile of their meaning produced by an artificial intelligence, and from this, I either feel a sense of fleeting satisfaction, or else find myself irritated and perseverating on their words for hours, or days.

Whatever the excitement or novelty of having all these foreign language reviews come trickling in, day after day, it was difficult to gauge whether the critics were even all that influential, or whether their opinions were indicative of anything important. Sure, there are a few major webpages that play the role of tastemakers. Occasionally, a blog reaches huge levels of prominence and bands succeed or fail based on their words. But the vast majority of critics are like the vast majority of musicians: of absolutely no importance.

Only the artists of greatest prominence attract the critics of greatest prominence. The small-timers, unsigned bands, underground bands, and the like, are covered by smaller blogs, or by the countless generic heavy metal webzines that look like every other heavy metal webzine. In order to get more attention, you want a good review from one of the influential blogs. To get reviewed by the more influential blogs, you need to first attract more attention. This is the Catch-22 of signal boosting your album through the internet.

I flipped through my notebook as we drove. My inquiry was sparked by the question of what exactly I was doing by bringing my music across the oceans to Europe. Now, after reading these reviews, the thought arose: what is the intelligible inner meaning of my band's music? What were we trying to transmit to the audience? Had I ever considered this question, or taken seriously the potential power of my art to affect the mind-states of others?

When we first formed Destroyer of Light, our style was almost endearingly straightforward and unashamedly cheesy. The lyrical content was the stuff of old horror stories. Steve wrote songs about virgin sacrifice, swamp creatures, vampire hunters. We'd come to the studio with a bunch of doom riffs, but during the whiskey-fueled recording session for the first album, we played almost everything at an upbeat rock tempo.

When the band first formed, Steve and Penny were foaming at the mouth to get out on the road. I was young, energetic and naïve. I was still listening to thrash metal, death metal and power metal. I was only marginally familiar with doom. I just wanted to rock, I wanted to headbang, go crazy. Thankfully, in Steve I'd found a frontman who also loved theatrics. There are plenty of doom bands that are content to just stand there. It usually fits the aesthetic of doom metal just as well. But that was never what a live performance was to us. As a performer, I always looked at the performance as something that had to exhaust me, something I had to work my ass off to bring to the audience. We saw that rock n' roll energy as key from the very start. Sometimes those stage moves were pretty cheesy in and of themselves. We'd raise our guitars, headbang in sync, get right up on the edge of the stage during the finale. But you should never be afraid to be cheesy during a performance. The only thing the audience cares about is sincerity. Give it your absolute, total being. Go crazy. If you're doing it right, you should be going out of your right mind. The audience loves that. If some hipsters stroking their beards in the back think that you're a philistine, who gives a fuck? You're not playing for them. You're playing for the people up at the front.

When we played at Psycho California in 2015, a reviewer writing for Invisible Oranges described us as "fast and unsafe." This is an unusual compliment for a doom metal band, a style of music which is supposed to be slow and ominous. I suppose, in a festival with a lot of doom bands, we seemed more of a rock band, and people have taken to calling us "doom rock" in the past couple years. Maybe that's what we are – I don't really know.

I suppose this is all to say that I'm not sure what it was we were communicating in those years. I don't think we even knew. We just sort of...

wrote horror stories, in the form of songs. I'm not sure if there was a unifying theme to it all, an emotional core to it, other than the general doom vibe. We just wanted to write good riffs and put on a fun show. In our foolishness, we thought this would be enough.

***

We'd originally planned on having a show that night. Valerio had tried to book one, but it hadn't worked out. By the time we'd arrived in Europe, he still hadn't booked it. Now, the day had arrived, and in spite of my foolish hope that we'd find a last-minute gig, Thursday had become a day-off. It was a disappointment, but I had to make my peace with it. After six hours, we arrived in Hamburg. Tonight, we could cut loose.

Davide found a secure parking lot for the van and rented out an entire room at the hostel. The rooms had nine beds each, consisting of three triple bunk beds per room: again, perfect. We had our own bathroom for the night to share between the nine of us. The showers were still communal; none of us used them. The most important thing, for me at least, was having a secure place to keep our personal items. A door that locks is good enough.

Nick rolled a joint with the weed we'd been given in Dresden, the night before. I lack the discipline to learn, but Nick had become fairly good at it. We sprinkled it with hash and mixed it with tobacco, in keeping with the European way. It was fine for smoking the cannabis here, which was not of the same quality as the American crop.

There was a metalhead bar somewhere in Hamburg that the Italians said was well known. Of course, Steve was game. The first order of business was food. We set out into the night searching for a quick bite within walking distance. The hostel was in the heart of Hamburg's downtown, in the red-light district.

We passed restaurant after restaurant with exorbitant prices. We decided to settle for a bar and grill. Hamburgers and fries would do just fine. It was basically just a yuppie sports bar. Their prices seemed high, but that didn't seem avoidable. It was sometimes hard to tell when one was traveling to a different city every day through Europe whether the prices were supposed to be normal or excessive.

Steve had received the money that Amberly wired to him by now, and I'd begun marking down the amount he was spending on my behalf on my phone's notepad. The burgers were pushing twenty dollars once you did the conversion and added in the extras for luxuries like cheese and fries. The beers were similarly expensive: around eight to ten dollars. The service was terrible; the food was sub-par. We waited for the better part of an hour for it to arrive. Their overpriced house beer was still exceptional compared to the normal American fare.

It didn't bother me. It was good to just hang, without having a gig later. Time was not a factor, for once. We had to converse loudly to be heard over the din of the bar. I sat next to Luca, who was usually in front of me in the van. We discussed the familiar topics: music, movies, what we'd seen so far in Europe, the norms of Europe versus America. Eventually the whole table was reminiscing about the show the night before, about the dour city of Dresden, about music. So often, we talked about music.

After dinner, Penny went back to the hostel and got some more sleep. The rest of the group headed through the packed and boisterous streets of Hamburg's downtown. It wasn't really raining, but there was just that mist in the air again. The city streets were wet with neon-reflecting puddles; the awnings drooled with rainwater. The bars were packed and overflowing. Laughter and shouting was in the air.

Eventually, we found the place. Ah, yes. I'd been packed into many such European bars when I went backpacking some ten years prior. The smells: the smell of humanity, in this case the smell of wet humanity, but also the smell of beer, and the sickly sweet smell of spilt liquor and mixed drinks. The extremely high-volume ambience of the chatter, far louder than the last place. The conversation was thick with the consonants and inflections of German. The heat and sweat and rainwater as bodies pressed against bodies. We eventually found a clearing towards the back of the place and began to plan our means of attack for getting a drink at the bar. True to form, everyone was wearing kuttes, leather jackets, spikes.

Fighting my way to the bar for a drink just so that I could stand around in this place and have inaudible conversations suddenly didn't seem worthwhile. I turned to Nick and asked him if he wanted to go out front. I gestured to Alex to follow us, telling him, "Hierba." I thought he heard me. Either he didn't, or my pronunciation was so bad he didn't understand me, or decided he'd rather be in the bar. Whatever the reason, he didn't come out.

The bar was positioned on a side street just off the main drag, so the foot traffic was not so heavy. We stood and smoked in the nook by the bar entrance. The little, covered stoop was just barely big enough for the two of us to stand in. It began to rain, drizzling sporadically as we traded the joint back and forth.

"Well, we made it man," I said to Nick. I smirked and clapped him on the back. "We're touring Europe. We're better than other people."

He chuckled somewhat uncomfortably. "I'm just happy to be here," he said.

I was being sarcastic. But I realized that maybe I'd meant it. Are we ever apart from the perception of others – or rather, from our own perception of how we're looked at by others? The quest to make your mark, to become great: the drive is there, and it's part of being an artist whether you want it to be or not. Neurons started to fire uncontrollably. The potential of greatness, what greatness really meant, why some people's names echo down through the ages and some fade into obscurity. What factors produce a person that makes a real impact?

"I was thinking of Martin Luther," I said.

"Martin Luther?"

"Mmm."

"What about him?"

"I don't know, I suppose because we're in Germany," I said. "I was just thinking about the drinking culture here, how it squares with the idea we have of Germans as strict and regimented... how does alcohol fit into that?"

"I'm not sure."

"It's just weird how, in America, we associate alcohol with sin. Probably because of the temperance movement. But not here. Here, alcohol has always been part of the religion…"

"And what about Luther?"

"He was a drinker, did you know that? He could put down steins of beer. They say he was a loud man, an extroverted man. There is something so German about that…"

I stopped for a second. I was losing my place.

"You were saying, about Luther?"

"Anyway you know how he translated the Bible into the vernacular…"

I paused, trying to get a hold of my thoughts.

"And the effect that that had…" I was really in a haze. "Well, not just the effect that Luther had. The effect of the printing press. The fact that Martin Luther happened right at the time when his translation could have the biggest effect. Suddenly, you didn't need a Church apparatus of people copying texts by hand in order to distribute them… anyone could distribute them…. He had fate aligned on his side… nobility to protect him… the the printing press, to disseminate his ideas… You know, not everyone really approved of the printing press when it came out? One of Luther's friends sent him a letter, telling him that by distributing his Bible in a language everyone could read, it would lead to chaos. He didn't think everyone having their own interpretation was a good thing, he thought it was terrible…"

"Keegan.?"

"Yeah?"

"Just shut the fuck up."

"Okay," I said.

We sat on the stoop, legs hanging out into the rain, and passed the joint back and forth until it was done. Before long, we were high as shit. I wasn't feeling particularly sociable.

"Want to head back to the room?"

"Yeah."

I sent a brief and mostly coherent text to Steve explaining that we were going to find our way back. I realized that we hadn't written down the address to the hostel, and tried to remember the route from memory. I hadn't really taken note of the route we took on the way there. Several times, when I was sure we were supposed to turn, Nick told me to keep heading straight. In the misty, neon dark, he found our way back.

The anxiety that I thought I'd conquered years ago was still there, rumbling beneath the surface of the mind's waves. It's always there; it never fully goes away. Certain substances can make it emerge, crest above the surface of consciousness. It's always a danger with marijuana, which improves the creative process, but risks stirring the beasts. Self-doubt, death-anxiety, the sense of vulnerability when in a foreign land, with no guarantee that if you speak to someone on the street, that they will even understand you...

Yes, I was anxious again. It was different though, different from the years before. I knew it now. I understood it. The familiarity allows you to steel yourself. If you're adapted enough, dispassionate enough, you can step outside the feeling of anxiety: utilize the memory of past panics and catastrophic thoughts, and realize that they are all transitory. They come and go. Thoughts appear to us as the most real thing, but don't have any permanent reality.

CHAPTER TWELVE - AALBORG

At the border of Denmark, the guards directed Davide to pull off to the side. Two soldiers wearing camouflage uniforms and berets approached the vehicle. Davide told us to start getting our passports out. He rolled down the window. They asked the usual questions – who we were, where were we going, and why.

"We're carrying two bands to a show in Aalborg," Davide said.

"You're carrying two bands?"

"Yes."

"How many people?"

"Nine."

"No one else in the back?"

"No, just nine of us."

"What's in the back?"

"It's all gear in the back."

"Passports."

We passed all nine passports to the front of the vehicle. We waited for about ten minutes. Finally, the border guard came back.

"Where are you playing?" the border guard asked. His tone was more interrogative than conveying a genuine interest.

"1000fryd," Doc said, pronouncing it, as I would have, 'one thousand fried.' Blank stare. "Here, I'll show you."

Doc handed his phone to the border guard, to show him the Facebook event page. The guard couldn't quite see it at the angle he was holding it. He squinted and came in for a closer look.

"Ah!" he said. He repeated the venue's name aloud, saying it, approximately, as "toosen flude."

I wondered if they'd notice my Danish last name, or say anything about it. Eventually, they passed the passports back to us. No one mentioned it. They waved us through. I think Doc showing them the show flier helped. Luca said that it probably helped just having four American passports, among the five from Italy.

I scribbled out our setlist into my journal as we drove into the country. We all had it memorized by now, but I wanted to remember it for all time. I inked each letter with care... Into the Smoke... Dissolution... Afterlife... Drowned... Burning Darkness... Luxcrusher... then began doodling around the edges of the song titles, entwining vines and twisting snakes around the lettering.

***

It wasn't until Destroyer of Light was tempered by many years on the road that our music began to become personal and introspective. I'm not sure if we qualified as 'artists' in our early years. We were more like performers. Rather, I should say that the art was more in the performance than in the composition. A lot of bands are like that: they are, first and foremost, performers. I don't say this to denigrate anyone, because some of the greatest bands of all time have been, primarily, performers – more so than composers or lyricists. Kiss is a great example of that. Iggy Pop. Sometimes a band is derided for this: The Sex Pistols are regarded this way in the punk scene today.

Anxiety and depression, the same feelings that had almost pushed me out of the band, proved to be my source of inspiration. Steve and Jeff, our bassist for about four years, were both struggling with addiction and depression when we wrote the songs on Chamber of Horrors and Hopeless, the releases that marked a change in the style and the quality of our material. The abysmal feelings started finding their way into the lyrics. The horror stories started to become more existential. We began to include more surrealism. Both Steve and I found a huge influence in The Twilight Zone, where the nightmarish and supernatural scenarios that confront the protagonists were often metaphors for the psychological.

A lot of this was subconscious. I didn't intend to write a metaphorical song when I wrote "Into the Smoke." It was just a song about a smoke monster. Well, an entity made of psychedelic smoke that seeps into your lungs and skin, possesses you, and takes control of your body, turning you into a forever-suffocating zombie.

During the time when the song was written, I was smoking a lot of weed, almost all the time. Anyone who tells you that you can't be addicted to marijuana is either naïve or a liar. More often than not, the way it happens is exactly what happened with me: my tolerance crept up and up and up until I was getting blazed from dawn till dusk just to feel anything. I started having paranoia. Weed had formerly calmed my anxiety. Suddenly, it was exacerbating it. I knew I needed to stop. But by this point, I had formed a psychological dependence. So what is the song about, *really?* Mental slavery. Dependence on a substance. It's about coughing, choking, panicking – and yet, coming back again and again for the same experience.

Of course, some of the songs were more explicit. "Drowned," one of Steve's songs, is roughly the same concept, only with lyrics that discuss addiction in a more straightforward way. The chorus of "Luxcrusher" was an unpoetic series of nihilistic declarations, ending with the couplet, "The human race has failed, we're better off dead / Give into sonic lust, turn off your head."

This music is what Nietzsche would have called, "decadent": an expression of despair at a dying and morally bankrupt world, and the liberation from suffering from this knowledge in hedonistic self-annihilation. There's a Greek myth that Nietzsche talked about in *The Birth of Tragedy*, about the nymph Silenus. Silenus was a demigod, and a friend of Dionysus. It was said that no man could capture him, so King Midas attempted to do just that. After a long hunt, he finally managed to capture Silenus alive. He then demanded that Silenus tell him, out of the wisdom of the gods, what would be the best thing for mankind. Silenus refused and remained silent for a long time. Finally, he told the king, "What would be best for you is quite beyond your reach: not to have been born, not to be, to be *nothing*. But the second best is to die soon."

2015-2017 was our Silenus period. For my part, I felt helpless, pessimistic, and emotionally fragile. My personal and familial relationships were strained. My relationship with my wife was strained. It sucked. The music was powerful, though. Why was it powerful? Because everyone feels these things at points in their life. It is powerful, and even enjoyable in some sick way, for a group of people to gather and wallow in that pessimism for a night. For many people, this helps discharge these abysmal feelings. The musical experience is therapeutic. But it's a double-edged sword. I don't think it helped my mental state, screaming out nihilistic creeds to the world every night. Those songs don't have the same effect on me now as they did back then, in the depths of my depression. But I remember sometimes feeling worse about myself and my place in the world when I thought about the fact that we were touring around propagating a message that basically boiled down to, "none of it matters, everything sucks, who cares if you die."

This is another old debate amongst the ancients. Plato said that a tragic poet would, from repeatedly exposing himself to the emotional states of tragedy, degenerate into a weak, fearful, and lachrymose soul. In the Platonic view, tragic art corrupts. Aristotle, on the other hand, says that negative human emotions are discharged through tragedy. In the Aristotelian view, tragic art is cathartic. It seems foolish to try and weigh in on which of them is correct.

I don't feel the artistic guilt I used to feel about our music for just that reason. Half the relationship with the audience is what they bring to the communion. The doom metal culture is about relating through mutual suffering. It's about seeing the beauty in sadness. It is made of people who find pleasure in nasty guitar tones and deafening noises. In an open society, all art comes with an implicit warning label. We're not controlling this emotional resonance thing anymore. Use momentary gods at your own risk.

VIII. Authenticity

Is the artist honest or dishonest?

Everything that an artist portrays, hides, emphasizes or ignores is what we call an artistic decision: this is the artist's dishonesty. This distinguishes art from the activities of science, journalism or philosophy, wherein intentionally obscuring certain elements would be considered a betrayal of the principles underlying these disciplines. The artist's dishonesty must concern us, for art cannot be fully separated from these other endeavors, e.g., journalism, a field which presupposes value in the truth. There is an irreducibly subjective element in all original writing. So too in all such arts and crafts. The photographer wants to bring certain things into greater focus; in doing so, he obscures other things. The poet composes an elegy to a deceased hero, and in doing so does not include a verse or two about their infidelities. Every inclusion is also an exclusion.

This is Nietzsche's view of the artist's dishonesty as we have considered it, and it was one of his fundamental problems with the artist. As to why he took this position, however, it is impossible to fully understand unless we have considered the position of Nietzsche's biggest influence, Schopenhauer.

Heavily influenced by the Buddhists and other ancient Indian philosophers, Schopenhauer concluded that desire was at the root of suffering. This is because mankind is always chasing after the objects of its desires. Simply in the act of desiring, a person suffers out of want. When we can't attain our desires, we suffer out of a sense of failure and deprivation. And even when we get what we want, we find that we are not ultimately sated, and new desires continue to arise. To ignore one's desires is an alternative to pursuing them, but trying to do this out of sheer willpower alone can cause people to fall into apathy, or depression; sometimes they snap, and relapse into their old vices with a vengeance.

The fundamental human drive, in Schopenhauer's formulation, is the will to live. But the will (desiring) is also the source of all our problems. This means that life itself is a problem for Schopenhauer.

The only salvation for Schopenhauer is the *negation of the will*: the refusal to follow after the objects of one's desires. The eventual goal is the transcendence of all worldly desires, wherein one finally finds happiness. For Schopenhauer, happiness is a *negative* principle: it is the *absence* of suffering. It can only be truly realized when we are freed from wanting.

The human condition consists of both the will and the intellect in Schopenhauer's philosophy. He argued that man is the zenith of nature, the one species blessed with a strong intellect, by which we can represent the suffering of the world to ourselves, and consciously turn and negate the will.

Schopenhauer finds the highest value in the intellect, and not in irrational willing.

To Schopenhauer, true art is not an outflow of passion, but a product of the intellect. Art is part of the intellect's ability to represent the world. This representation of the world is, Schopenhauer argues, roughly the same process whereby our conceptual symbols represent the world to us. The will itself is blind desire, but with the intellect we can come to gain an understanding of the world through our representations. By means of artistic contemplation, one can become a "will-less subject of knowing," like a clear mirror that reflects only the object, and is drained of all subjectivity. The subjective is where Schopenhauer sees the world as will, and thus the ability to transcend this world is to be released from ceaseless desiring and suffering.

Schopenhauer believed that, in art, the beginning of our separation from the blind willing of the animals begins. The work of the artist and the enjoyment of art become a form of rapture from the pain of desire. This is because art is the representation of forms that have no will, and are not themselves objects of the will. We can contemplate the form of an apple through a painting of an apple, but the painted apple is not part of the world of willing (and, therefore, of suffering). Our hunger is not directed at the painted apple. We enjoy the painted apple as beautiful without desiring it, Schopenhauer argues, because we know it is a mere representation. Schopenhauer loved the Dutch realist painters, who painted scenes from ordinary life. They painted still life and portraits. He said they had achieved the highest form of art.

Artistic pleasure is therefore defined by the dispassionate contemplation of the world as idea, or *representation*. (This is another standard for what is beautiful, for every aesthetic theory must include one.) We may remember that pleasure, or happiness, is a negative principle to Schopenhauer: which means that aesthetic pleasure (the sublime) is the *absence* of willing through the contemplation of art. We might consider all that we've considered so far about ulterior motives for doing art: for example, making art for a financial gain, or for vanity, or for popularity. It is exactly because True Art has nothing to do with any of those worldly desires that Schopenhauer finds it to be a source of happiness.

Schopenhauer's view of art is anti-realist. He attempts to account for the idea of the artistic genius as madman by referring to Plato's description of the wise man who has left the cave and its shadows and seen the light of day: such a person, Plato says, will be regarded as mad by those who have never left the illusions of the cave. But this kind of "madness" is not the madness of the passions that Socrates attacked, but rather a kind of eccentricity, a radically different view of the world, as a result of having perceived the Platonic forms. It is, in fact, a false designation of madness placed on the wise man by an ignorant society. Schopenhauer's view of the world did not hold the indulgence in one's emotional world to be a good thing, and thus he argues that the true good of art is actually the transcendence of such subjective feelings. Everything that is subjective in art, Schopenhauer opposed on principle.

His definition of an artistic genius was someone so absorbed in their art they were unconcerned with the world. We can't call such a person a "subjective artist." The everyday affairs carried out in the normal business of life are mostly the toils of attending to our desires, which is exactly that which Schopenhauer considers to be "subjective": for what could be more subjective than the subject's preferences and desires? In the language of Buddhism, which is Schopenhauer's major influence, the human being is a mere series of aggregates, rather than an individual subject. The intellect allows for the rational consideration of the human being as merely consisting of empty forms, not as a willing subject. The world of the empty subject's desires does not belong in art, in Schopenhauer's view: rather, art becomes the very realization of this emptiness.

Where Schopenhauer agrees with Socrates, the Stoics, and many of the figures of the Enlightenment, is in the way he separates reason from the passions, and the mind from the body. While he would have denied a supernatural "immortal soul" (since all beings are equally part of will and indivisible from it), he nevertheless conceived of the "mind" as separable from the unreasonable animal instincts and physiology – the parts of the self that are driven by the painful desires. Whatever it is that is able to use the intellect becomes synonymous with what we would call a mind. The rational mind had to be capable of divorcing itself from the emotions in order for a truly dispassionate art to be possible.

Nietzsche was deeply influenced by Schopenhauer, but had scathing remarks for this view of art. If we define the subjective world as all of those petty, everyday wants, fears and imaginings, Nietzsche agreed that the artist should overcome the subjective. But where Schopenhauer saw the transcendence of individual concerns through dispassionate reason, Nietzsche saw art as a powerful force for which the artist was a mere conduit. Nietzsche's studies of the Greek Dionysian rituals surely presented a stark contrast with the view of art Schopenhauer expressed.

Nietzsche felt that the quiet contemplation of the still life painter and the wild, pounding rhythms of Dionysus were both serving a clearly different function in society. And yet, we call them both, "Art". Clearly, both *are* art. Their mutual definition as art demanded an explanation. And yet, as we have considered, there are no perceptible commonalities between sweaty, entranced dancing to the beat of drums, and a Rembrandt.

Nietzsche categorized art according to whether it aimed at individuation or dissolution, creating the Apollo and Dionysus dichotomy. From our anthropological and linguistic investigations, I would conclude that this is a differentiation of the bleeding edge of the artistic experience: the Dionysian, which is purely emotional and sensory – from the artistic expression once it has cooled and hardened into a symbol, concept or narrative: the Apollinian. Dynamic Quality, versus the static hierarchy of objectified qualities. The myth-making faculty in man, and the impulse to reify these myths – to make them ossify into fixed images.

Schopenhauer, on the contrary, would have declared that art really could be practiced "objectively". Following from the ideas of Schopenhauer, the artist would become simply a craftsman. In this respect, it is a return to the way Socrates viewed art. The artist practices a technique: in the case of the painter, he paints, in the case of the sculptor, he sculpts, etc. What the true artist produces, in Schopenhauer's view, is not a subjective product. The extent to which he renders reality accurately is the extent to which his art is an authentic representation untainted by the artist's dishonesty.

Thus, Schopenhauer contrasts the false, subjective artist against the objective True Artist. For Nietzsche, on the other hand, True Art is made by one who is "One with the primordial artist": *the will*. Nietzsche didn't think we ought to separate subjective from objective in artistic expression at all. Where he located the biggest error in Schopenhauer's entire philosophy was in trying to separate the intellect from the will. It is the same mind-body dualism that plagues the Western mind.

Schopenhauer acknowledged the intellect as an outgrowth of the will, and Nietzsche would have agreed. But Nietzsche doubted the power of the intellect to motivate the will, to turn upon it and negate it. This is a fantasy, he concludes, the expression of a desire to repose in nothingness. Art cannot be purely subjective, because "the subjective" to Nietzsche exists not within the world of the will, but only within the conceptual world of the intellect.

The ego-consciousness and all its self-image, its self-serving motivations and conceptual prejudices: this is the subjective world that Nietzsche says is thoroughly unartistic. The calculating mind is where we find error – and here, it should be noted, Schopenhauer and Nietzsche agree. The possibility for error in intellect is so much greater than instinct. Yet, where Schopenhauer, like all other philosophers, thinks we just need to employ reason in the correct way, Nietzsche thinks that *the rational world is a false world, and irrational passions and instincts are the true person*. The intellect imagines itself to possess more power than it actually has, as if it controls the lion's share of the self. It shits above its ass, one might say.

Nietzsche writes, in *Thus Spoke Zarathustra*, that the body is the true self, the source of a "subconscious", itself the source of consciousness. Our deeply rooted instincts reveal more about ourselves than our post hoc rationalizations and narratives. The reason Schopenhauer's view of art is untenable, then, is that the idea of a "dispassionate intellect" is actually a contradiction in terms. There is passion and there is intellect, to be sure. Intellect is a product of the passions – here Nietzsche and Schopenhauer agree – but, Nietzsche goes further and says that the intellect is *inseparable* from the passions. Whereas Schopenhauer sees the intellect as something distinct and sovereign, Nietzsche sees it as something indistinct, something suffused with will, and completely driven by unconscious impulses.

Artistic expression, as it is an expression of an emotional state, is "subjective" insofar as these emotional states come from a thinking subject's body. It is experienced as a divine madness because it confronts the ego-consciousness in all its alterity. But artistic expression is also objective to some extent: only, it is not a depiction of "objective reality." *Art is authentic to the extent that it honestly represents the artist's world – whether inside or outside – as he lives it.*

The problem for Nietzsche is that the contents of our soul, even when honestly expressed, might still only be a manifestation of what Pirsig would call a static pattern. This is what it means to be "backward-facing". Moved as we are by deep feelings more than by hard facts, the static patterns that shape our artistic expression are selected by irrational means. The feelings will tend to be rooted in nostalgia, in what is familiar, in what has been always been valuable as far back as we can remember. Nietzsche's accusation was that the artistic impulse makes the artist dishonest in this very specific respect, following the decline of religions. Because we come to art looking for feelings conjured in a bygone era, art is inevitably tainted by these nostalgic and wistful states of mind. Nostalgia is capable of profoundly warping our perception of reality, as our reality is indelibly filtered through memory.

Every perspective is absolutely honest, in that it is a reflection of who and what we are, and how we experience the world. And yet, every perspective is dishonest, because it represents a falsification of reality – whatever is in the limited sphere of attention of the artist. We can manifest beautiful representations of utter falsehoods, especially when some religious or political dogma has colonized the psyche. If we give up the artist to dishonesty, then he is no better than a propagandist.

All art is a form of propaganda: why couldn't this be the case? But there is something dissatisfying about this conclusion. Perhaps it is contradicted by the simple fact that we can distinguish it from genuine art. At the very least, we feel we can identify cases where the propaganda is clear-cut and intentional, and cases where we don't believe the artist was consciously attempting to manipulate us. For what it is worth, I don't believe this difference is as well-defined as we would like to believe.

Nietzsche himself understood this: that there is a difference between the genuine artist and what he called a "magician" with the senses. He later criticizes his mentor, the great composer Richard Wagner, in just these terms: he is a man who knows how to manipulate the audience by contriving the emotional impact of a given scene. In modern terms, James Cameron and J.J. Abrams both create films which are almost *scientific* in how perfectly they're tooled for the purposes of playing upon the heartstrings.

The counterfeit artist recognizes the power of emotional resonance and the divine madness it brings on, and tries to manufacture it artificially. They seek to hone their artistic technique in order to achieve the maximum transmission of feeling possible, but with no expression of soul beneath it.

There is something cynical, and even sinister about this: when the "artist" is doing this by rote and does not feel the divine madness himself. This means that they were merely imitating the artistic expression of others, and not actually attempting to communicate something from the depths of their subjectivity. The propagandist has the ability to manipulate and stand apart from one's feelings and instincts, and therefore try to push the feelings of others into channels of their choosing. This expression of the self is given to us by fundamentally deceptive people, who know that their outward expressions are a falsification of the inner content. This is another terror of mind-body dualism, the monstrous offspring born of our severing of thought from feeling.

***

The view of Denmark from the highway was flat. Fields, some colorful flowers, thickets of trees here and there. It was not the Scandinavia of my imagination, with all the forested mountains and fjords. It reminded me more of Holland. The sky remained a dull white, and the rain was never far from us wherever we went.

At the first rest area, a somewhat irritated older woman spoke flawless English with us. She conducted her transactions with us as quickly as possible. I did a quick conversion in my head and realized I'd spent sixteen dollars on a chicken sandwich. I wolfed it down. Strange to chew on something that was somehow dry and soggy at the same time. I left the store quickly thereafter, wanting beer and cigarettes and road snacks, but unwilling to pay such a high premium for them. I'd just have to wait.

I was the first outside the diner. It was late morning, light still dimmed by the loitering mist. I strolled up the grassy gnoll behind the diner's chain-link fence, the wet grass dampening my shoes and the hem of my jeans. As I patted the grass off them, I felt how dirty they were. The jeans were probably starting to smell by now. There were some light streaks – from cigarette ash smudged across them, or spilled food, or beer, or whatever it was. We hadn't even had a conversation about doing laundry.

It was wonderfully cold. There were pretty yellow flowers covering the land just behind the diner, separated from the rest stop by a fence. A windmill in the distance. The sun still hadn't emerged from behind the white curtain.

***

We reached Aalborg, which overlooks the waters of the Limfjord. It wasn't a large city. The Lutheran church towered between the sea of red rooftops. Like many European cities, the houses were painted an assortment of pastel colors, and it was greener and less densely packed than the large, European metropolises we'd seen so far.

1000fryd was another D.I.Y. venue. We were greeted warmly by the staff. Everyone who worked the club were volunteers. Coincidentally, someone from Davide's hometown of Pescara worked there. She came out to tell us where to put gear, then rode with Davide to show him where to drop off the vehicle.

"That's crazy," I remarked.

"Isn't it?" he said. "Small world."

We unloaded into a covered "patio" – what looked to be a repurposed garage or outdoor commons area. It was basically just a rectangular space set into the first floor of the building, consisting of a few chairs, a couch, and a locking gate; it was otherwise open to the elements. Once we had everything out of the rain, we took the gear inside and then up a set of stairs. This led to an upstairs hallway. To get into the green room in the back, there was a door with a keypad lock.

Inside, there was a fridge full to the brim with beer, a selection of sodas (I didn't recognize the brands) in glass bottles, and bottles of water; there was a crockpot full of what looked to be curry, a kitchen with dishes and cutlery, and a circular dining table. A door from the kitchen opened into the bunkhouse: a large loft with bunk beds, cots, couches, tables, and windows overlooking the little alleyway beside the place. It was a veritable band palace.

After load-in, they told us the food upstairs should be ready. Each band got one shelf in the fridge. Everything was so well-organized, and by anarchists no less. I took the opportunity to make a long call with Amberly. I figured that I'd probably be able to talk with her for her whole morning commute to work. I told her about the show in Dresden, about how awesome the venue was in Aalborg.

"Seems like things are going a lot better," she said.

"They are," I replied. "It helps to have a good show."

"Yeah."

She was quiet for a moment.

"What is it?"

"I don't know…" She paused. "It's just not the first time you had issues with how a tour was going…."

"Uh huh…"

"You just seemed like you were doing really bad the other day. And now it seems you've completely flipped around."

"Yeah... I guess I have..." I said. "Well, the first couple days really sucked... But now, I don't know... Things are looking up."

"Okay..." she said. "It's just that sometimes... you seem to forget about how bad things were. And when the tour ends, you don't ever bring up the problems. You complain without communicating, so the same thing happens time and time again."

"I know."

"So. Don't forget this time."

It was easy for a romantic like me to get caught up in compulsive optimism, and gloss right over the negative bits. I could be totally negative one day and forget about it two days later. Sometimes you could forget how risky or stupid something was because it all worked out in the end. You might forget the past four nights of drudgery and hell-drives because of a single good show. That's how important issues go unaddressed, thoughts and feelings unexpressed. Small problems swim beneath the surface. They grow and grow until they swell into monsters, nourished on silence.

After the call, I returned to the kitchen to find everyone gathered around the table. The food was ready, and there was plenty for everyone. I don't know what the dish was. Someone said it was something local, but it tasted like curry anyway. It had potatoes, peppers, onions, some kind of lentil or grain.

We discussed the next day, and Davide booked our ticket for the ferry. To reach Sweden, we'd travel via ferry from Fredrickshavn to Gothenburg, and the full journey would take about three hours. Then, it was still a half day's drive to Stockholm. With all said and done, based on the ferry schedule, we'd need to leave 1000flyd the next morning by 6:00 AM in order to catch the 7:30 departure. If we waited for the next one, which was hours later, we wouldn't be able to make the next show. Thankfully, Davide was on top of it.

I retired to the loft. The club beneath me was starting to fill up – I could hear more muffled voices and commotion below. I think most of my bandmates and the Italians had gone downstairs by now. Penny, and then Davide came up, I think, found a bunk and went to sleep. I was half-asleep myself, and shut my eyes again as soon as they came into the room.

I thought about getting up from the couch, and climbing into one of the large, soft-looking mattresses, but I didn't find the energy to move myself. The daylight trickling in from the window was the daylight of late evening on a dreary day. It was pale and blue. There was the gentle patter of rain against the glass. The occasional car engine passed by on the streets below.

***

In my dreams, I often found myself traveling. I would be in some city or small town that I did not know: some place I've never been, or rather some amalgam of scenes and places I've visited, or seen on television, or in movies, or in video games. Apocalypse dreams were common, also – a dream where I was journeying with some small group of survivors and a random assortment of friends or loved ones, through the ruins of a fallen society, looking for somewhere safe. I still have them, sometimes.

But after years of touring, being on tour is a much more common theme than the apocalypse. After all those memories of touring were uploaded into the old noggin, that is the new story that the narration of the dream creates. I've read that the stories in our dreams are narratives added as post hoc explanations to the sequences of events and images and sensory experiences conjured up at random as we sleep – that dreams are a sort of "defrag" process, a dump of excess information. Your brain is sorting through all the information you've taken in during the day, or over recent memory, and is discarding what is not important. In the course of this defrag process, your sleeping mind experiences a bunch of seemingly incoherent sensory inputs. Meanwhile, memories and people from all over our past are sometimes associated with a given set of sensations, and appear within the sequence. The conscious side of the mind can't handle the chaos of this random sequence, so it makes up a story – which is actually not so different from the way the conscious mind interprets the world while we're awake.

So, it would make perfect sense for my conscious mind to think, when dreaming, and finding myself yet again in some strange city, "I must be on tour right now." That is the explanation that most readily matches my experiences from waking life. So now, most of my dreams of traveling have the narrative explanation of touring interposed upon them by my mind.

The weirdest is when I have tour dreams while on tour. Usually these are anxiety-laden, and involve all the day-to-day fears: of engine trouble, showing up to a club to find our gear doesn't work, or that we've somehow traveled to the wrong city, or going on stage and forgetting all the songs. Waking up from a tour dream to find that you're on tour is somewhat surreal. It takes a few moments longer when you wake up in some foreign setting: to recall where you are and what you are doing. It is always a shock. In my dreams, I'm exploring. Always. Looking for the next horizon. The events are not as interesting as the settings.

***

Art's task is not to represent the external world, but to falsify it in the course of a different, more important task: the representation of the internal world.

We have two forms of dishonesty: the kind found in True Art, and the kind found in True Dishonesty (propaganda, cynical art, mere entertainment). The first is the act of expressing a subjective reality, wherein the artist honestly tries to represent his or her own inner world, and in the process falsifies the outer world. We've called this the artist's deception. This *is* dishonesty, but it is honest dishonesty. Then, there is the separate question about the act of representing a subjective reality that does *not* match one's inner, subjective experience: under this category we might classify art done by rote, art done for financial gain, or simply, *imitation*. This is True Dishonesty.

Even in the case of the dilettante, who is nothing more than an imitator, we might distinguish an honest type of imitation from a dishonest one. We don't think that the advertiser who imitates a popular stylistic trend in his advertising was made to feel something, do we? That he is honestly trying to convey a feeling from his own soul? No. But he knows how the style he imitates is effective at causing feelings in others, and uses this manipulation of feelings in order to sell products. The process is not truly an artistic process because the creator is not resonating anything from within. This is a different case from the amateur artist who sincerely feels something that he wants to express but is stuck habitually in imitation of his influences because of a lack of command of the technique.

Tolstoy, in his essay on art, argues that art done by rote, or for cynical reasons, that which he calls "counterfeit art," cannot have the same degree of infectiousness as True Art. Tolstoy writes: "There is one indubitable indication distinguishing real art from its counterfeit, namely, the infectiousness of art. If a man, without exercising effort and without altering his standpoint on reading, hearing, or seeing another man's work, experiences a mental condition which unites him with that man and with other people who also partake of that work of art, then the object evoking that condition is a work of art. And however poetical, realistic, effectful, or interesting a work may be, it is not a work of art if it does not evoke that feeling (quite distinct from all other feelings) of joy and of spiritual union with another (the author) and with others (those who are also infected by it)."

The "infectiousness" here is part and parcel with the mimetic quality of art. To Tolstoy, art must truly bring about a state of communion (emotional resonance between artist and audience, through the medium of the artwork). It is this spiritual union, which Tolstoy describes as joyous, that is the *sina qua non* of True Art. This set of definitions makes the question of authentic or honest art fairly easy to answer. If the infectiousness is present, it is art; if infectiousness is not present, it is not art.

Tolstoy even uses the principle of art's infectiousness as a judge of the quality of the art. Tolstoy writes: "And not only is infection a sure sign of art, but the degree of infectiousness is also the sole measure of excellence in art. *The stronger the infection, the better is the art as art*, speaking now apart from its subject matter, i.e., not considering the quality of the feelings it transmits."

In his imitation, the artist is confessing that another artist has captured him, captured his attention and his creative focus. One imitates because he experiences an expression of someone else so profoundly that he *must* express the same thing himself. This is art's goal, after all: to transmit feeling. When art achieves its goal, then one who experiences an artistic expression actually *feels the same feeling!* Emotional resonance is achieved. The imitator is one whose psyche has been effectively colonized by another artist. In the imitator, we have the example of someone who has been made to feel what the artist feels.

This makes the sincere imitator who never overcomes his influences an inferior artist, but still an artist. He remains forever inferior to the artists who captivated him, and whom he never escapes the imitation of. The quality of his craft may be poor. As Tolstoy says, the quality of the feeling itself may even be poor. But the poor artist is nevertheless an artist.

The cynical propagandist, however, is excluded from being an artist. He may be a master of his *craft* – that is to say, the techniques of whatever medium he is using to achieve his ends. We may permit that there have even been some political propagandists who so sincerely believed in the moral and the aesthetic pushed by their political ideology that their propaganda might have approached genuine art. And there may have been genuine artists who have occasionally indulged in cynical propaganda. But while all artists engage in deception, only honest deceivers can be included among the ranks of artists.

The crime of the propagandist is not that he lies, but that he turns art into a craft. If one is serving a momentary god or a Muse, then however much he may imitate or borrow from others, he is an artist. His art will naturally be *motivated*, and directed at creating a reality out of the artist's own values. So long as his work flows out of emotional resonance, however, it remains that seeking of emotive communication, and the bridging of self or other. If one is serving Mammon, and shaping their artistic expression with the ulterior motives of profit, power, politics, or simply because of a cynical desire to please an audience, drawing on nothing of what they deeply feel in order to do so, then such a person is not an artist. The propagandists are parasites on the mythological power of art.

***

It was an early show. 1000flyd attracted the typical anarchist D.I.Y. spot crowd. There were girls with one side of their heads shaved, Vikings with dreadlocks and hemp hoodies, dudes with Mohawks, dyed hair and piercings, punks, artists and weirdos of every stripe. The bathrooms were covered in pro-gay, pro-progressive, anti-fascist cartoons and graffiti. There were fliers saying, "No human is illegal: refugees welcome," rainbow flags pinned to the walls.

The show that night was in the running with the previous night for the best show so far. Destroyer and Obelisco performed to a packed house. Small houses are easy to pack, but it feels better to pay to a small packed house than a big and half-empty one. The attendees were enthusiastic and full of energy. These people were here to enjoy themselves and enjoy the music.

I was over the jetlag and had my own energy back again. I had to reign in my performance a bit from the night before. I tried not to thrash around too viciously. I still headbanged, but kept it more restrained, by putting my whole body into the motion. It didn't feel as bad as it did on Wednesday, but it was still hurt and inflamed. My own body mostly dictated the level of physicality I could use. I felt the pain sharply whenever I jerked my neck too violently.

We stayed up for hours after the show, mingling, smoking cigarettes, drinking, dancing. I spent a lot of my time outside where the smokers were. It's a good general practice if you're bumming cigarettes on tour – either because you're broke, or you're a fake non-smoker (both of which applied to me at the time) – to bum from outside the van enclave. It increases your total goodwill for when you need to bum one from a tourmate later, and you might as well skim as much charity off the local economy while you're there.

I bummed a rolled cigarette from a tall, Danish hippie. We began talking, and naturally I mentioned that I was Danish-American, and my last name.

"My grandparents said that Denmark was the only place where they checked into a hotel, gave the name Kjeldsen for the reservation, and were asked, 'Which one?'," I recounted.

"My family goes way back here," he told me. He paused, looking away a bit shyly as he rolled the cigarette. "I am ashamed to say this, at all, but I am actually incredibly Aryan."

I didn't quite know what to say. I understood perfectly well why someone would make such a qualification, as we westerners all have negative associations with anyone who talks about their "Aryan" blood. I just kind of shrugged and smiled. He went on to tell me how a distant ancestor was basically a small feudal lord, who was always fighting the Germans who would raid his lands.

I walked in after the long conversation on the patio to hear a thumping rhythm, then the words, "Boys, Boys, Boys", sung by Sabrina. It was that pop song from the 1980s. I scanned the room. Steve and Andrea were standing over by the DJ, grinning. This was their doing. The whole room was dancing. I grabbed another beer.

I stayed up too late, given how tired I was. I eventually wandered up into the loft again. The thumping of the bass through the speakers and the ambient noise of people downstairs was plenty audible up through the floorboards. At first it was distracting. But eventually, there was something almost soothing about it.

***

Nick and I stood in front of the venue in the early light of dawn. It was foggy and overcast, just as the day before. We had to use up everything before crossing international borders once again. Nick rolled a cigarette that was mostly tobacco, but he used the last of the hash and crumpled it throughout. All the weed we'd acquired was now gone, and this was the last of the hashish. We shared it between the two of us and Alex. The hash-cigarette was a bit rough to draw on first thing in the morning. It was basically just like smoking a filterless tobacco cigarette, and the hash did not exactly cut down on the harshness.

Davide pulled up in the van, and we all piled inside. It was a forty-minute drive to Frederickshavn, where the ferry would depart. We pulled up to pay our fare and show our passports for border crossing. In the narrow lane, each of us got out of the vehicle and walked around the side to show our passport to the lady in the booth. Each of us had to duck under the driver's side mirror on the way back. The border checker spoke Italian with the Italians and English with the Americans, switching flawlessly.

When it was my turn, I handed her my passport.

"Finally came back home," I said, smiling.

She looked at the passport, looked at me, and smiled. She said nothing other than, "Thank you," and I circled back around the front of the van and climbed back inside.

The ferry had five decks, and was larger than any I'd ever been on. There was the level that we drove onto, where we parked the van and left it with the other autos. The level above had a few duty-free shops and cafes. The food was a buffet price – too expensive. I settled for a coffee and a sandwich – which was also too expensive, but the price of a coffee included unlimited refills. I determined at that moment to drink as much coffee as possible for the five euros that I'd paid.

We all lounged tiredly in the swiveling, cushy chairs on the deck. The lounge was full with people huddled in their different parties, charging their phones and keeping warm. Outside, the sea winds were biting and cold.

Once we got underway, I went out. Doc, Luca, and Alex eventually came out to take some pictures as we departed. We each had a cigarette. Being out in the elements was refreshing. Cold, free air, beating against my skin, and blowing my hair to one side of my face or the other. I pulled the hood of my black hoodie over my head, and nursed the coffee that steamed into the frigid morning. We watched the coastline disappear into mist.

I found my way onto one of the higher decks. The sea was a foreboding, silvery blue. It was like a mirror reflection of the grayish-white of the clouds. I pondered the frigid depths beneath. I always think about what it would be like to plunge in. What would happen if I suddenly went over? If the ship capsized? Wouldn't the shock simply stop one's heart? Don't we always – when we look at a cliff, or the ocean, or any kind of abyss – think of just throwing ourselves in? Where the imagination always seems to go. There is a neologism, *lachesism*: the longing for the clarity of disaster. Is that what this feeling is?

Eventually, there was nothing to see. It was all white mist and endless waters. I imagined these ferries made this trip multiple times a day. The captain and crew probably made the route hundreds or thousands of times a year. It seemed so odd, so impossible that one could navigate through this opacity. It was all the same, an endless sheet of white cast over the icy seas, in every direction I looked.

CHAPTER THIRTEEN
STOCKHOLM

Three hours later, the mist parted. Gothenburg appeared. Nick, Steve and I greeted the shores of Sweden from the upper deck of the ferry. There was a castle on a peninsula jutting out from the shoreline; the old buildings topped with verdigris-green roofs. Eventually, the white curtain of mist was fully cast aside, and I took in the full view of the city. It was a place of mostly modern architecture, with a few eye-catching historical edifices planted within.

It was late morning. We made port. The calls were going over the intercom to disembark. We joined the herd of people shuffling down the flights of stairs. But the crowds of people who were still aboard all seemed to be disembarking by foot. We went down the flights of stairs to get to the elevator leading to the parking level. We rode the elevator down. On that floor of the ferry, there was no one else other than us in the bands. I could tell everyone was nervous about this, but we were all silent about it.

When we got to where the van was parked, we discovered to our horror that Davide's van stood alone in its lane. The crew working the ferry shouted at us, irate. One of them shook his head at us, making eye contact as we piled into the vehicle. We all half-jogged over to the passenger side and piled in as quickly as possible. We must have fit the image of irresponsible musicians.

"Fuck," someone said.

"Did they say it was time to disembark? I didn't hear shit."

"No, nothing."

"I didn't hear any announcement," Davide admitted.

We had to wait a couple minutes – three of us hadn't made it down yet, having gotten separated on the way down to the auto deck. The crew came and yelled some more, and after an agonizingly long time, the rest of our party showed up. Davide hurriedly started the van and drove us off the ferry. All the crew we passed gestured at us, pointing, shouting, laughing.

It was five hours to Stockholm. The highway took us through Boras, on a route running along Lake Vattern. After a while, we were out in the country again, driving through wooded hills and pastures. We had a lot of ground to cover if we were going to make it to load-in on time, so we kept it to a single stop that day. The gas station was in the middle of the woods. The highway wasn't very well-traveled; it felt like we were in the middle of nowhere. As was the pattern, even when Davide insisted that we had to keep our stop to just ten or fifteen minutes, we ended up lingering for twice that time.

I bought another expensive, mediocre sandwich and sat at the picnic table with Nick, Penny, and a couple of the Italians, throwing my crumbs to the birds pecking around at our feet. Andrea walked over to the sign designating the exit to the parking lot, reading, "Ausfahrt." We watched as Doc snapped a picture of Andrea, bending over and obscuring the part of the sign that said "Aus", so that you could just see the arrow reading "fahrt" pointing outward from his rear end. Laughter echoed into the open sky.

IX. Private Art

There is an obvious problem with the idea that art is essentially communication, because that would mean that art always seeks an audience. The challenge to this explanation is *private art*. We must consider private art in the most literal sense of the term: art created with no intention of sharing it with the world. If such art does end up being shared, it is only after the artist's death, or after a stark change of heart in regard to the work of private art. Francisco de Goya's Black Paintings would be one famous example of such private works of art. For another, Marcus Aurelius also left mankind a masterwork of literature simply by writing notes to himself that he never wished to make public.

What is troublesome about private art is that its contents cannot be created for the purpose of communication, supposing that it is created with the intention of never communicating it to anyone. If art is communication, then this apparently presents an inconsistency in that model. Private art would be a meaningless endeavor, and yet many people find enjoyment or a sense of release in their private art.

There could be any number of motivations for private art. For example, the new artist: an amateur who is not confident enough to show their work to the world. In this case, the artist recognizes that they don't have mastery over the techniques yet. There is a sense of social shame from producing something ugly: art that resonates with no one, or worse yet, resonates in the wrong kind of way, provoking ire, or criticism. The worst art is that which provokes laughter at something intended serious, or vice versa: where the emotion, feeling, or state of mind one wishes to transmit is actually received in the opposite manner. No artist wants to be a laughingstock or a charlatan. There is always a social consequence for miscommunication.

But this kind of private art is no mystery. The amateur artist makes art for the sake of improving their technique; he has no intention of debuting the product because his artistic expression is a work in progress. This kind of private art is art done in the course of practice.

Another example of the private artist is the hobbyist, who practices an art but with no intention of *ever* progressing to the point of displaying it publically. Such a person is not working up to a public, communicable expression, but is satisfied to keep their works to themselves, whether they be paintings, songs, poems, short stories, or whatever. And yet, the artistic expression still occurs, albeit in a private form, and the private artist keeps making private art. I've known a few writers who were like this. Some of these writers eventually published under pseudonyms, some have still never published at all, to my knowledge.

Even this type of private art remains somewhat intelligible in my model of art as communication. In this case, there is a drive to communicate something emotional, but also a feeling of shyness or embarrassment, and this feeling of shyness overrides the need for expression to the broader world. Most people who don't show their art to others lack confidence in themselves and their work. As to why this would be the case for some people is an interesting psychological and social question, but it doesn't pose a problem for my explanation of art. One could argue that in the cases we've considered, the amateur artist wishes to communicate their inner contents, but cannot find the courage to do so, just as many people do not find the courage to communicate in the linguistic form.

Still, we cannot have done with private art with these explanations, for there is something deeper here. What is most interesting to me about the concept of private art is that artists themselves often praise this view of art, either implicitly or explicitly. We may remember the common utterances I cited at the beginning of the book. "It's all about the music." – "It's just rock n' roll!" – "It's punk rock!" – "Art is creativity for its own sake." – "I don't care what the audience thinks." There is some sense in these intuitions, especially when we examine all that we have concluded about art so far. But these statements seemingly disavow the importance of the communion of art, and stress the primacy of a one-sided subjective expression.

I have argued that art is the authentic communication of our inner world, however much these representations might falsify the outer world in so doing. I have also argued that art is counterfeit when the representation of this inner world is done not from an emotional need, but from pragmatic concerns of profit or fame. The natural conclusion that many will then draw is that private art is actually the sincerest form of art, because it is a form of art in which there cannot be any pragmatic concerns. The objection could then be raised that we haven't proven the necessity of an audience at all.

Perhaps we can hone the problem of private art with a thought experiment. The question I put forward is this: whether we believe that an artist would continue to make art if he was confined to a desert island, with no one else to appreciate the work. We can easily imagine that some artists would not. At the very least, most artists would not push themselves to produce work of the same caliber of beauty or excellence without the social pressures. On the other hand, the opposite intuition seems just as valid: that most artists would continue to make art even if the possibility of the audience was removed. When people find themselves isolated – in prison, in solitary confinement, in long-term seclusion in the wilderness, or whatever the case may be – many occupy their time with artistic expression. In some cases, this is done with the artist's knowledge that he couldn't share his art with the outside world if he wanted to.

This thought experiment seems to incline our intuition in favor of the existence of private art. If our hypothesis is that art is a form of communication – the expression of which arose communally, and the very substance of which is communal – then doesn't the notion of private art, of art done for its own sake, fly in the face of that? We have argued that art and language are parallel forms of communication. If there can be no private language on this account, then presumably there can be no private art. From all appearances, the private artist threatens to unravel the whole theory.

And yet, a bit of sober reflection should reveal to us that the private artist is not so problematic. First of all, we engage in private linguistic communication all the time. While there can be no private language, this doesn't mean there cannot possibly be conceptual thoughts expressed through language that are nevertheless kept to oneself. The rejection of private language doesn't invalidate the possibility of, say, the last living speaker of a language that is dying out. Such a person would have a 'private language' in that he is the only one who can speak it. In the desert island example, one might talk to himself, as well as make art solely for himself. But this does not mean that art and language are not communicative.

Language is not a system that the brain forms on its own, as an individual invention or conception. One can use language to express things to oneself that are never shared with others: the impossibility of a private language does not mean the impossibility of private meaning. Meaning is the content: that which the language is meant to convey, not the language itself. The language shapes the form of that content – maybe its very essence. This means that all true meaning is shareable, even if it is not shared.

The common example of using language privately is the private journal. There is no contradiction, in principle, with the idea of language as indelibly communal, and the journal: committing language to the page with no intention of communication. We may regard private art as akin to a private journal. Just as we use the socially-developed forms of communication, via languages, to express things which we only express to ourselves, the same holds true for art. We paint paintings for ourselves alone, we write stories for ourselves alone, we sing songs in the shower for ourselves alone. This obviously raises the follow-up question, *why?* – and for this, we might also consider why it is that people keep private journals.

The private journal and the private artwork are both forms of expression for therapeutic means. What is it for something to be therapeutic? Therapy, in the literal sense of the word and as it is conventionally practiced, takes the form of one person communicating information to another – personal information, profound and traumatic events, and deep emotional problems. The mere communication of this inner content is by those same means a form of treatment. The mere expression comes with the relief of psychological baggage. The private journal is much the same. The mere act of expression acts as a surrogate for communicating with another human being.

This is not strictly speculative. Art is done for therapeutic reasons even in clinical, psychiatric settings. Mental patients are encouraged to paint, journal, write poems, or express themselves. Sometimes, the therapeutic use of self-expression goes beneath the foundations of art, and returns to the rawest forms of emotive expression. Consider, for example, "primal shout therapy" in which the patient is encouraged to scream as long as they want to, as loud as they want to. This type of therapy is, in fact, the inspiration behind the song, "Shout" by Tears For Fears. Both the founding members deal with mental health problems and underlying anger issues. In shout therapy, you dredge all of that up to the surface, by means of the most primordial and basic artistic expression: screaming.

Let us consider the temptation, in light of the previous chapters about the social pressures on the artist and concerning the questionable honesty of the artist, to designate therapeutic private art as the most authentic art possible. Perhaps art, like language, arose communally, but is only truly authentic when expressed to no one but one's own self. One speaks most honestly when he thinks no one else is listening – that sort of sentiment is at play here.

But this reveals yet another moral prejudice: *that man is most honest with himself.* That is not at all clear, has never been demonstrated, and I would say that in many cases we have evidence to the contrary. Often, what therapy is intended to remedy is man's own alienation from himself and his own emotions.

This is sure to be an attractive stance to those of us who have been raised in an individualist society. The intellectuals we looked up to were existentialists, concerned with the liberation of the one from the tyranny of the many. We would love to say that authenticity is self-authenticity and a disregard for how others might feel. I cannot say that this even goes against my own intuitions. There are always some truths that we reserve for ourselves.

Keeping art private keeps it "pure" in our conception of it, free from what Tolstoy would have called counterfeiting, or what Schopenhauer would have called subjective concerns. But we should really ask: to what degree are these declarations about art a *defense mechanism?* They shield the private artist from ever having to grapple with his lack of confidence or insufficient technique. Even the artist who does share his work with an audience and finds that he is dismissed or ridiculed can reject the audience as unimportant. I am not denigrating the reclamation of art as being intensely personal: merely pointing out that this assessment of art is irrational, just as art itself is irrational. It is no surprise that our artistic impulses would resort to irrational means in order to justify themselves!

To put this another way: *of course* the Muse would whisper to you that it doesn't matter what the audience thinks, for the only thing that is important is to express the divine inspiration. If the audience is a hindrance to the Muse in using you as a conduit for this inspiration, the Muse will direct the artist to ignore the audience. In the case of truly private, therapeutic art, we must then conclude that *one is communicating with oneself.* What does it mean to communicate with oneself?

***

It was late afternoon when we entered Stockholm's downtown. It was a Saturday night, and the city was alive with energy. There were beautiful, blonde people with high cheekbones everywhere one looked. The venue tonight was an English pub: the sign read, "Copperfield's." Weird, to spend our first night in Sweden at an English pub. Steve spotted the promoter, standing out front. It so happened that the promoter that night was an American, someone from Baltimore that we'd met on one of our U.S. tours. Strange, the people you run into on the road. The doors of the van opened. Everyone started piling out.

"Are we getting out? I thought we were going to stop at the hostel first?"

Steve didn't say anything, he just kind of stared at me. I stared back. He turned and walked away, and went over to talk to the promoter.

When he and Davide came back a few minutes later, they told us they had details on where to park the van and our accommodation. There was a secure parking lot provided, but it was several blocks away. We'd need to load in gear first. As for the accommodation, Steve told us they'd procured a hostel for us. The two bands would be staying in two different rooms; we wouldn't have a whole room to ourselves that night. We'd be going to the hostel first to drop off personal items and bags, then unload gear at the club, then Davide would take the van and park it.

Honestly, I was pissed. I didn't feel good about the accommodation at all. But everything we did was to save money, to minimize cost in light of our abysmal revenue. The room in the hostel didn't have any lockers. I decided to just leave my personal belongings in the van. Better for the peace of mind. Of course, if I did that, I wouldn't have my toiletries with me. I hadn't showered now for about three days. I told myself that one more day wouldn't make that much difference. I made the last-minute decision to bring my shoulder bag with me. I decided I'd just stash it with the gear. I didn't want to be without my books for the whole evening.

We loaded gear up a set of carpeted stairs, past an upstairs bar and seating area. The place was open, but relatively quiet. More people were downstairs. I don't think the upstairs was open yet. There was a little storage room adjacent to the kitchen, the shelves full of boxes and cleaning supplies: there, we stacked the speakers, amps, guitars, pedalboards, drum set.

There were a couple of bartenders in sharp, black button downs and slacks who stood there chatting, leaning against the counter. Didn't seem like they had much of anything to do. The promoter got the soundguy, and they both sat down with Steve and I. The promoter made sure that everyone got a meal from the kitchen, and asked who was vegetarian and who wasn't. The soundguy was wearing a hat that said, "Blue Ruin."

"Is that a reference to the film?"

"What?"

"Blue Ruin."

"Oh," the soundguy answered. "That's a band."

"Oh. Never heard of them."

"It's the name of a movie?"

"Yeah. Same director who did Green Room. Maybe the band is named after the film?"

"I don't know. I haven't seen his movies. Are they good?"

"Do you like over-the-top violence?"

"Actually, no," the soundguy said.

The conversation turned to the show. The soundguy prided himself on having been able to pull off all these metal shows at this venue. The sound ordinances were strict, he explained. It required everyone who performed there to dial back their volume. He asked us to trust him to control most of the volume through the PA. By this point in the story, you can probably guess how I felt about this. He promised us that he knew what he was doing. He said he would make it sound rich, full, loud – at a lower volume. He said he knew the acoustics of the room. I wondered if he sat down over a meal and explained this to all the bands, or if the promoter had warned him about bands like us.

They put us in touch with a local who would bring weed. The connection arrived just after the doors opened. The promoter and I went off with him, walked around the corner from the pub, and turned down a side street. We burned one together, I paid him for the product, and he and the promoter headed back inside.

We still had a few hours to spare before showtime. I texted Nick to meet me outside the venue. We walked past the McDonalds on the main drag. There were homeless people sleeping right in front of it, on the sidewalk. This did not fit my perception of Northern Europe, which I'd generally conceived of as a post-poverty paradise.

We turned onto a sidestreet and entered the Kronobergsparkens: a series of concentric paths that intertwined about a hilltop that rose up in the park's center, overlooking a sloping, grassy field. It made for some steep, uphill inclines for power-walking. We reached the top. Nick shielded the flame from the wind as I lit the joint. We passed it between the two of us. We watched the twilight dissolve into night, as we stood alone at the apex of the park, under the shadowy tree branches, swaying in the wind.

We talked. Mostly about politics. I'd become rather enamored with the universal basic income movement as of late. There was even a candidate running on that issue in the Democratic primary. Nick had been willing to hear me out on the subject, but I could tell that he was skeptical. I was doing my best not to launch into a high rant as he stood there, on the highest hill.

"You seem to have a fairly positive view of human nature," he said.

"I think the cumulative effect will be greater than the sum of its parts..."

"You think that people are going to use that money to go out and start businesses, learn new skills, that sort of thing? I think a lot of people are just going to keep sitting on the couch and playing video games. UBI will be injected into people's arms."

"Maybe so," I said, "Maybe some of them. Most of the work is done by a small group of hyper productive people, anyway. With automation, we aren't going to need everyone to work. If 85% of the workforce is displaced... it doesn't matter if we only need 15% to do all the work anyway."

"I worry about the 85%," Nick said, with a note of finality.

We both found we had nothing else to say, really. We'd probably expressed more about our own temperaments than any facts to evaluated objectively. Politics is always like that. The conversation ended. We lingered there for a short while, taking the reprieve from the breakneck schedule at any possible opportunity. Silence was nice.

***

The human being is not a unity, governed by a solitary ego-consciousness that controls the emotions and makes voluntary, rational decisions, as in the conception of an immortal soul, or of a "mind driving a body." On the contrary, the self is a multiplicity of drives, emotions, and subpersonalities. Nietzsche argued that a drive is the "leading string" of the notions of the consciousness. Our desires and valuations originate in the body, within the unconscious physiology, and are pushed into conscious channels by these drives.

The psychoanalyst Carl Jung wrote, in his book *The Undiscovered Self*: "We welcome to find anybody who is not influenced and indeed dominated by desires, habits, impulses, prejudices, resentments, and by every conceivable kind of complex. All these natural facts function exactly like an Olympus full of deities who want to be propitiated, served, feared and worshipped, not only by the individual owner of this assorted pantheon, but by everybody in his vicinity... we have got accustomed to saying, 'I *have* such and such a desire or habit or feeling of resentment,' instead of the more veracious 'Such and such a desire or habit or feeling of resentment has *me*.'"

In the early psychoanalytic school, the individual was divided into the conscious and unconscious mind. The conscious mind consists of the ego-consciousness and all of its rational conceptions of the world. The unconscious mind is all the feelings, drives, and instincts that the ego-consciousness is not aware of. This does not mean it cannot *become* aware of them – but as soon as a feeling comes to the attention of the conscious mind, it is no longer unconscious, by definition.

How is it that the unconscious mind is able to bring forth its contents into consciousness? According to the theories of Carl Jung, the self communicates its unconscious content to its conscious mind through artistic expression. Thus, we may say that one of the needs served by art, perhaps even a primary need, is self-communication. This is what we are doing in therapeutic art, and why even private art is a form of communicating.

Artistic expression is how we bring forth our raw emotional data into an intelligible form. By intelligible here, I mean *emotionally intelligible*. Since the symbols and their emotional resonance developed communally, we express our emotions within the previous channels laid by our long history of emotive expression. In order to recognize our emotions, we translate them into an artistic form as we bring them into consciousness.

Artistic expression exists at the edge of the raw sensory and emotional chaos solidifying into a definite, objectified vessel. Art lives at the border of consciousness and unconsciousness, of the objective and subjective, of the known and the hidden.

Jung's book, *The Archetypes and the Collective Unconscious*, provides a direct window into how this process develops. Jung's research references a literal therapeutic example – of art produced for the sake of the patient's own mental convalescence. The example is, arguably, not strictly private. The art was republished in a book, after all. The patients gave permission only after the fact, however, and under the condition of anonymity.

Mandalas were always a fascination for Jung, as he felt that they exemplified the universal religious symbolism that he argued came from humanity's collective unconscious. By "collective", Jung did not mean that the unconscious minds of humankind are all linked. This type of supernatural interpretation of Jung's theory is wrong and all-too-common. Jung believed, on the contrary, that the collective unconscious was the inherited set of symbols and archetypes that would be the same for every single person regardless of culture or nationality. This is a controversial enough claim all its own, but it has nothing to do with an unconscious psychic link shared by all human beings. Jung took the common use of certain symbols and narrative archetypes as evidence of this. Jung's patients would draw mandalas spontaneously during their therapeutic drawing and painting.

Jung: "The pictures come as a rule from educated people who were unacquainted with the ethnic parallels. The pictures differ widely, according to the stage of the therapeutic process; but certain important stages correspond to definite motifs. Without going into therapeutic details, I would only like to say that a rearranging of the personality is involved, a kind of new centring. That is why mandalas mostly appear in connection with chaotic psychic states of disorientation or panic... At all events they express order, balance, and wholeness. Patients themselves often emphasize the beneficial or soothing effect of such pictures. Usually the mandalas express religious, i.e. numinous, thoughts and ideas, or, in their stead, philosophical ones. Most mandalas have an intuitive, irrational character, and through their symbolical content, exert a retroactive significance, like icons, whose possible efficacy was never consciously felt by the patient..."

We can leave aside Jung's claims about the collective unconscious. It would seem that, through the artistic expression of mandalas, Jung's patients were able to bring the chaos of their psyche into some kind of orderly, comprehensible form.

He relates the stories of patient after patient who drew images and symbols that resembled Tibetan thangkas or Eastern Orthodox Icons, and who experienced a state of calmness or understanding. As part of the process, they gained heightened awareness of themselves and their emotions. Jung emphasizes that the technique of the patient does not matter. Their forms and lines are not very well expressed, even when the resemblance to a religious symbol is clear – and, if anything, *it is better* if the patient is lacking in technique, and not knowledgeable about the religious subject matter. The more ignorant and unskilled the person is, the better the artistic impulse can express itself in the rawest, most emotive form.

"I tried to paint this dream," one of his patients writes, "But as so often happens, it came out rather different." The patient had dreamt of walking through a dark, disagreeable city with one of his friends, until they finally came to a park. In the center of the park was a pond with a red-flowering magnolia tree standing on an island in the center. It was bathed in impossible sunlight. "The magnolia turned into a sort of rose made of ruby-colored glass," the patient wrote, "It shone like a four-rayed star..." The symbolism of a rose, or a ruby, shining as a sort of four-rayed star within the center of a mandala is the classic symbolism of western alchemy, which Jung claims the patient had no knowledge of.

As Jung's patients often engaged in therapeutic artwork by painting their dreams, the connection to dreams is also of interest. The dreaming mind is a continual well of inspiration for artists. From H.P. Lovecraft to Salvador Dali, we can find artists of every medium who delved deeply into their dream imagery for artistic inspiration.

Nietzsche suggests in *Human, All Too Human* that dreaming is a state of mind not dissimilar to the experience that primordial man must have had while awake. The dream is the "magical world of myth and ritual" that

McLuhan describes. The first shamans looked to their dreams as a source of religious folk teaching. Shamans were also the first actors: they allowed multiple spirits to inhabit them, and therefore played many roles (another example of art and religion springing out of divine madness near the dawn of history). We might recognize now that the shaman was acting as a conduit for momentary gods. In dreams, all of the traits of mythological thinking are present. Things that happen in succession are 'caused' by one another by that token alone, in both mythological thinking and in dreams.

In mythological thinking, and dream thinking, correspondence is the rule. If fire is hot, and fire is red, then the color red is hot and the color red is fire. This is the rule in astrology, alchemy, and folk magic systems the world over. In both dream and artistic expression, one delves into their unconscious mind, which is the domain of such irrational correspondences. One perceives images and scenes that do not carry any apparent conscious meaning, and yet they seem profound in the dream. Dreams manifest these intuitive correspondences into imagery. Perhaps the conscious mind learned its skill for visual art from its experiences in dreaming, wherein it encounters the unconscious.

Jung writes about a patient who drew a manadala featuring a Kundalini serpent coiled three and a half times around the center of the picture. She was, yet again, trying to draw that which she had originally seen in a dream. "The dreamer had no notion of what was going on in her, namely the beginning of a new orientation, nor would she have understood it consciously. Also, the parallels from Eastern symbolism were completely unknown to her, so that any influence is out of the question. The symbolic picture came to her spontaneously, when she had reached a certain point in her development…"

There are dozens of examples like this one, too many to relate. Again, the point is not to substantiate the collective unconscious theory, however interesting it may be to our inquiry. The spontaneous act of artistic expression from people who were untrained in any particular art, and uneducated about any sort of religious symbolism, produced religious symbols which they found to be of profound emotional significance.

The patients experienced an emotional resonance within themselves – they experienced thoughts and feelings as a result of engaging with their own work that were not even clear to them when doing the actual painting. Art is used to comprehend the incomprehensible. Buried experiences that presumably stirred beneath the surface of consciousness for decades could in some cases be accessed by patients through artistic expression.

The feelings and experiences described by Jung's patients, as a result of their art therapy, are not dissimilar from spiritual struggles, religious experiences, or feelings of pious reverence and awe. The artistic significance of the paintings often gave the patients an appreciation for religious art, which they had never felt before. They had become religious artists themselves, now having partaken of the mythological mind-state that was at the forefront of all religion.

We now have the framework to incorporate private art into the model of art as essentially communicative. The private artworks of people, done either for explicitly therapeutic reasons, or for reasons possibly even unknown to themselves, are done out of an impulse for expression. In the case of private art, *the intended audience is oneself.*

In some cases, there may even be an imagined audience in the mind of the artist. The oldest audience is the gods; the spectator of all our deeds is the divine. Perhaps this is what the desert island artist does, or the artist in solitary confinement. When communication with other human beings is withheld from us, art is one of our ways of coping with this deprivation. There is hardly anything crueler than withholding human interaction and community from a human being. That art can serve as a sort of surrogate for this feeling of community speaks to the power of art, not to the existence of art that is non-communicative. The isolated artist creates out of the same need that leads Tom Hanks' character in Cast Away to create Wilson. It is a means of preventing a slip into insanity during prolonged solitude: his artistic act is to create an audience.

Art is always the communication between the conscious and the unconscious mind of the artist. It is the relation between the two – the interaction between conscious technique and unconscious emotion – that produces art. In the case of most art, communication with the audience (the social world) is the surface goal. But the communication with the self-audience is included even here. In the case of private art, it is not that anything essentially different is happening; communication still exists, and an audience still exists. We communicate within our own psyche because our consciousness is a microcosm of the community. Our consciousness developed within a communal net, and therefore mimics a community within itself.

This is why the pianist Glenn Gould said, "I believe that the justification of art is the internal combustion it ignites in the hearts of men and not its shallow, externalized, public manifestations. The purpose of art is not the release of a momentary ejection of adrenalin but is, rather, the gradual, lifelong construction of a state of wonder and serenity."

Gould contrasts the substantial inner world with the superficial public world. But this is not as interesting as the fact that he has intuited the dynamics of art: as first occurring as a communication within. Art originates from an expression of inner feelings newly realized. Those who appreciate the private and the personal in art have recognized this as the origin, as the primal communication within the self: the deepest level of communication. The internal brings forth the external communication. Gould is careful to distinguish this from a purely Dionysian feeling of "release." Art is not a wasteful discharge of energy. And yet, it springs from this internal friction and the need to outwardly manifest what is unexpressed within. Even the constructive and self-reflective art of the painter or composer begins on the razor's edge between unconsciousness and consciousness.

***

The soundguy was surprisingly good. He coaxed a powerful sound out of us while keeping the show at a relatively low volume. I think this was probably the only time I can recall that a soundguy had made such promises, then actually made us sound good. The local openers, a band called Nest, warmed everyone up appropriately. They blasted a catchy, fuzzy, mid-tempo doom groove. That seemed to be popular in Sweden, in those days. There was an enthusiastic crowd, if not a large one.

While they played, I hung out with Doc and Luca in the gear room. They ran through their scales, tuned their guitars. I noticed that Doc ran all of his guitar pedals through individual power adapters. I couldn't believe I hadn't thought of it before.

"Could I borrow that power cable?"

"Of course," he said, "I'll give it to you after our set."

The soundguy recorded both the touring bands. It was the only show of the tour that was recorded, something that I'm glad for. We'd hit our stride. Hell Obelisco was a raging maelstrom of energy that night. Alex pounded out the barbaric, prehistoric sounding rhythms, layered with Doc and Luca's churning guitars and Andrea's shrieks.

When we took the stage, the audience was more than ready. The vast majority had no idea who we were before that night. The amps hummed on and the feedback swelled. Steve began the opening riff of Into the Smoke, and Penny pounded out the toms signaling that the headbanging was about to begin. We had the crowd from the very first moment. It had been the right decision to borrow Doc's power supply. The delay pedal sounded so much richer, so much better than when I ran it on batteries. We didn't play flawlessly, but it was the most energy we'd brought to a show so far. We were locked in, in sync with one another, in sync with the energy of the crowd.

***

The question now concerns the other extreme: what about the celebrity artist? What about the "stars"? What do we make of the artist who is an inherently *public* artist?

The acquisition of fame is deeply unappealing to many artistic people, and yet it lies at the heart of any successful artistic career. To succeed as an artist means to reach the widest audience possible. Certainly, many artists have more humble goals. Most artists will tell you that their goal is merely to create enough of an audience to provide a sustainable income. I am inclined to believe that this is true (it is true in my own case). But this means that there is a genuine contradiction that runs through the heart of the artistic path, because rarely do artists strike this balance. Practically speaking, it is feast or famine.

Many artists come to have a complicated relationship with their own audience – some even come to despise their audience. In many artists, I've detected what one might call a thinly veiled contempt for their fans, and especially the critics. The intense social pressures on artists might make this outcome unsurprising.

The audience is demanding. They demand beauty – that is to say, artistic quality, or artistic value. Artistic value is the facilitation of this emotional resonance: this alchemy of feelings by which the audience itself feels gripped once again, moved once again, cleansed once again. They are cleansed because the emotional resonance of very powerful art brings forth the same experience for the audience as it does for the artist: the manifestation of that which was lying beneath the surface, unconscious, into the light of conscious reflection. In the case of shallow, purely sensuous art, simply forgetting one's self-consciousness for a while will do the trick.

As our techniques have advanced further and further, we have created art that is more and more powerful. The same momentary god never has the same power twice: once it is reified into a symbol, once it becomes a familiar image, melody or story, it becomes deprived of the power it once held. Art demands that new and more powerful gods continually overthrow the old pantheon.

Thus, there is a real danger that the artist can lose himself to the audience. The artist in this case becomes a mere conduit for the most resonant states that they are capable of expressing. They attune themselves ever and ever further to the wants of the audience, and over time their expression ceases to become even their own. Or, worse, they become a panderer: they begin consciously manipulating their audience, to continually give them new highs. They become deceivers or propagandists, having begun as true artists.

The most rebellious artists go the opposite direction of their audience's wants – and sometimes they suffer for this. Occasionally, you strike a vein of some emotionally powerful expression that the audience didn't know they wanted, until they wanted it. Once one has attained a sort of immortality or god-like status, they can get away with irritating their audience to a great degree.

The most tortured among the famous artists kill themselves, either intentionally, or by way of drawn-out, unconscious, habitual means. This is usually achieved via drugs or alcohol. We might consider all the members of the infamous "27 club," the unusually high number of famous artists who have died at age twenty-seven: Jim Morrison, James Dean, Jimi Hendrix, Kurt Cobain, Janis Joplin, Amy Winehouse, and so on. The case of Kurt Cobain is particularly interesting, given that we have his suicide letter, and comments he'd made to his friends: that he hated fame and wanted more than anything to go back to being an anonymous musician. He missed the days of playing in dive bars. He faced the reality that he actually *couldn't* go play a show like that if he wanted to, not anymore. Kurt Cobain's art had brought him fame as a byproduct, and the fame killed him.

This realization – of the power of the audience to overwhelm the artist – reflexively leads artists back to the response that so many of us cultivate: the detached, dispassionate approach. The disregard for the audience. "Art for art's sake." The ever-potent defense mechanism: which always boils down to, "it is irrational, just don't think about it."

I continually push past this response because we should all understand by now why human nature prohibits art from being a strictly private concern. The famous artist who thinks he is holding onto his individuality by asserting that he does art for its own sake without a care of what his audience believes nevertheless continues making art and showing it to the audience. Thus, this statement, of "Art for art's sake," is an article of faith, a magic talisman held up against the chaos that is implied by the idea of emotional resonance. One must hold up the amulet of "Art for the sake of art" against the powers of vanity, against the social pressures of the audience, against the threat of losing yourself.

Our claims about the artist here are not so different from a relatively uncontroversial understanding of the philosopher. Does the logical truth depend on what the philosopher's audience believes? If an audience is too uneducated to understand a philosopher's words, does the linguistic coherence of his ideas depend on what the audience perceives? Of course not. His truth is his truth, regardless of who else believes in it. Similarly, to the artist, his beauty is his beauty, regardless of whether you understand it or not.

But can a famous philosopher, then, who gives a lecture before a crowd of students, claim that he *does not care* what the students think of his lecture? Again, of course not. Anyone who gives a linguistic presentation – a political speech, a philosophical argument, a declaration of intentions, a scientific lecture, or even recounting a personal anecdote – must hone their diction, practice their delivery, make certain to speak clearly, and argue their case as persuasively as possible. If a philosopher gives a lecture that the audience finds confusing, muddled and unpersuasive, the philosopher cannot fall back on, "Philosophy for philosophy's sake." He simply gave a bad lecture. If he cannot communicate his philosophy, then his philosophy doesn't matter.

Thus, the disturbing conclusion: *Art cannot be separated from the audience.* The philosopher therefore laughs at the artist whenever he gives the pretension of not caring what the audience thinks. The philosopher must rule against the artist and declare that vanity and the force of popular opinion are very much involved in the communal project of aesthetics. This complicates the artistic life, and makes the artist uncomfortable, especially if he understands how the ulterior, pragmatic motives in making art can be harmful to art itself. The artist becomes nauseous, unable to be sure whether his work is truly free of propagandistic motives or falsifications of his inner state. Perhaps most or even all art is infused with it, even if its core is True Art: like impurities in iron ore. Perhaps there is art that is like pure steel – but how can one tell?

The artist must express a genuine emotional truth in order to be a True Artist. It is for the sake of his all-too-subjective truth that he engages in artistic expression. This artistic truth is what the artist tries to preserve when he declares that he does art for art's sake – damn the audience. But emotional expression demands an audience. Emotional resonance only occurs in a relationship. There is no expression of artistic truth without resonance. To the degree that an artist shares his art, *he is seeking an audience*, whether he claims to care about that audience or not.

***

Next morning, I slept longer than everyone else. The room was pitch black when I awoke. I fumbled around in the dark to dig my phone and wallet out of my shoes, and struggled to stuff my legs into my jeans. My eyes adjusted to the light, enough to perceive that all my bandmates had gone.

First thing's first. I went to piss. I regretted that I'd left all my clothes in the van, because the thought of a shower sounded wonderful. Too bad. Come to think of it, I wasn't sure I even possessed any clean clothes – everything I'd brought was covered in dried sweat by now. I decided against it, and gathered what few things I'd brought down and headed upstairs from the basement hostel. My shoulder bag was really starting to dig into me as I hauled it up the stairs. It was like hauling a miniature, portable library. I always brought too many books with me on tour.

I found my way to the pub. It was just on the other side of the block. Copperfield's had opened the restaurant for the morning, and Penny and Nick were already there. Their table was open to the morning air, as the outer façade was open and there was no wall between the restaurant and the street. I sat down and joined the two of them.

"What's the plan?"

"We're hanging until they get back," Penny said. "Steve's out walking around with the Italians. When they get here we can load up and leave."

I rubbed on my neck and shoulder as I sat there, and realized that maybe I'd been incorrect in blaming the cramped conditions of Stracchione's van for my neck. I probably hadn't helped matters by carrying all that weight around in a shoulder bag. Oh well. Yet another instance where there was no going back. I'd brought the books, now they were mine to haul around.

Penny was trying to get in touch with Steve via text and getting no response. None of us had a good signal. Steve had not given many details about where they were, or what they were doing. Penny mashed the keys on his phone.

"What's wrong with Steve?" I wondered aloud. "I tried to ask him something when we were getting out of the van yesterday and he just stared at me."

Penny shook his head.

"You know how he gets. He gets weird on tour sometimes, man."

"Yeah, I know how he gets." I said. "Is it that hard to acknowledge that someone said something? To say, 'yes', 'no', or 'I don't know'?"

"Apparently it's hard," Penny said.

"I hate being ignored," I said.

"It's like he's someone else," Penny said. "Sometimes he gets into that weird tour funk, where he just clams up."

"It's fucking annoying."

"Say something to him."

"He's probably tired," I said. "I'm tired. We're all tired."

"He can still convey basic fucking information."

Eventually, he got a text back from Steve. He was at an electronics store. He said was looking to pick up another adapter for our phone chargers.

By happenstance, Nick had bought the very same thing, earlier that very morning: a second power adapter was sitting, still in its brand-new box, on the table in front of him. Penny typed a message to Steve as quickly as possible and tried to tell him not to buy another one. He sat there, watching, as the messenger app tried its hardest to send the text, but the progress bar lingered near 90% without the message sending. Finally, it goes through, but no read receipt. Sure enough, Steve shows up with an extra power adapter ten minutes later.

"I was trying to tell you not to buy another one, goddamnit. Nick just got another one…"

"Jesus, dude," Steve said. "I didn't get your message. I'm trying to help us out here."

"Well, if we could just coordinate what we're fucking doing."

"Goddamn, okay, I'll return it…"

"I'm not asking you to return it…"

"Well I might as well return it…"

"What's going on with you?" Penny asked. "You're being all weird."

"What?"

"You're not telling us about the arrangements until the day before, Keegan's asking you questions and you're just staring at him..."

Fuck. Steve looked over at me. I really wished Penny hadn't said that. But it wasn't his way to keep things from being aired out. I just didn't want to give Steve the impression we were talking shit about him behind his back. The first time I spoke, I immediately backtracked.

"It was just weird yesterday. I told Penny that when we got out of the van and got to Copperfield's, when I asked you about the arrangements, you just kinda stared at me..."

"I didn't hear you, dude." Steve said, irritated.

"Okay, well..." I started, but Penny talked over me.

"If you're gonna be the go-between, be the go-between," Penny said. "But you have to explain shit to us. It doesn't have to be complicated."

"Okay," Steve said. "If you want to know something, you gotta ask me –..."

"How hard is it to just tell us?"

"Alright, fine then. I'll try to keep you in the loop."

"That's what needs to happen." Penny said.

"Not acting like myself." Steve repeated. "I don't know what you're talking about."

Nick didn't speak throughout the conversation. His nose was buried in his book the whole time.

***

As soon as we began the day's drive, we received more bad news. Even though they'd booked a show in Boras, it had been nothing but radio silence from the promoter in the past weeks. Now that we were on the road, heading to the venue, we were contacted, through Facebook, by one of the local supporting bands for that show.

Steve relayed their story to us all: this band's account messaged us, and said that the promoter said that his girlfriend broke up with him. He said that his girlfriend robbed him, stole some money, and his computer. But he hadn't contacted the touring bands, or made any announcement on social media. He'd simply cancelled the show, and informed no one. The local opening band had found out about it from the venue that very morning. When the promoter finally responded to their messages, he told them he was too distressed to come into work, and furthermore he couldn't find any friends who would run the show for him. They then relayed this information to Steve and Doc, who relayed it to all of us in the van.

What a story for our inquiry in this book! – bad communication can be utterly destructive in and of itself. Not only was this story second-hand, no, third-hand information, distorted by its numerous tellers each in turn; but, furthermore the central piece of the story was the complete lack of communication on the promoter's part. Poor communication was the crime of the promoter, and through his poor communication he had materially fucked us all over. The local bands were embarrassed on behalf of their own scene. Steve and Doc agreed that anyone who calls himself a promoter and behaves this way is no promoter at all.

We pulled off the highway about twenty minutes outside of Stockholm. We followed the exit into the parking lot of a Burger King. There was some kind of carnival or something, in a nearby park, right across the street. Some of us went inside to order food and charge our phones. It was a Sunday morning, and there were children everywhere – playing, running about, screaming, shouting. There was plenty of commotion from the kids inside the restaurant as well as out. The Burger King's menu offered fried Halloumi – I'd never seen that at a Burger King before. It was seven euro, but I decided it was worth it.

Steve, Doc and Davide were all on their devices – phones, laptops – trying to find out if a last-minute show was possible, or if there was any way to salvage this one. It was unlikely they'd find anything, but they had to try. I think Davide was just trying to re-plan our route in light of this new development.

When I was done eating, I went out to the van again. No one else was there. Soon, we'd be on the road again, crammed together again... Pressed forward against the seat in front of me, or with my cheek stuck to the cold glass of the window, amongst the breathing, snoring, and jostling of eight others...

I stretched out across the entire backseat. Hadn't actually laid down in the van yet, this tour. The door was open, and my feet hung off the edge of the bench seat. I jammed my bag under my head, and shut my eyes. I could hear the cars passing by from the highway, shrieks and laughs of children echoing the distance. The breeze.

Ah yes. This wonderful feeling.

CHAPTER FOURTEEN
STOCKHOLM - COPENHAGEN

We waited longer than we should have waited. After a couple of hours, we had no choice but to start driving. If we didn't, we wouldn't be able to reach *anywhere* by this evening, supposing a show did miraculously happen. Maybe we'd wrangle something in Boras, or in Gothenburg. But the chances of such a thing became vanishingly small by the minute.

By this point in the tour, it didn't feel like we'd been in Europe merely for a week or so. It could have been a month or a day, but it didn't feel like a week. I felt I'd known the Italians a long time. The days had stretched on and on, and yet our time with them felt as though it were all about to come to an end all too soon.

The road took us into the forests of Sweden. The highway began to twist and wind, through seas of pine and rolling hills. As the hours passed, and the woods thickened, and no word from the outside world was received, we all made our peace with the fact that our Sunday night show had been canceled.

Funny, the reversals of fortune. They can happen so quickly, when every single night is so important to your overall success. We'd been on top of the world the past few days, but the cancellation of this show was probably the biggest disappointment of the tour so far.

Hours later, we pulled off into a rest area, part of a large park. It was the edge of afternoon and evening. There were cabins nearby, upon a hill next to the parking lot, all shaded by towering pines. We relieved ourselves in the log-built outhouses. We loitered for a while near a gently sloping hillside next to the van.

We made our battle plans there, the nine of us sitting, lying, standing on that grassy hillside. Davide was seated next to me, laptop in his lap, and looked at the best options for where to spend the night. We decided to drive straight through to Copenhagen. There was no show planned for the next day, Monday, when most clubs were shuttered anyway. Davide booked a hostel in Copenhagen, securing two rooms for ourselves at a very cheap price (especially for the notoriously expensive Danish city). We'd take the ferry the next morning, into Germany. Our Monday drive would take us across the whole of Germany once more.

Thankfully, on this same evening, Steve received confirmation that we'd successfully booked a show for the following day. This had been the first show to be cancelled while we were on the road, and we'd now had one miraculously handed to us. At least we'd have a final show with Hell Obelisco, albeit a Tuesday night.

Some of us wandered down to the shore. Just down a rustic pathway between the regal pines, there was a small lake, one of the countless little lakes that cover Sweden. Little birds with black feathers and white beaks jabbered and fought over the crumbs from our chips and sandwich bread. With nowhere to be now, the sense of urgency we felt at the beginning of the day was gone. There, we smoked cigarettes and threw stones in the water.

I can't remember who told me – I think it was Doc – but it was Alex's birthday. We didn't really have any way to celebrate. Just some booze in the van. Even though I'd felt that I'd made peace with the show getting cancelled, I suddenly felt much worse about it. This would've been Alex's birthday performance. Hell of a fucking birthday present.

The sun sank a little lower by the minute. An empty dinghy bobbed lazily on the waters. The breeze was cool, but the day's lingering warmth had not yet departed. The air was the perfect temperature. There was no one else at the rest area, no one there at all except for some campers we'd passed on the way down to the lake's shore; but the sounds of their voices were gone now, and there was not another soul in sight other than the nine of us.

The wood larks flitted back and forth in the pines above us. I laid down in the grass next to the waters, and I looked up and studied them, the laughter and chattering amongst my tourmates audible and intermingling with their chirps. I listened intently to the bird calls, straining to lend them my attention: the chirps and twitters repeated in little rhythmic patterns. There were so many different phrases. I thought of Igor Stravinsky, crafting his compositions while studying the bird songs of the Ukraine. How can beauty be so arbitrary, such that certain combinations of wavelengths simply produce good feelings? Why do the birds sing so sweetly to us, as well as their own kind? Are the birds traveling musicians as well?

The German word for an outlaw is vogelfrei, which means "bird-free," or "free as a bird." An outlaw is someone outside the bounds and therefore the protections of the law: a criminal so bad that they can be shot on sight. The comparison between traveling musicians and outlaws has been made before, by the 'outlaw country' genre if no one else. Funny that the Germans, usually thought to be such a disciplined and orderly people, would have such a poetic, dare I say beautiful, word for the criminal drifter. I would have expected such a term to come from America, where we have always romanticized the open road and the outlaw, because we romanticize freedom. We like the rugged view of freedom: freedom as a trade-off, something bought at the high price of self-sufficiency and danger.

Were we people of disrepute, of the low morality of an actor or the dishonesty of a poet, we modern musicians? I suppose the term "free as a bird" does fit the modern touring musician. But Skynyrd ruined that analogy for all musicians by writing a song called "Free Bird" that has now been obnoxiously screamed at every musician for the past few generations. I'd never use the term in English. If we keep it untranslated, it is a good enough term. Vogelfrei.

***

Perception of time is different while on the road. I remember our first month-long tour. I was sitting in a coffee house with Jeff, somewhere in Atlanta. He remarked that, even though it was only three weeks ago, the kick-off show in Austin felt like it was three months ago, and he was right. It was exactly how I felt.

I have my theories as to why. The first factor is the normal rhythm of waking and sleep is disrupted on tour. When you sleep in an unfamiliar location, your quality of sleep is diminished. Oftentimes, when we're on tour, we're drinking and smoking, which affect the quality of sleep also. You tend to make up for it by sleeping during the daytime. Since the best time for this sleep is in transit, this sleep is also irregular. This means that, while on tour, your overall average level of fatigue is higher than normal.

Everything is a little more dreamlike when you're tired all the time. Moments stretch on. And sometimes it is not just an illusion: sometimes the day actually does stretch on. Some days, you wake up at seven AM and don't get to sleep until five AM the next day. Other days, you nap for hours on end in the middle of the afternoon, in and out of sleep in a van that is always shaking and rumbling against the pavement. Or, perhaps you depart in the early afternoon in America and play a show that night in Bologna, twenty-six hours later.

I think the most significant factor is being in a new place, every day. In the normal course of life, the experience most people have is that we awake in a familiar place. We do familiar things, such as make coffee, take a shower, eat breakfast, make the same drive we always make, go into work, go home, unwind with some TV, and so on. On tour, you still do most of those things, but they're no longer familiar. You wake up in an unfamiliar bed. If you want coffee, maybe your host has some, maybe not. Maybe you have to go find some, in an unfamiliar city. When and if you shower, it is in a different shower every night.

As such, on the road, you still have some regularity to your schedule in that you can count on most days to consist of waking up, driving, playing a show, and finding a place to sleep. But every day the drive is different, every night, the people are different. Because you spend every day confronted with novelty, your brain has less opportunity for forgetting. In the normal course of life, where everything is the same and little stands out except for a few exceptional events, your brain is inclined to blur everything together to save space. It determines, week after week, that no new, relevant information has been introduced, and the weeks and months just sort of bleed into one another. Our sense of the passage of time is dependent on our own memory, and how our memory represents the passage of time to us is therefore malleable according to all the ways in which memory is malleable in general. With the regular tempo of a commute, a job, and familiar forms of recreation, whole weeks, months and even years blend together in an undifferentiated mass. Time therefore seems to expand on tour, because every day is more memorable.

Every day has its own repetitive pattern to it; the tour experience is not *completely* novel. You get used to a new routine. If there were no routine, and we were left to our own devices, it would require a great exertion to continue putting ourselves in novel circumstances. But we have a schedule to keep, and shows to make. That there are predictable patterns to every day on tour only makes the experience more somnambulic.

The tour life is freedom, found in the act of letting go and surrendering to limitation. Once the route is planned and the shows are booked, you must follow the course that has been set. There is no going back or changing anything. There are no decisions for you to make over the course of the day, other than the trifling choices you have, in the details of when and where to procure food, where you'll sleep, when you'll stop to piss. None of these decisions are made individually, but collectively. One's subjective whims are sublimated to the overarching goal.

***

In the past few years of Destroyer of Light, our artistic vision shifted once again. I'd like to think we matured. We began to include more influences from outside the heavy metal subgenres. Steve and I were fans of New Wave, and included stylistic nods towards bands like The Cure and Tears for Fears in our leads and guitar tones.

In the period after Nick joined the band, we became a little less concerned with even adhering to the doom label. Nick was an eclectic weirdo in his musical taste. His interest in music that one might call 'heavy' didn't come through the musical lineage of Black Sabbath or Judas Priest. Nick's interests were more in bands like Daughters or Swans. His joining the band just so happened to coincide with our inclinations at the time, which were to throw any and all genre limitations out. We stopped caring about the traditional doom formula, and decided that anything goes.

Mors Aeterna was a concept album, about a protagonist who dies, and finds himself in the afterlife. The seed of the idea was when Steve wrote a song about a man who was dead, but didn't know if he was dead or alive. It's one of the deepest existential fears. It reminded me of a passage in the Bardo Thodol, which I was reading around the same time. The Bardo is also known as the Tibetan Book of the Dead, and the passage it reminded me of is as follows: "When the consciousness getteth outside the body, it will ask itself, 'Am I dead or not dead?' It cannot determine. It seeth its relatives and connexions as it had been used to seeing them before. It even heareth the wailings. The terrible karmic illusions have not yet dawned."

In the Bardo Thodol, the description given of the afterlife is that everything the departed consciousness encounters is simply their own mind, or their own nature – depending on which translation you use. This was the jumping-off point for the album's concept. Every demon the protagonist encounters, every dead loved one, every pleasure or wonder – all of this is actually just a reflection of his own consciousness. The journey of the album is the story of his gradual discovery of this fact. Even when he ends up in hell, it is just his own sense of guilt and self-recrimination that is causing him his suffering. The release from this is found in letting go, and learning to love the void.

This concept roughly reflected the way I thought about the world at the time. When one stops looking to the heavens to find the source of human beliefs, we discover that all our mental suffering has an origin in the natural world. Our biggest metaphysical problems are human inventions. All the hells anyone has ever written about came from the recesses of the human mind. We're the authors of all the guilt we impose on ourselves, all the pangs of conscience, all the social shame. We cling on to these things because they're tied in with our sense of self and of free will. We want to feel anchored or moored in this ever-changing existence. But, as payment, these prejudices and heavy feelings will weigh you down.

When we finished the recording, it was my favorite thing I'd ever made up to that point in my life. It was a new aesthetic for Destroyer of Light, and a new phase in our artistic development. With Mors Aeterna, I finally felt as though we'd expressed something real, something meaningful. It wasn't as if our previous albums were inartistic drivel or something, but now I felt as though our artistic evolution had actually led up to the expression of some feeling about the human condition. I'd wondered if we might have a chance to rake our nails across eternity after all.

Now, this tour of Europe was the first serious tour to promote that release. Our first truly artistic achievement – ...and was it all turning out to be a disappointment?

X. Barthes is Dead

And we have killed him!
Now that we have redeemed the audience, another crucial component of this new understanding of art remains: we must resurrect the artist. The answers to these final riddles will be adumbrated in the course of answering my antipode, Roland Barthes – the author of the notorious essay, *Death of the Author.*

As regards the idea of, "the death of the author," Barthes' essay specifically discusses authorship – which is to say, literature. His ideas can easily be applied to the whole of art, however, and have been. For the purposes of this inquiry, we can understand the "death of the author" to mean the "death of the artist" and use these two terms interchangeably, since literature is a form of art, and the same concerns Barthes raises about literature can be applied to any other artform. If authorial intent in a literary text can be rejected from consideration, the same arguments that Barthes uses would apply to artistic intent in any type of artistic medium.

Barthes wished to eliminate the study of the author's life and motivations when studying his work. He argued that the work is a separate thing from the creator of the work. To the extent that the author has an opportunity to voice his intent, it is sufficient to look within the work of art itself. Therefore, we should not consider "authorial intent" in interpreting a work. No amount of adding onto the text with additional information will change the fact of how the audience engages with the text.

To Barthes, *the text is all there is*: the work of art has a life and intent of its own. By 'text' we here mean everything contained with the work of art, whether it be a book, film, painting, song, etc. This means that the facts of the author's life, the author's stated motivations, the events surrounding the writing of the work – all of this is irrelevant to understanding the work. This is the underlying meaning when Barthes says the author is dead.

Authorship attempts to impose a limit upon the text. And yet, it is impossible to know the exact intentions of the author. Even if we think we do know those intentions, the suggestion that they should play a role in our artistic interpretation means that we should necessarily look outside of the text for meaning. If we accept this proposition, we must conclude that we cannot have the same degree of insight into texts which have no statement of authorial intent, or of whose author we have no information. The texts that do have documented statements of authorial intent would be analyzed differently than those that do not. Barthes argues that this is an absurdity.

The result of authorial intent, in Barthes' view, is that the text itself – and experience of the reader, in the immediate moment – loses its status as primary. The text is no longer the whole of the artistic output. Barthes argues that this means that the text cannot have a life of its own, and is forever limited by whatever conscious intentions the author had when writing it. The idea of deferring to authorial intention can therefore produce sloppy and incomplete interpretations, however easy and clean it may seem.

The example Barthes uses to attack authorial intent is Balzac's Sarrasine. The protagonist of the story falls in love with someone whom he believes to be the ideal woman, but who is actually a castrato.

Barthes writes: "Who is speaking in this way? Is it the story's hero, concerned to ignore the castrato concealed beneath the woman? Is it the man Balzac, endowed by his personal experience with a philosophy of Woman? Is it the author Balzac, professing certain 'literary' ideas of femininity? Is it universal wisdom? or romantic psychology? It will always be impossible to know, for the good reason that all writing is itself this special voice, consisting of several indiscernible voices, and that literature is precisely the invention of this voice, to which we cannot assign a specific origin: literature is that neuter, that composite, that oblique into which every subject escapes, the trap where all identity is lost, beginning with the very identity of the body that writes."

In Barthes' view, one's life is not even his own. The author's influences will consist of his culture, his upbringing, random experiences in his life, his relationships, his religious and ethnic background. However many books a man may author, man does not author himself. Therefore, looking to the author's conscious and stated intent is hardly the whole story. In effect, the text does not even belong to the author because his influences are not his own.

Barthes coins the term *scriptor*, to replace the term author. Who is the scriptor? – he is a mere conduit. This kind of description of the artist may sound familiar by now. To Barthes, the writer is merely a body. He cites the examples of earlier societies, which we've also considered, where the shaman or spiritual 'mediator' was the first storyteller, but one who is himself not responsible for the story he tells. He is merely a conduit for the divine – a vessel for *genius*, in the sense that we have been using the word. Again, we find the concept of divine madness as a means of explaining art.

The scriptor is the instrument by which the momentary god, or the Muse, expresses itself. This is coupled with a view of mankind that is not dissimilar to the Buddhist view – that the self is an illusory phenomenon, and the individual is really just a collection of aggregated physical and mental states given labels by cognition. Barthes therefore interprets the divine madness model of art very differently from my own view of art, as communion between artist and audience. Barthes extrapolates the concept of divine madness into *a refutation of the artist*.

It is in this type of insight that I find the most sympathy with Barthes, just as I found sympathy with Schopenhauer in his idea of the artistic genius as naturally a bit "mad" – in spite of the fact that I ultimately disagree with Schopenhauer as to why this is. I agree with Barthes insofar as he argues for the de-subjectification of art, to use the language of Schopenhauer. Art is not a product of an individual's reason; it is not even the product of the mind, in the way that we usually think about the mind anyway. The techniques one might use are developed by the conscious mind, yes – but once again, we must separate the artistic expression from the craft. To Barthes, it is a body possessed by a spirit that produces the story, and after it is discharged from his hand, it is an externality, over which he no longer has any say. This is the Socratic view of the rhapsode, the dramatic poet. As Whitehead said, pretty much all philosophy is just a footnote to Plato – and Barthes once again proves this rule.

But Barthes goes further. In Barthes' view, *the story is only ever written in the here and now*, every time it is engaged by a reader. Any reader will bring to bear his own subjectivity on the text. Without the subjective experiences of the readers', which shaped them, they would not be able to even comprehend the text. Their subjectivity is their very toolkit for even understanding it. And so it is that every last subjective interpretation becomes "correct" – or, to speak more correctly, the idea of correctness or incorrectness of a literary interpretation becomes nonsense.

Barthes recognizes art's irrational character, the alterity of the artistic impulse from the conscious self. It is as though Barthes wants to save art from becoming reified and objective – which is to say, deprived of its emotional power. By declaring that the text is written again and again in the reading of it, he is pointing to the emotional resonance experiences of the audience in their engagement with the text. Authorial intent, when made into a rule of interpretation, threatens to make the art into something static.

However noble Barthes intentions may be, he is still just a nobly intentioned killer – for, unlike Nietzsche, who merely declared God dead as though he were the physician at the scene, Barthes here takes Chekov's gun and empties it into the author – all authors, everywhere. The author didn't die of natural causes: Barthes is a murderer. For all my agreement with Barthes, I oppose him in this, and reject the idea of making ourselves into scriptors only. The result of Barthes' idea, if taken seriously, and taken through to its practical conclusions, is to sever us all from the real experience of art.

If we say that the conscious intentions and meaning of the author are irrelevant, then how can *any* interpretation of a work's meaning be relevant?

Any literary criticism imposes a limit on the text: this essentially means that we should ignore not only the author's interpretation of his own work, but all interpretations. All of them become limitations on what others might wish to interpret, and thus we end at a place where no one can communicate anything. We cannot take the right of conveying his meaning away from the author without taking this right from everyone. If my interpretation of the text imposes a limit on your interpretation, and yours imposes a limit on my interpretation, and we adopt this rule of delimiting the possible interpretations, then never shall any two interpretations meet. Thus, we must be willing to accept the limitations that another imposes on a text if we wish to see their perspective. If we accept this, then we must consider that acceding to the limitations of the author's interpretation of their own text, at least as an act of mediation or 'meeting in the middle', is the very essence of any attempt at communication with the author.

If the author is merely a scriptor, a body through which an artistic impulse flows, then surely we cannot say that the reader is the true author any more than the author is. The reader is simply a body; why is the reader not merely a scriptor as well? If both are merely scriptors, then who is writing the text? This does not require us to posit an essentialist Self to become the author. But we are forced to concede that, even if we accept Barthes' idea that the text is written anew, the text is only written through a *relationship*. Relationships exist between living beings, not dead ones.

The Muse is not actually a foreign entity, but an expression from the unconscious depths of the artist. The momentary god that seizes the author results in a work of art: it is thus mediated through a particular conduit. That work of art is possible only through the raw material of unconscious feelings and conscious memory. Even Jung, with his collective unconscious, asserts a personal unconscious for each person, which is unique to them. To some extent, the idiosyncrasies of each author, and the fact that we can recognize these across multiple works of the same author, refute the author's non-existence. This is the author's style, which exists not only in a single text, but across multiple texts, and attests to the author's life. The author's *style* is what lives, and it is the living style of the author that stands as a refutation to the author's death.

Even though the real content displayed on a television is the broadcast – something formless for which the television is only a conduit – *one cannot on that account get rid of the television.* You need a conduit, and the conduit affects the display. We find that different televisions display the image differently: some have different dimensions, different degrees of resolution, different light and color balances, different technological means of displaying light and color. Even if we say that the artist is only a conduit, we cannot on this account have done with the conduit, insofar as it shapes the message. We can therefore enrich our reading of an author with a study of the author's life.

Some might say that all that is unique to the artist has to do with technique, and therefore craft – and I think this is perhaps an unarticulated premise beneath Barthes' work. But this is, again, where he missteps: for what we must consider when we consider "authorial intent" is not merely the explicitly stated, *conscious* intent of the author. The *intent* behind the work of art is all that which we have been considering: the life of the author, their habits, their memories, the contents of their personal unconscious, their leitmotifs of thought. The true artistic intent is determined by the need for communication between one's personal unconscious, and the conscious world – the conscious world existing within the collective, social net of consciousness. In short, this is the work's *meaning*. We should regard any work of art as a form of communication with that author, and a way of engaging emotional resonance with them, such that the artist lives in their resonance with us.

Art is not linguistic communication, even when that art takes place within the linguistic medium of literature. The artistic meaning of the work is not conveyed as one conveys information. It is, at base, a purely emotional meaning that the author felt, and wished to convey. One could argue that this emotional meaning – which comes from the artist's subjective experience – doesn't "belong" to the artist only in the most abstract, philosophical sense – in the same sense as the Buddhist means that they don't belong to the self, insofar as *nothing* belongs to the self. But to the extent that the word "self" means *anything*, this is what the self *must* mean: the sum total of our memories, relationships, feelings and experiences that we carry with us, and which form the raw material of any artistic expression. Every individual reacts to powerful emotional states in different ways, and the same experience or emotional state can result in completely different forms of artistic expression from two different people.

Barthes is right in attacking authorial intent in the superficial sense that there can never be a settled interpretation of a work of art. Certainly, it is endlessly debatable. But the same is true of religious texts, philosophical texts, or even the U.S. Constitution for that matter. The arguments about interpretation can go on forever. Barthes does not want the author claiming any special ability to decipher the story simply because the author told the story. Given that artistic expression delves into the unconscious, where not everything is rational or comprehensible to the artist himself, it is even plausible that an author could be unaware of the hidden layers of meaning in his own text. But none of this changes the fact that the raw material of the art is the artist: his work is his own flesh and blood.

This touches the deepest problem, the heart of my disagreement with Barthes: in declaring the author dead, Barthes must first affirm that the author's "self" resides in his rational ego-consciousness. This means the self is not found in the body, in the unconscious mind, in the life experience, nor in the emotions. To me, this is exactly where we find the self!

The author is "just" a body? But we're all just bodies! Barthes must first set up a mind-body dualist view of the author, which is a strawman, then uses a Buddhistic negation of the self to knock it down. It is a false dialectic from the beginning. But more importantly, it runs exactly contrary to the true meaning and teleology of art in the human condition. Barthes would not only kill the artist, but by this same act – kill art itself.

***

We drove into the darkness. I managed to get several hours of sleep. I jerked awake as we pulled into the parking lot and the van's motion finally stopped. It was so easy to sleep now, when it had been so difficult before. The hostel in Copenhagen was an unassuming house in a suburban neighborhood. We were booked in a room on the first floor. No one was there to greet us. We'd simply been sent a code for the keypad.

I claimed the first use of the shower before anyone else. I changed into my last set of relatively clean clothes. Either we'd find a Laundromat soon, or I'd begin recycling my dirty garments. After I showered, I wanted nothing more than to collapse into bed. But just then, Amberly called. It was around two or three in the morning, but it was late afternoon for her. She must have been on her drive home. I answered and walked outside.

I was barefoot, and enjoyed the feeling of the cold sidewalk beneath my feet. I paced as we spoke. Even though nothing much had happened that day, there was a lot to talk about. The absurd story of the promoter and his runaway girlfriend. The cancelled show. More complaining about the record label. This was ultimately the label's fault, after all, having booked the tour and set up that show in the first place.

"So, how are you feeling?"

"I don't even know at this point, babe," I said, rubbing my eyes. "I feel like I should be more upset than I am. There've been so many ups and downs. Alternating successes and failures. Getting upset over it seems harder now. I almost feel... immune."

***

We awoke the next morning to strange sounds coming from the room on the other side of the wall. It sounded like a woman. At first, I thought she was shouting. Then it sounded like moaning. We giggled as we put on our jeans and got our things together.

"Someone's having morning sex!" Penny said, laughing.

Nick left the room to go to the restroom. Then, we heard louder, more frantic shouting from outside. Sobbing and groaning that didn't sound like the throes of ecstasy. Shortly thereafter, the woman came running into the hall. She asked for help, at first in German. Nick apologized to her in English, and she switched to English.

"My husband is having a seizure!"

Nick went into the room at her behest. He did his best to help, moving the man away from the nightstand where it looked that he'd already hit his head. He said there was blood everywhere in the room – a lot of blood, in fact. An ambulance was called.

The man's episode soon ended. Shortly thereafter, he was lucid. In spite of the pool of blood that Nick described, the man said he felt fine. The ambulance had already arrived, however, and it was just in time to block our exit from the hostel, right as we were ready to depart. The paramedics went inside, and we waited out front while they checked the man over. Davide told me stories about driving the band Pallbearer, and their show with Chelsea Wolfe. Steve and Andrea were talking about horror films again, I think. I bummed another cigarette, and stared down the street, studying the details of every house and tree and fence and parked car. There was an endless horizon that remained forever tugging at the bounds of my perception.

***

We had the whole day to cross Germany – from the north to the south – and reach the city of Kassel. Davide chose Kassel because it would put us within only a couple hours of Basel, and our final show with Hell Obelisco the next day. We spent a few hours that morning in Copenhagen. The first order of business was to visit a record store downtown, just near a large plaza. Steve wanted to visit there because it was owned by the guitarist for King Diamond. The internet said the shop opened at ten. We managed to find a parking spot on the same street that morning, and arrived at ten, more or less on the dot. They weren't actually open. We loitered about on the street, until the owner showed up, about fifteen minutes later or so. I went in with Steve, Penny and a few of the Italians to browse for a bit. I quickly lost interest; the selection was incredibly obscure.

Eventually, we ended up going our separate ways, and wandered about the streets around the plaza. It was a pedestrianized zone, crowded with shoppers and tourists, the windows and patios and doors of all the shops open, the smell of fried food in the air. It was the first sunny morning I'd experienced in Scandinavia. After walking for a bit, I started to work up an appetite. I texted Penny to see where he was. He replied that he was at a café nearby. Baked goods and coffee; it sounded perfect. Just off the plaza.

Eventually, I spotted Penny, sitting with Andrea, Doc and Alex. I was out of cash. Penny offered to pay. We both had a coffee and a croissant. As we ate, an older Danish man of large stature, with long hair and a beard sat next to us. He had an old and friendly dog on a leash, that flopped down on the cobblestone next to him while he waited on his espresso. He made us for tourists and was eager to talk with us in English. He was even more excited to find out that we were musicians. He himself was a folk musician, he said. He played traditional Danish music during festivals, at the nearby historic city of Christiana. What joy music brought to this old man's life! What a joy it was for him to find out that we were traveling musicians. I doubt he would have enjoyed the music we were making, but who knows? In any case, just knowing that there were young people traveling the world and playing music was enough to brighten his day.

He told us we simply must visit Christiana – I told him that, unhappily, even as we had no show that day, we really didn't have time. We had a lot of ground to cover. His dog rolled over onto its side and began snoozing amidst the hustle and bustle of the plaza's weekend crowds. We said our goodbyes and went to meet up with the others near the statues in the square.

This ferry ride was much shorter than the last one. We reached the opposite shore in about forty-five minutes of travel; the whole affair took no more than an hour or so. The food was more affordable, too. I bought a sandwich to save for later, and more coffee. I'd already had a decadent amount of coffee and baked goods that morning, but coffee was as good a drug as any for getting through the day. Caffeine is my most powerful vice, the one most approved-of by society. Especially in Europe.

On the long drive, the road once again took us through the forests, hills, and fields in the heartland of Germany. The drive took eleven hours in total. The journey was fueled as much by German beer as by petrol. My neck was finally starting to feel better. The stinging pain was mostly a memory. There was only a dull soreness. Over the day's long course the sky turned to gray, the hours dragged on, and we drove through scattered storms. Somehow, the time passed insensibly, and I fell asleep in transit again.

CHAPTER FIFTEEN
KASSEL - BASEL

It was pouring rain when we arrived in Kassel. A neighborhood hostel again. We talked on the way there about looking for something to do in town, but that had been earlier in the day. Now, everyone was tired and downtown was a long ways away, and the drive had taken longer than projected, as usual. It was almost midnight; nothing would be open at that time on Monday anyway. Having booked the hostel in advance, we knew we had shelter. But we hadn't stopped nor eaten for hours, we were mostly out of food and the prospects for dinner seemed bleak.

We ran in from the downpour and made our way to the front desk. The front desk doubled as a bar, as the lobby was also the hotel's restaurant, common room, café, and even a venue – there was a stage opposite the bar. Many hostels are like this. The lighting was dim. It was quiet, other than the sound of rain on the windows. One table was occupied. There was a man with long dark hair and a beard, eating dinner with a young blonde woman in a red sweater. They both looked college-aged. Other than the two of them, the place was deserted. The man got up, wiped off his mouth with the red cloth napkin, and walked behind the bar. Davide approached him, speaking Italian.

The young man handed him some paperwork for the reservations. He was answering Davide in Spanish. Davide would say something in Italian, or ask a question in Italian, and the Spaniard would think for a moment then answer him in Spanish. Or maybe it was some combination.

I was walking beside Davide as we carried our luggage up to our rooms, and asked him about it.

"Yes, he was speaking Spanish," he said.

"You could understand him?"

"Mostly," he said.

Once again we would share our rooms with strangers. As I turned the key and pushed the door open, pouring light into the pitch-black room, a few of our roommates for the night stirred, and rolled to turn their backs to the open door. I plugged in my phone and stashed my things under the bunk bed.

I didn't know what everyone else was planning on doing, but I wasn't in the mood for sleep. I was hungry, and wondered if there was a vending machine in the lobby. I went downstairs to the café area, bringing with me my bag, my books, and notebooks. Best case scenario, I could get some snacks and get some writing done.

As soon as I opened the door to the lounge, however, the Spaniard got up from his table again. He started speaking Spanish to me.

"Esta cerrado," he said.

Cerrado, I thought. *Closed*.

There were no vending machines anyway. I wondered if there was some other common area where I could go. The last thing I wanted was to be in a dark room full of other guests who were trying to sleep. I'd been in close quarters with others for too long, and I was feeling solitary. More than that, I'd been asleep all day and was wide awake whether I wanted to be or not. I had to keep my mind off my hunger by plunging into reading and writing. I stalked down the hallway, hauling my portable library in my bookbag, the raindrops pattering their rhythm against the windows, wind thrashing the trees in the darkness outside.

I went back upstairs, and found that my keycard wouldn't buzz me into the hall. I tried three times and finally got it to work. Unexpectedly, I ran into Davide. He whisper-called out my name, "Keegan!" so as not to make too much noise in the hall, and gestured for me to follow him. I did so.

He'd just returned from talking with one of the staff here. Thankfully for us, there were leftovers from dinner that night. The staff was more than willing to give it to us. The leftovers consisted of a quinoa dish with tomatoes that had an odd taste to it, some pasta that was good enough with olive oil, salt and pepper, as well as salad greens, vegetables, bread. It wasn't exactly a gourmet meal. It didn't matter. Somehow, there'd appeared before us enough food for nine grown men. With the beer we'd bought earlier that day at a rest area, the meal felt luxurious.

Through pain, camaraderie. It had been barely more than a week, but now we were close friends. Laughter, stories, arguing amongst ourselves. I wasn't feeling solitary any longer.

***

Barthes' real motivation is revealed in the conclusion that there is no correct understanding of the work. Literature is a complex style of artistic expression. It involves the use of the intellect to a great degree. It may seem on the surface, then, that the correct interpretation of the narrative is an intellectual process. But however technical or intellectual the medium, the artistic expression itself is irrational, as we have established.

Barthes' problem is, at bottom, *the equivocation of 'literary criticism' with the artistic understanding of a text.* The artistic understanding that is achieved by a powerful work of art happens on a completely subjective, emotional, immediate level. Barthes, to his credit, puts forward a theory that attempts to preserve this – but this is unnecessary, because there is nothing, shy of banning artistic expression entirely, that can interfere with the emotional resonance that art creates. Whether the interpretations the audience produces are "correct" or not, it is always true that we relish in authoring the text anew as we engage with it. There is also nothing Barthes can do about the emotional resonance of artworks diminishing over time, which is the thing I think he hopes to prevent. This is because rigidification is also a perfectly natural development. As emotionality is discharged into a symbol, an image, or a sound, it eventually becomes deprived of its subjective emotionalism and rigidifies.

When one engages in literary criticism – a vice which I have even indulged in myself, from time to time – one tries to "decode" the text and determine the *subtext*. This is really what Barthes is trying to say can have no incorrect interpretation. Subtext is not merely contrived by the author, this much is true; but is it open to endless debate as to what the subtext of a given text is, as Barthes would claim?

The true meaning of a text is not anything conscious; it is not a political message or a moral of the story; it is not a religious allegory carefully plotted out, or a character study developed in order to make a point. It may be contained in some measure in all or none of these aspects. The deepest meaning is an emotional story, usually a resolving of contradictions or overcoming of a dilemma – one feeling overcoming another feeling. The true artistic meaning is the expression of this play of feelings. All the conscious processes that went into its production cannot alter this meaning, and the author cannot consciously dictate the meaning.

Authorial intent is not the arbitrary and final say on this meaning; on the other hand, it can *reveal* the meaning. Neither is artistic meaning governed by the strict subjectivity of the audience, nor can the audience's new authorship of the text be ignored. The true meaning of a work is not subject to change according to the interpretations of critics. Our rational analysis cannot touch it. We can describe it, in the same feeble terms we use to describe any emotions – I say feeble because our definition of anger would be devoid of meaning to one who had never experienced anger. If a work of art criticism wanted to truly speak the language of emotions, it would have to become a work of art itself to be up to the task. This is why all art criticism, all literary criticism, is simply playing on the outskirts of the core issues of art. Only art can truly interpret art. Most art critics are deeply inartistic people, and the more rational analysis they bring to bear, the less artistic their art criticism becomes.

The experience that a work of art communicates is not subject to debate. This does not mean that there are not demonstrably true or false descriptions of the emotional content, in terms of the intellectual honesty or insight into the emotional resonance. The *experience* is what captivates us and interests us about a work of art. We can analyze what causes a feeling. We can analyze where it occurs in the brain. We can analyze the things the feeling is associated with. But the experience is inescapably subjective. We may dispute the author's exclusive claim on the conscious meaning of his work – whatever moral point the author is making or whatever allegory he wishes to carry out. But the *artistic meaning* cannot be argued with.

No one else had the feelings and experiences that Balzac had: only Balzac had them, only Balzac lived them, and only Balzac expressed them. The self that the Buddhist negation of the self cannot ever dispense with is the locus of feeling, the locus of experience. In Buddhist metaphysics, this is called *citta*, the mind. The mind is here understood as a vector of thoughts and experiences. Therefore, the Buddhists argue against the concept of the self, but they don't argue against a locus of experience. They don't argue to people that they aren't *really* suffering – quite the opposite.

The subjective, sensory experience is unmistakable as the most immediate reality. In the language of Pirsig's metaphysics of Quality, the edge of perception is Dynamic Quality, and it is so real that it actually transcends the subjective/objective split. The transmission of this "inner life" is the true aim of art. The emotional resonance of art is valuable to us for this reason and this reason alone. By missing on this question, Barthes misses what all art truly is.

The entire point of communication is to make real the inner contents of your world to someone else. Art is a means of overcoming the split between self and other. Barthes and other literary critics would have us communicate with the end of merely imposing our own ideas on what someone else is saying. In terms of linguistic communication, this is known as "not listening." Literary critics are simply bad listeners.

Communication is a two-way street: it requires the artist just as much as it requires the audience. If one means to express suffering, and the audience experiences joy, *then either the artist has failed or the audience has!* And yes, there is such a thing as the failure of the audience.

We do not like to imagine that we might not understand a work of art because it is above us. There are works of art that some people are not educated enough to understand, or not attentive enough to understand. But is it not the peak of arrogance to always assume that it is the other way around? That if we find a work of art obtuse or confusing, that it is the artist's fault? Let us dispense with the conclusion that it is valid to interpret joy where suffering was expressed. This is not permitted by sane people, and yet Barthes' argument demands it.

A masterpiece does not become less a masterpiece for the ridicule of fools. The extent to which the audience can faithfully represent the author's intent in their own psychic experience is the extent to which communication has occurred. The fool's reading is only its own retelling of the work in the most general sense. In a more important sense, it is merely an incomplete work – a poor facsimile, a conduit that is receiving a distorted signal, the aforementioned failure of the audience.

Tolstoy writes: "Art, in our society, has been so perverted that not only has bad art come to be considered good, but even the very perception of what art really is has been lost." I bring up this quote because there is a side-effect of Barthes' argument: if art is endlessly open to interpretation, then there cannot be good or bad art. One man's good art would be another man's bad art, and vice versa. It is now fairly common for people to reject even the possibility of judging the quality of art.

Most people aren't capable of thinking critically about the art they consume these days. Most of us realize that much of the art we consume, if we consider it dispassionately, should be categorized as "bad art". It's like junk food. Just like people with unhealthy eating habits, we rationalize our unhealthy artistic habits.

The various arts all straddle the line between artistic and purely technical these days. There is so much art produced for mere entertainment, where the emotions are cynically manipulated and nothing meaningful is communicated whatsoever. Meanwhile, the most intellectual forms of artistry, such as filmmaking and literary authorship, have become so self-aware, so self-conscious, that the medium has basically become a playground for the mind. This is, broadly speaking, what Nietzsche predicted about the two directions of art: high art becomes desensualized and lower art becomes sensuously vulgar and excessive.

People love to discuss what works of art "really mean." Why this love of art criticism? Because people use art criticism the way they use art: as a form of entertainment. This is all so much easier when we can banish the artist from the discussion – that is the effect of the Death of the Artist doctrine.

It is only in a climate like this that we could sustain such a volume of critics of every stripe. There is a whole cottage industry of internet film critics these days.

Rather than saying that the artist's intent should be weighed and balanced against our own interpretation – which might actually lead to something like a meeting of the heart or mind with the artist, and the possibility of the resonance with the artist, the communication for which sake we are moved to do art in the first place – Barthes says to kill the artist. Who would create such a psychotic ideology? This is, of course, because literary criticism is Barthes' craft, and he wished to validate it.

This should tell us all we need to know about the real motivations behind Barthes' interpretation and its popularity: Barthes, a literary critic himself, wanted to open the floodgates to every kind of literary criticism. The literary critics will then further desensualize the art of literature into a wholly symbolic, intellectual exercise. Notice what happens in the final analysis: *only* the literary critic is permitted to speak about the meaning of art; the artist himself is excluded from the discussion about his own meaning.

Barthes' objection to putting a limit on the text reveals his psychological preconceptions about authorship. What the anarchists and existentialists have sought above all things is limitlessness – to take the finite boundaries imposed on mankind by nature or society, and eliminate them. This may have once been a noble goal, when blind tradition ruled, and the institutions of society were devoted first and foremost to the task of indoctrinating new generations into the limitations of said tradition. The abolition of a number of harmful limits on mankind was a righteous thing, especially those limits created by accident of birth, caste, religion, or ideas of what nature or God demands.

But let us be realistic about limitations. A painting is not limited by putting it within a frame. It is limited by the edges of the canvas, which every painting must eventually reach. We are not adding a limitation by understanding the author's intent, the details of his life, or his cultural context: these limits already existed, and the understanding of them can only help in fine-turning our reception of the artist's meaning. These are all enrichments to our understanding, not detriments. That such facts may trample on our subjective whims is really no objection.

There are a million limits on every single work of art. The artist's intent is merely one more to consider; but it must be considered. Barthes' dream for limitlessness in art is just a dream. The individual is, in reality, limited. Art is a *human* phenomenon, and humans are limited.

These interpretations of art tempt us because art is at the edge of the creative world that seems to have no limits. The unconscious roil from which we draw up our artistic inspiration always confronts us in new and mysterious forms. Even if Barthes' arguments were not correct, perhaps his *instinct* was: *that art is at its greatest power in novelty.*

***

It was an overcast, humid morning. We congregated in the restaurant. There was a discount on the breakfast if you'd stayed at the hostel. Most of us decided to eat there. We sat at two tables relatively close to one another. I chose to sit with the Italians that morning. For all the cursory internet study of the Italian language that I'd managed on the trip so far, I didn't pick up much of the conversation. Occasionally, Luca, Doc, or Andrea would address me, but mostly they talked amongst themselves. I tried to just listen, to pick up the sound of the language, its inflections.

While Davide checked us out, we goofed off in front of the hostel. Some of the guys took funny pictures in front of a statue of a colorful, red, fantasy-style dragon that stood by the front doors. I watched and smoked. Andrea came up to me. We started talking.

"The last song that you play," he finally asked. "The one that you sing. What is the name of this song?"

"Luxcrusher," I said.

"Lux crusher," he repeated, pausing between the two parts of the title. "Incredible song. Brutal."

"Thanks, man," I said.

"I would love to sing this song with you."

"Yeah," I said. "Yeah, at the last show! That would be fucking awesome!"

I told him I'd write out the lyrics for him on the drive, that way he could look them over while listening to the studio version of the song.

***

The final date had originally been planned for a city in southern Germany. Of all our shows that fell through, this was the only one that we'd actually managed to salvage. Help came from Jeff Henson of the band Duel – another band from Austin with whom we'd been friends for many years. They'd toured Europe quite a few times. When Steve put the word out that we were looking for a show somewhere in southern Germany, or in Switzerland, Henson messaged Steve. He found us a venue in Basel, at an underground venue called the Hirschneck.

Our contact there was Michael. He was Duel's soundguy for their European tours, and ran the sound at Hirschneck. He'd toured with Duel throughout Europe and even come with them to America. He was an older fellow, bald with a goatee, wearing leather. He looked more like a biker from the south than my mental image of a Swiss person.

The venue was in Basel's old town, just a short walk from the Rhine. It was an incredibly old building that served as a neighborhood restaurant and tavern. Virtually all the streets and buildings in that part of town were ancient. Hirschneck itself is situated inside/beneath a building that was built in the 1300s. It had survived numerous fires and calamities, according to the staff. It appeared like an ordinary tourist-friendly restaurant, with outdoor seating and cozy inside tables and booths – and the menu listed food and drink that cost the usual Swiss premium. Someone could easily spend upwards of a hundred dollars on food and drinks for two people.

The inside of Hirschneck was full of patrons, a mix of yuppies and well-to-do people with younger hipsters. Michael secured us each a meal from the restaurant. We pushed together two tables to fit the nine of us at a single table. On offer was spaghetti with Bolognese sauce, or plain red sauce for the vegetarians. He poured us all beer from the tap.

After the meal, Doc and I stood out front. It was quiet that night in Basel. I bummed a cigarette from Alex. We stood in the twilight calm, watching the intersection of the old streets. "I cannot believe this," Doc said. "I'm ashamed."

"Sorry?"

"I told my mother I would not eat Italian food when we were outside of Italy…"

"And…? What, the spaghetti?"

"Yes."

"What, it wasn't good?"

"Spaghetti Bolognese," Doc said. "There is no such thing."

"Ah," I said. "And you're from Bologna."

"Yes."

"But we eat Spaghetti Bolognese in America. This isn't a real dish?"

"No," he said. "This is an insult to us in Bologna, that people serve spaghetti noodles with Bolognese sauce. And on the last day," he concluded. "After avoiding it this whole time… I eat fake Italian food."

There was a particular kind of noodle that had to be eaten with Bolognese sauce – though I cannot recall which noodle it was. Doc was adamant about this. But, of course, a touring musician doesn't refuse a free meal from their host. Doc may have been Italian, but he was also a touring musician. You had to take what the venue had to give you, then you thanked them, ate it, and were grateful. All the same, I found the Italian devotion to a traditional food culture to be admirable.

After we were done eating, they showed us the accommodation. The apartment was two stories up from the restaurant. They told us that in the darkness of night, the three flights of stairs were plunged into pitch-black, so we should use the flashlights on our phones. The stairs were steep and creaky. The apartment itself was a single room; a dozen or so comfy mattresses were laid out on the floor. A single table and some chairs stood near the single window. There was a sink just outside the room for water or hand-washing. The only toilets would therefore be all the way down at the bottom of the stairs. I made a mental note to pee before bed.

It was an early show. Very few turned up, except for the staff, a couple of patrons from the bar up above, and one of Hell Obelisco's friends, someone Doc knew from the old days who now lived in Basel. It didn't matter. We played our hearts out to a mostly empty room. Andrea joined us on stage and sang with me. Those who were there enjoyed it. It was as good a night as we could have hoped for as a last-minute set on a Tuesday. And that was that. The last gig together.

After the show, Nick and I sat at the small wooden table up in the loft, near the window. It overlooked a street in the old town, a church, and the park. I opened both the wooden shutters and let in the quiet noise from the street. I imagined people sitting here, looking out into Basel, at different periods in history, for hundreds of years.

Davide came and sat next to us. He'd come up here to wind down for the night; understandable, as he had the longest drive out of all of us the next day. I don't remember how we got onto the topic, but we talked about the opera. Nick asked Davide what he thought of opera, and Davide answered that he had a great appreciation for it. The Italians were full of surprises.

Nick showed me, on his phone, the address for Nietzsche's room. Of course! We were in Basel. Nietzsche taught at the university here. According to the GPS, it was a thirty-minute walk from here. Nick planned to go in the morning, on his jog. We were leaving early in the morning, which meant getting up even earlier. *Fuck it*, I thought. *You're here now, for one day and one night* I told him I'd join him. After a while, we rejoined the others in the downstairs bar, and started drinking.

After this brief reprieve from activity, the staff told us that downstairs would be locked in the morning. Therefore, we just had to haul everything up from the basement and into the back hallway. That way we could just move everything into the van come morning, and get out as early as possible. We hustled to get all the gear onto the ground level.

We were all drunk by this point in the evening. Penny and Davide were already upstairs, sleeping. Nick went up shortly after we finished with loading. It was one of our few chances to party, and Steve was of course taking the opportunity to give our run with Hell Obelisco a proper send-off.

Doc, Alex, Andrea, and Luca stayed up with us. There were four or five people from Hirschneck there, too.

The bar upstairs closed; downstairs, we began smoking inside. A bottle of peppermint schnapps was opened. I was offered a shot. I drank one shot, and washed it down with a Swiss beer. Quollfrisch. I was offered another shot of schnapps; I drank another shot of schnapps. Each shot was invariably a toast with four or five others. Another bottle of schnapps was opened. Another shot was poured. Things began to blur a bit.

Michael and I drunkenly talked about international politics for a bit.

"It is all a comedy show!" he said, laughing. He was right. It was all too absurd to talk about.

Luca disappeared upstairs, and Andrea. Then Alex. I remember asking Doc a question after the fifth or sixth shot. The music was loud.

"What?" he said, his accent thickening with intoxication. It was much harder to expend the effort to communicate with one another under the influence of all that beer and schnapps. A joint was passed around.

Eventually, it was just me, Steve and a few of the guys from Hirschneck. After an hour or so more of drinking, I had to bow out, and stagger my way up the stairs again. Steve remained downstairs for.... Well, even he doesn't remember. I didn't know what time it was when I finally went to sleep. As my head hit the pillow, swimming in drunken blackness, I had the anxious realization that I'd forgotten to piss before lying down.

**

Nick woke before I did. My alarm went off along with his, as he was getting ready for his jog. My head was pounding; there was a searing pain behind the eyes. I snoozed the alarm. I couldn't bring myself to rouse any earlier than I absolutely had to.

He left without me. He sent me pictures of the placard that hung over Nietzsche's room, and the surroundings at the old university. I somewhat regretted sleeping in, and having missed a philosophical pilgrimage. All the same, I would not have enjoyed the excursion.

In what felt like no time at all, all the alarms started going off. Penny was the smartest out of all of us, I thought, having turned in immediately after the show. He didn't seem fatigued at all. We all took our turns brushing our teeth, and slowly filtered downstairs while Davide went to bring the van around.

Steve was the most ruined. His eyes, normally set into dark, deep circles, looked even more fatigued and bleary than normal. We all reeked of cigarette smoke, weed, beer. I was glad I'd taken the opportunity to shower in Copenhagen. I hadn't bothered in Kassel; the previous night it hadn't been an option, which meant I was now on day three of uncleanliness once again.

Davide went to pull the van around. I made it downstairs, took a much-needed piss, then loitered outside. A couple of the guys were still up in the loft, packing. I figured I had a couple minutes. The Rhine was right there. I walked down to the shore. The stone steps lead right down into it. It was cloudy, opaque water, but flowing incredibly quickly. The massive amount of water pushed and flowed with an enormous power, channeled into such a narrow width. Colorful historic buildings overlooked the river, painted those pastel colors – gold, pink, beige, blue... I thought about jumping in right then and there. But my bags were already packed in the back of the van. I wanted to swim, but I didn't want to get wet.

CHAPTER SIXTEEN
MILAN - VIGONE

We had to cross the whole of Switzerland that day. This would take around four hours, then we'd drive another two hours or so to get to Milan. Once there, Davide would drop us off, then take Hell Obelisco back to Bologna. After that, he had several hours to drive on his own, back to Pescara. The Italians all had a much longer day than ourselves. But for us, the tour would continue, and we'd play our final four shows in Italy, starting that night in Milan.

I fell in love with Switzerland that afternoon. The highway takes you through the mountain valleys that cover the country. The Alps were wreathed in mist that morning, and it seemed that on every mountain slope there was a waterfall. In the domain of the mountains, I grew more and more detached. My stress over the tour had more or less dissipated. The frustrating search for artistic validation didn't seem as important. I felt like I was near to eternity: or, at least eternity as far as human beings were concerned. In the valleys and fields below, man had constructed civilizations, destroyed them, rebuilt them, and repeated this process *ad nauseum*. Meanwhile, the mountains remained as they were, unchanged, over countless generations. Nick was sitting in the front of the van. There would be no way to talk over the road noise, and with a whole row of Italians sitting between us. But I thought of Nietzsche's description of the moment when he first was struck by the idea of eternal recurrence. I sent a text message to Nick: "Six thousand feet above men and time."

The highway took us soaring over Lake Lucerne, its crystal-clear waters glittering beneath us. We crossed the longest automobile tunnel in Europe, which was sixteen kilometers in length and seemed to go on for an eternity in the orange-lit cavernous darkness, until finally giving way to more mountains and valleys. We stopped at a rest area. Under blue skies, at some rough-hewn stone picnic tables, we smoked the last of the weed we'd been given, ate Swiss cheese, and reminisced about the time with our Italian friends that was all but over. I took off my shoes and felt the morning dew on my feet. In the distance, the clinking of a cowbell indicated one of the Alpine cows roving around nearby.

***

Hours later, we pulled up to the venue in Milan. It was mid-afternoon, and it was actually hot. Back to Italy indeed. There was a café across the street, selling the ubiquitous one-Euro-espresso-shots. Steve paid and we each took a shot, and washed down with mineral water. We talked and carried on for about ten, fifteen minutes or so. But the Italians had a schedule to keep, Italian time notwithstanding.

We unloaded all of our bags, the backline gear, and our guitars. We took a farewell picture, and said our goodbyes. We all hugged. I told Andrea how awesome it was to share the stage with him. I told Doc we'd be waiting when Hell Obelisco made it to America. Alex and I had but few words to exchange, for the language barrier had never been overcome, but I thanked him for the cigarettes. Last, I said my goodbyes to Luca, who had sat in front of me most days. He seemed to be their quieter one, like Nick.

For their part, the Italians had taken to calling Nick, "Dr. Jekyll and Mr. Hyde," since his persona on stage was so different. Steve had of course endeared himself to all of them, as was his nature. He had the natural magnetism, the natural charisma.

"Davide," I said, shaking his hand "You're the best driver we've ever worked with."

"Thank you," he said. "I had fun, it was good meeting you."

"No, you don't understand," I said. "You made this thing possible. You held this tour together for us."

"Thank you."

"Thank you. Have a safe trip home."

Not with a little apprehension, I watched Davide Stracchione's van drive off for the last time, and join the procession of traffic in downtown Milan. We were once again on a city street, with all of our gear and our luggage on the sidewalk, in the heat of day. Vulnerable again. Quietly, we waited.

***

Alex arrived an hour later. We exchanged hugs and greetings. It was funny how familiar he seemed, solely on the basis of having met him a week and a half or so ago and having spent a little less than a day with him. He of course asked how the tour had been going. I wasn't sure what to say.

"Some ups, some downs," I said, and left it at that.

I could have said that it was exciting, that it was boring, that it had gone off the rails, that it had been predictable, that it was contemplative, or that it was chaotic. These descriptions are all true and none of them make sense with one another. How could I talk about it? Besides, Alex knew and worked with the people from the label. How could I explain the nuances to him? Express my discontent? Somehow express how incredible it all was in spite of all these things? No. I would say nothing negative to Alex. He was like our host; we were his guests in Italy, and guests shouldn't complain.

Instead of communicating any of that, I showed him that I could now say, "Piacere di conoscerti" with confidence. I'd spent some of the time in the van studying the basics of Italian, in anticipation of coming back to this country. Or, at least what I could study with the limited cell coverage that was available to me.

While we waited for the venue to open, Alex drove us over to a three-star hotel and we checked in early. The van was not exactly luxurious, but it felt that way to us after a week and a half packed in like we had been. I'd been hoping that the last few days would offer some relief, dreading the prospect of ending the tour in Italy and looking to that as the one silver lining. This rental was even more spacious than the van he'd had when he picked us up from the airport, and we were better at loading gear and luggage now. And we had less. Less luggage, less people.

When the clerk first greeted us, he must have made me for an American, and immediately began speaking English with us. Alex replied to him in Italian. The clerk apologized. Alex said it was alright, chuckling slightly. Even though he told him he was Italian in Italian, and the clerk apologized in Italian, I understood all of this mostly from their body language and inflections, not because I could actually keep up with the Italian they were speaking.

We left our luggage up in our rooms. I'd imagine that we'd have time to get some rest, but when all was said and done, we didn't have that much time to ourselves. After what felt like no time at all, the hour for load-in came. We headed back to the venue.

After loading in gear, I stepped out onto the patio, craving a cigarette or a joint or a spliff, or really just something to smoke. Unfortunately, I had nothing. Evening gave way to dusk. Storm clouds began to blow in, and the wind kicked up, blowing cigarette butts and plastic bags around on the patio area near the sidewalk. It seemed like a storm was coming. But the rain never came.

Wednesday night in Milan didn't feel so different from a venue back in Austin on a Tuesday night. It was a decent-sized stage, a metal divebar aesthetic, lots of band stickers on the walls. Then, the band we would share the stage with for the next few days arrived. The Great Electric Quest was a rock band from San Diego. We'd run into them more than a few times on the road. The first time I spent any real time with them was during a festival in Sioux Falls, South Dakota, called Stoned Meadow of Doom. We'd shared a bottle of whiskey in the downstairs vending machine nook of the hotel.

They arrived in a hatchback. The first thing I noticed was that the steering wheel was on the wrong side. The driver's side was the right side of the car. We said our hellos, shook hands and hugged. There was Buddy on guitar, usually wearing a baseball cap, with long, straight brown hair and some of the best technical chops I'd seen. There was Tyler on vocals, with his bushy mutton-chops and denim vest; he had a taste for the theatric, and was a lead singer to the core. There was Mucho on drums, with a physique like a bodybuilder and a reputation for long drum solos. There was Jerry on bass, recognizable by his leather jacket and long curly hair. With them was Kerube, Buddy's fiancée who had come with them to sell merch.

These guys were, essentially, cryogenically frozen in the 1970s and only recently thawed out. Their frontman Tyler was probably a match for Steve when it comes to the pure rock n' roll mentality. We would be touring together with G.E.Q. for three days. They'd been in Europe for a couple weeks now, and they had several more to go. They'd spent most of their time in Britain so far. It seemed like a small vehicle to tour in. But if you could rely on the backline gear provided by the venue, what did it matter? Again, I found myself thinking that I might have enjoyed that kind of thing at nineteen or twenty.

I asked Tyler about the car.

"We got it in Britain," he said.

"Umm…Isn't that dangerous?" I asked. "You're driving on the wrong side now."

"Nah. It's all good," he said. "Maybe. I don't know."

"Why did you rent a British car anyway?"

"We didn't rent it, we bought it," he said. "We're going to be here for a couple months, and it was cheaper to just buy it, so we did. Had to use someone else's info though, a promoter in Britain, friend of ours."

They'd racked up a couple speeding tickets whilst driving around Europe, Tyler explained, as many of the speed-traps are automated. If you're speeding, and the computer's camera catches your plate and the radar determines that you're going over the speed limit, you're mailed a ticket. These citations had all been sent to the guy who bought the vehicle for them.

"He's been calling us," Tyler admitted, taking a swig of his beer.

"What are ya'll gonna do?"

He smiled and shrugged.

Meeting someone who you know when you're traveling abroad, even just an acquaintance, is a bit of a surreal experience. It was comforting, at least. The venue fed us for the evening and provided some free drinks. We drank Italian beer and ate pasta together. There wasn't anyone else in attendance, other than a pair of local metalheads, and we spent most of the night chatting and catching up with the G.E.Q. gang.

I was starting to worry that concluding the tour with four days in Italy hadn't been such a good idea. The few people who came out seemed enthused about the music, so there was that. Kerube tried to snap a picture of the fans who did come out for their Instagram. One of them, wearing a leather jacket with patches, adamantly declined the offer. He hurried to get out of the way of the camera.

"I do not want to be photographed!" he said.

***

The next morning, Penny and I awoke to the sound of banging on the wall. Or was it the ceiling? A continuous pounding – was it a hammer? Was there construction going on?

It continued. After an indeterminate number of minutes, I sat up in bed, blinking and rubbing my eyes. It was bright and sunny outside. It could have very well been three in the afternoon for all I knew, I was so disoriented. I leaned over the side of the bed and dug around in my shoes, where I usually kept my phone. It wasn't even eight in the morning yet. Penny, on the other bed, drew the covers over his head. Nick was already gone, presumably jogging. Steve was staying in the other room, with Alex.

Penny tried banging on the wall with his fist. It stopped for a bit. We both wrapped ourselves up in our blankets again. Five minutes or so later, the banging commenced again. Penny groaned. I swiveled my legs off the side of the bed and pushed myself up into a sitting position, looking about the room as I searched for the location of the sound. It was coming from just beyond that wall, and upwards. Probably people on the roof. I decided to try some rudimentary Italian.

"Silenzio!" I shouted, angrily, as loud as I could.

The banging stopped again.

By now, I was awake anyway. The restroom was really nice. Italian hotel bathrooms always have a bidet. It's a foreign practice to us Americans, but

I'm completely in support of it. The showerhead was refreshingly forceful. I took my first shower in days, and stepped out a remade man.

I fiddled with the balcony door, which was behind two door-sized wooden shutters. I finally got it open, and stepped outside. I could hear some people talking, albeit faintly, and the sound seemed to be coming from the roof, but I couldn't see upward from that angle. Must have been the workmen. At least they'd stopped hammering. The morning air was refreshing even in a city the size of Milan. I couldn't even see the city itself. The balcony overlooked a small courtyard with a brick floor, chairs artfully arranged around potted plants. Vines climbed up the old stone walls of the hotel, creeping around the windows and arches. The sounds of the city were not deadened entirely within the courtyard. One could still hear the occasional siren pass by, and shift with the doppler effect, the ambience of automobiles humming in the distance.

I met Steve and Alex downstairs. They were drinking espresso and talking about metal albums they liked from the past couple of years. There was a little espresso bar, in a little nook with a window looking into the courtyard on the ground level. At the counter was the same, middle-aged, mustachioed man who checked us in. I think you could get a shot for one euro pretty much anywhere in Italy. Nick soon arrived from his jog, and I put down a two-euro piece for my second shot and one for him. Within ten minutes or so, most everyone from both bands had congregated downstairs. We swapped stories and planned the day.

It was a mere two hours to Vigone. We weren't performing in Vigone, per se, but on a small farm just outside of town, beyond the village limits. There are countless little towns in Italy on every road, every few miles. You'll pass through one village, with stone walls and red roofs and a single little bar with some two or three ancient men sitting at a plastic table, smoking and chatting. And then you pass a sign with the name of the village, but now a red strike through it, indicating you're leaving the village, sometimes less than a minute later. Then, more farmland.

We had to make a stop in Turin on our way to Vigone. Our destination was a rehearsal space and gear rental shop. Alex knew the technician working there. It was where the Marshall cabs we were using came from, as well as the drumkit Penny was using. I borrowed a power supply for my delay pedal; the guy gave it to me for free and made me promise to return it. Penny needed something fixed on his kick pedal. Buddy from Great Electric Quest was also looking to get one of his guitars worked on. The gear rental shop had some kind of relationship with the record label.

While the others finished up inside, I loitered outside with Tyler, Jerry, and Kerube in the parking lot across the alleyway from the shop, under a row of shady trees planted on the sidewalk. I bummed a cigarette from Jerry. The church bells tolled out that it was three o'clock. Shortly thereafter, a procession of middle school aged kids spilled out from a nearby walkway. The apartment buildings towering nearby were stereotypically Italian – with clothing hanging out to dry from every balcony, arrays of garments and towels of every color fluttering in the wind.

The technician said Buddy's guitar would take a few hours to fix. Great Electric Quest headed to a nearby record store while they waited. We decided we'd meet up with them later, at the venue.

We piled into the van and Alex took us the final thirty minutes or so. We traveled between green and golden fields, through one little town after another, until finally one of those little towns happened to be Vigone. The road wound through narrow streets that twisted and turned among old stone walls and eventually led us to a parking lot, beneath a church and an old clock tower, in view of a local park. Vigone had its own little piazza. Alex explained to us as we climbed out of the van that this place was once known for raising horses. Hundreds of years ago, it was the site of the royal stables. Now it was merely one of many towns on the outskirts of Turin.

There was a bar, obviously a thoroughly local establishment. It was just around five o'clock, and the patrons were families and older folks. The working day was done and everyone was out at the picnic tables enjoying a glass of wine or beer. Clouds of cigarette smoke hovered over the patio and dissipated into the wind. In the park nearby, families were enjoying the afternoon; children ran and skipped while their parents walked behind, linked arm-in-arm, carefree looks on their faces. The people in the Italian countryside all have that look, that disposition. Serenity.

Steve inquired as to what kind of wine we should have. Alex recommended that we ask for a Barbera. Nick and I went inside to procure some.

"Posso avere un bicchiere di Barbera?" I asked.

The bartender didn't have Barbera, but held up a bottle of Nebbiolo. I accepted this choice – who was I not to? Alex told us when we brought it to the table that this was another wine from nearby. Just as there is no other kind of beer quite as pure, natural, refreshing as German beer, the same can be said of Italy when it comes to wine. I don't claim the most refined pallet, but even a charlatan can immediately taste the difference.

He poured us five glasses, and Nick and I carried them out to the patio. Penny sniffed his glass, took a little sip, then tossed back the glass and gulped most of it down in a single swig. Alex burst out laughing. "This is not how Italians drink wine!"

"It's not how Americans drink wine either," I said.

We lingered at the little bar in the piazza well past six. Earlier, Alex had said that six was the time for load-in. But none of us really cared. Not even me.

***

Some time later, we drove another ten minutes or so, taking us out of the town and down a couple backroads. Alex turned the dirt road, leading to the farmhouse. The driveway took us around the building and into a grassy lot. There were fir trees, and other red-roofed farmhouses off in the distance, but it was mostly just fields as far as the eye could see. I looked around and assessed the surroundings: there was an outhouse for a restroom, there was a cooler that was currently empty, picnic tables and chairs set up just outside of a locking gate, which led to the yard.

The house itself was two stories, and framed half the yard at a ninety-degree angle. It was made of brick and looked old. The host, who lived there, had converted what was once the shed into a recording studio. The venue itself was a separate building, adjacent to the outside area with the tables, where the patrons could smoke and hang out. Inside, there was a plain, rectangular room with some band posters, two PA speakers, a "stage" – not a stage, but simply a section of the room for the band to stand in. Normally it served as a rehearsal room for bands in the area.

Great Electric Quest hadn't shown up; we'd figured they would have beaten us there, given how long we spent at the bar. We didn't have a phone number, only Facebook messenger. This meant we were reliant on our cell coverage, which was fickle. It was probably fine. They were likely just taking their time, as we'd done. I wondered how difficult it would be for them to find the place. I decided not to worry about it.

We were in the home stretch. We'd passed the point where the most grievous problems could arise. I walked out of the compound and onto the dirt road. It continued out into the field. A little dirt path continued off the road for autos and tractors, and into the field itself. It looked like the owner had not grown crops here for some time. His interest was more in music than farming, after all. This is apparently the story of this generation of Italians: the kids aren't interested in the traditional ways of life any more. The sun dropped lower and lower in the sky. I felt lost to all the world, but only for a moment.

***

Great Electric Quest showed up just before sundown. Shortly thereafter, Valerio arrived. He was tall – even taller than me – with a long, raven-black ponytail, and beard. Here was the booking agent who had been the source of so many problems: the routing that made no sense, the absurdly long drives, shows set up with irresponsible promoters that were cancelled or under-promoted. He was friends with the owner of the venue, and had started his booking career by setting up shows there. We exchanged pleasantries, through the language barrier.

Of course, I had the thought of saying something to Valerio, but what would I have even said? I couldn't really talk much to Valerio in any case, since he barely spoke English. Again, I realized there was nothing productive in venting my frustrations. Furthermore, he was somewhat in the position of host that night. Valerio brought us pizza, in the local style. It was on some sort focaccia bread of different varieties. There was an incredibly spicy variety I was particularly fond of. Soon, the cooler was filled with beer. We all ate our fill of carbohydrates, which was the theme of many of our best European meals, and then drank even more. How could I complain?

My expectations for the actual show attendance had been, admittedly, quite low. The Thursday night show in the middle of nowhere surely could not have been any better than a Wednesday night show in Milan. But once again, Europe surprised us. By nightfall, maybe thirty or forty people showed up. There were families there with kids, there were teenagers, some college and high school aged kids, a couple older metalheads in attendance. I thought I even recognized some people from the tavern. In absolute terms, this is not that many people, but relative to our expectations, it was wonderful. They filled the outdoor commons area, and packed into the venue room when it was time for bands to perform.

I watched as G.E.Q. did their full set, complete with the drum solos, the guitar licks, Tyler's maniacal energy. We did our thing, exactly as we always do it, and headbanged and thrashed and created storms of feedback. The show felt good.

I called Amberly around five in the morning. Back in Austin, she'd just gotten off work. I paced back and forth in the blackness of night, eventually wandering off from the party, into the field.

"I can hear the bugs!" she said.

"Can you hear the dogs, too?" I asked. They were barking and roughhousing in the yard.

"Yes, I can hear the dogs," she said. Amberly grew up in the country. These were the sounds of the countryside at night.

At the very end of the night, Great Electric Quest wanted to go into town to get more wine. I thought it was, frankly, a terrible idea – though I said nothing. Steve was initially going to go with them, but ultimately decided against it. I was glad. I'd have worried about him. All of us went inside and upstairs, to bed.

***

When I awoke, I wandered over to the bathroom and took my second shower in two days, which was a first for this tour. It felt luxurious. I dried off, wrung out my hair, wrapped the towel around my waste and walked over the window. I opened the shutters, managed to unlock the stubborn latch on the window, and slid it open. I looked out over the dirt driveway that led up to the country road. The thickets of trees, the fields. The farmhouses in the distance, mere pale silhouettes.

When you first awake in a strange place, you don't always immediately recognize your surroundings, and consequently, your brain has to reload the program, recall where you are and what you're doing. It was a strange realization: that I was awakening in the Italian countryside because I was abroad, touring with my doom metal band. What a surreal reality to awake into.

Our host, whose name I don't remember, awoke shortly after Steve and I. He offered us espresso. I thanked him and gladly accepted. His cat wandered out into the living room and began rubbing on my legs. Our host put on some heavy metal records, beginning of course with his own band. I smiled and told him I liked it.

With the doors to the balcony and the windows laid open, the morning air and the chirping of the birds blended into the living room's atmosphere. I looked up the phrase in Italian, and asked him if I could play with his dogs. He led me downstairs to the yard and let the dogs out. They didn't seem to "play" very well, and seemed a bit confused by my attempts. I guess they were just farm dogs. Or maybe there is a double language barrier when an American *homo sapien* tries to communicate with Italian dogs.

CHAPTER SEVENTEEN
VIGONE - VERCELLI

We all gathered in the courtyard of the farmhouse after our morning coffee. The members of G.E.Q. told us about their night. After heading into town to get more wine, they'd shown up at the bar and ended up getting drunk with some of the locals. Then, the locals took them joyriding through the streets of Vigone, and out into the farmland, tearing through the village streets with breakneck twists and turns.

"It was fuckin' *wild*, man!" Buddy said.

"I don't even know what time we got back here," Kerube added.

I was doubly glad that Steve hadn't gone with them.

It was another warm, humid afternoon. We'd traveled together on the highway yesterday, but today we had a few stops to make, and decided to split up. We made our plans to meet up with G.E.Q. that evening, at the bed-and-breakfast that our label set up for us in Vercelli. We parted ways.

That night was supposedly the big show. It was an Argonauta Records Showcase, in the hometown of the label's owner, Gero. Though Great Electric Quest wasn't one of Argonauta's bands, Steve had gotten them on the bill. Gero's band and another local group on the record label would be joining us, and Destroyer of Light was headlining. Even though Vercelli was on the other side of Turin, it would only take an hour or so to make the drive there.

We decided to devote the first half of the day to sightseeing. It was the only chance we would have for such touristy behavior. Steve wanted to visit Villa Scott, a place where one of Dario Argento's horror films had been filmed. Nick suggested we see Nietzsche's room in Turin. I'd missed out on seeing his room in Basel, and I figured this would be as good a pilgrimage as any. Alex then suggested we drive through a national park to see the king's hunting lodge, a site that was on the way to Turin.

After a stop at a grocery store for food and wine, the road took us from the farmland into a forested area, where patches of trees thickened and thickened until they congealed into an army of arboreal sentinels. At the edge of the land once designated as the king's copse, there stood a barracks of sorts for the king's guard. It was a large building. Alex assured us that was nothing compared to the actual lodge. True enough, the palatial structure we encountered after rounding the corner of a long semicircular turn was probably bigger than some presidential estates. We parked under the shade of the trees planted along the main road, which stood just by the parking lot. We walked along the grounds, and up to the gates, which were closed to the public. The grounds themselves were impressive. It was almost a miniature city, centered around the lodge. It was commemorated by a towering statue of, presumably, the king on horseback.

By the time we reached Turin's downtown, it was early afternoon. Traffic was heavy. Nick remarked that Turin was perhaps the most aristocratic city he'd ever encountered. The styles of architecture that characterized the historic portions of the city certainly conveyed this grandeur. The king's lodge had colored those impressions. Though it had been sunny out at the lodge, now it was overcast, and a light drizzle was just starting to come down.

Downtown, there were shops and cafes, crowds bustling beneath their awnings, lining either side of the street. Down the center of the road was the tramline. A line of commuters was waiting on the raised central platform, just to the left of us. I was sitting in the back seat behind Alex, my face pressed against the window.

There was an older gentleman, his nose buried in a newspaper, leaning casually against the railing; there were two or three older women, all dressed as fabulously as possible, with bright nails and glinting earrings, bejeweled sunglasses and designer purses; there was a middle-aged couple, smiling at each other; there were four or five young men, college aged or younger, laughing and chatting, carrying their books and papers underarm; there was a mother holding the hands of her two children on either side; there were a few chaps with quaffed hair and cologne that I could smell just by looking at them; at the end of the platform, there was a young couple, who just so happened to embrace and lock in a passionate kiss just as we flew past them and the platform disappeared from sight.

XI. What is Beauty?

The knowledge of art's origin and function leads us to understand it as communicative and therefore communal. The degree to which a work is expressive of the irrational and emotional side of the human psyche is the degree to which it is artistic. Art is the expression of the subjective, the attempt at communion of certain emotional states, feelings and experiences – this is what we call emotional resonance. In spite of the artist's attempt to kill the audience, and the literary critic's attempt to kill the artist, this resonance, which is the *telos* of all art, can only exist as a relationship between artist and audience. Private art is still communication, but communication within one's self, and it is within this private communication between conscious and unconscious that the spark of the artistic process begins, ignited by the divine inspiration of the Muse, or, to speak plainly, the play of feelings within. Art can facilitate this bridging between self and other because it exists on the edge of the subjective and objective, the conscious mind and the unconscious impulses, between what we feel and what we understand.

My friends, way back in my college days, dismissed aesthetics as a fool's errand: as a simply subjective endeavor that could never have any value. But this inquiry of ours is not a declaration of subjective preferences: this is not my explanation of what *I* find beautiful. On the contrary, the contextualization of art as a form of communication provides solid ground on which to consider the core question of aesthetics: namely, *what do we mean by beauty?*

This, of course, raises the old problem of deriving an "ought" from an "is" – if we are continuing with the idea that every aesthetic implies an ethic, and vice versa. While we may not take this as a hard and fast rule, it seems inescapable that the question of "what is beautiful?" remains in the same category as the question of "what is good?" – insofar as both are subjective and thus cannot be derived from objective fact alone.

The ought/is problem can be re-evaluated. The contrast between art's biological, social, and historical context, versus the question of artistic quality, can be reconsidered. I will refrain from making prescriptive and universal statements. We can talk about aesthetic value judgments in the same sense that we talk about ethical value judgments. One can classify ethics as relative; yet we can make sense of an ethical statement by making it conditional upon certain (subjective and relative) axioms.

The first condition is the communicative quality of art as its original quality, its essential quality. Without this quality, there is no art, for whatever lacks this quality does not deserve to be called art. Not everyone will accept this condition. I could conceive that there could be new, absurdist uses for art. There have been movements such as Dada, Zen, and postmodernism that have (at least allegedly) repurposed art and language for uses that could be considered absurd, or even opposed to the functions of communication. We might include the modern poet in this regard.

But to excise the communicative quality from art is to attempt to redefine terms that are already in common use. Thus far, I do not believe there's much that we've said about art that contradicts what we conventionally mean by the term. The anthropological context of art can only enrich that understanding. We may have had to part with a few cheap and pithy expressions concerning *what we think we mean* by art – mainly those which are motivated by unbridled individualism. We have seen, for various motives, that people often wish to separate the art from either the artist, or the audience. But this is impossible. At best, such a conception of art is an intellectual exercise. It has nothing to do with the creation of art or the experience of art.

We speak of artistic quality as the degree to which art fulfills its purpose in human existence. Under this definition, we can therefore include under the definition of "beauty", the portrayal of things that are considered ugly or disgusting, so long as such a portrayal is not mutually exclusive with fulfilling the purpose of artistic expression. A quality work of art is by definition a quality expression. Whether an expression is high quality or not depends on whether it finds emotional resonance with the audience. The inevitable conclusion now presents itself: *beauty is a relationship*.

The quest to define beauty as if it resides solely in the work of art itself is futile, just as it is futile to consider it merely a subjective statement of preference. Beauty must reside in both the work of art *and* in the beholder. The work of art preserves something of the artist, insofar as it manifests and represents the expression of that artist's emotional reality. But a message written in language, for example, cannot communicate anything to those who cannot read it. A stone tablet with the most sublime poetry or the most significant message would be irrelevant and meaningless in a world after the extinction of mankind; to those animals who happened upon such a thing, it would be just another rock. There must be a beholder in order to appreciate what is beautiful.

This is not as simple as the old adage referenced above, that "beauty is in the eye of the beholder": this is another pithy expression that leaves out half of the story. Beauty exists just as much in the work – which is to say, within the artist, whom the work represents – as it does in the beholder of the work. It is not solely an ersatz quality that the beholder gives rise to, since the work of art possesses the power to draw forth the soul of the beholder through its emotional resonance. The work of art is in many ways the active force.

The word beauty has many meanings confounded under a single label. It is primarily defined by the common understanding of beauty, and thus exists as a linguistic concept to represent what the culture at large finds to have artistic or aesthetic quality. In yet another sense, beauty is therefore comparable to love. Love in the romantic sense is comprehensible only as a relation between two people. In the case of artistic beauty, it is only possible between subject and work. And yet, the word love has also always confounded multiple ideas and feelings and definitions within a single label. The folly in our thinking about both is that a relationship can be established between different things and thus produce a different emergent property.

The terms "love" and "beauty" are descriptions of a type of relationship between things, not essential characteristics or substances.

Now that we have established this concept of beauty as another condition, can we then get down to the ugly business of distinguishing good art from bad art? We must give the Socratics of the world their due, and admit that the endless hunger for novelty in art has led to greater and greater complexity in art, and therefore greater command of technique – and thus ever more dangerous forms of expression. In determining proficiency in a craft, there are immediate, observable traits of good craftsmanship and bad craftsmanship. While these may not always be immediately apparent to laypeople, they are always noticeable by fellow craftsmen. This is as simple as the recognition of a master's brushstrokes – in total control, able to produce the slightest or smallest mark as well as sweeping, powerful strokes – or, for that matter, the recognition of a master's keystrokes at the piano. We distinguish art as better to the degree that the technique is better – this element of distinguishing good art is not mysterious and should not be regarded as merely a statement of preference.

There is an analogy in language. We may not be able to come up with a bright line at which point a person fits the description "articulate." But we can distinguish easily between an articulate speaker with a large vocabulary, and with command of the techniques of public speaking, from someone who is inarticulate, unskilled, nervous or crude with their language use. This level of skill can be evaluated independently from the message, even as it affects the message and is itself a part of the message.

The same holds true in art. We can tell the difference between a piano virtuoso and a man who has never played before, and this is a factor in distinguishing good art from bad. We can measure piano players against other piano players, and we can survey the techniques used in playing the instrument in order to gain an understanding of who has the best command over the instrument. We cannot separate the expression from the skill of the piano player – and yet, how beautiful we judge a piano performance has nothing to do with the technical knowledge in its playing. Skill can be evaluated separately from whatever artistic message the pianist conveys. There are session musicians who have a mastery of their instrument but do ever not compose any of their own songs. Technique is nurtured in the process of artistic expression but exists independently of an artistic expression.

Some works of art give rise to beauty, though without the artist possessing much in the way of technical skill. But even the completely uneducated artist must have some command of technique even if that technique is unorthodox or idiosyncratic: technique is the grammar, the syntax, the articulation. It is the means of artistic creation, and it stands in that sort of relationship to the end of creating beauty. While we may think it denigrating to refer to something as a mere means to an end, we'd do well to remember that *without some kind of means we cannot achieve any ends.*

The question of what is beautiful concerns itself with those ends, however: the emergent relation between artist and audience. This is the sense of unity that Tolstoy mentioned, which in the most beautiful works of art culminates in a sense of joyousness. This relation is the point of all artistic communication. As beauty is a relationship, it only emerges when the work finds a beholder.

Wherein, then, do we find the highest aesthetic value? Where is the most artistic quality located? What type of art is the most beautiful? To speak of what is beautiful indicates one of two possible meanings: either it is a statement of the strength of the relation a given work of art has with an individual beholder ("What *I find* to be most beautiful"), or a description of a work of art as forming the most possible relations ("Widely considered the most beautiful painting of all time"). We may take the first as a mere "statement of preference." The second possibility is also problematic: it implies that art is just a popularity contest. The vapid pop singer, under this definition, would be producing the most beautiful art solely on the basis of how many records they'd managed to sell.

Both definitions of beauty, as a mere statement of preference, or as a mere popularity contest, may seem excessively cynical, but these types of evaluations are all we have for considering art, in the wake of analytical philosophy, logical positivism, and the like: the dismissal of any question as to what art is, what it does, and what its value is. Might we reconsider the question, what is beautiful, in a different way?

When someone talks about what he or she finds most beautiful on a personal level, this is only a "statement of preference" insofar as a declaration of love or a proposal to marry is a statement of preference. We ought to all know better by now. Romantic love is as much chemical and physiological as it is psychological. With the term preference comes the connotation of whim or triviality, when nothing could be further from the case with our romantic relationships. They form the basis of that which ranks as most valuable to human beings – family, community, love – but love does not happen by arbitrary whim or by conscious choice. It is something *felt*, something that strikes with a powerful magnetism and commands the subject by means of the most intense and motivating feelings. Consider all the crimes, even heinous crimes, which have been committed in the name of love, not to mention all the self-sacrifices and renunciations. Love causes behavior considered crazy behavior by any sane person who is not so afflicted.

Beautiful art is much the same: one does not decide by conscious consideration or by flippant whim what to consider beautiful. It simply happens; the feeling is there, the experience is real, and the relation is created.

Similarly, while we may consider the momentary popularity of a vapid artist (or a counterfeit one), we might also consider that vapid art performs its function just as much as art that concerns itself with deep and existential questions. People need a safety valve for their emotions and irrational passions, and they are just as well-off dancing to the pounding, repetitive beat of electronica as they are doing anything else, so long as they achieve the needed momentary release from self-consciousness. Whether or not we agree with Nietzsche about the splitting of art – into purely sensual, versus overly symbolic – is beside the point. Dissolution of the self is a useful function, and while we may rightly attack vapid art as "bad art" for its clumsy, overwrought technique or shallowness of subject matter, it is not bad at the social function it performs.

Furthermore, it is only short-sightedness that would lead to this cynical view: of the collective definition of beauty as being a mere popularity contest. Vapid art may win the day seemingly in every age. But the forms of art that are least sophisticated and most popular at a given moment are dominated by trends, which come and go. Trends rarely leave a lasting impact on societal consciousness. The popular zeitgeist changes the standards of beauty every few years, always seeking novelty: for we know that novelty is good at capturing and holding one's attention.

The forms of art that are most dissolutionist and based on sensory experiences are dominated by novelty. These forms of art are therefore guided by cycles of popularity in which genres of artistic expression rise, fall, and are resurrected. The aesthetic philosopher really shouldn't concern himself with the vapid art that is popular in his current day and age, for one's lifetime is but a blink of an eye when it comes to the history of artistic expression.

The vapid artist and the counterfeit artist are always eventually conferred to the wastebasket of history, forgotten almost as soon as the trend goes out of style. Tolstoy writes of how we will eventually reject all counterfeit attempts at art: "As soon as the spectator, reader, or hearer feels that the author is not writing, singing, or playing for his own satisfaction – does not himself feel what he wishes to express – but is doing it for him, the receiver, a resistance immediately springs up, and the most individual and the newest feelings and the cleverest technique not only fail to produce any infection but actually repel."

What is beautiful then, is not a mere statement of preference of a single person, but the deeply felt relationship between someone and a work of art. And the art that is most beautiful is not that art which is the most deeply relatable to a single person – or even to an entire society. Rather, the great works of art are those that endure through the ages, and are preserved through multiple generations and forge relations even outside of their original cultural context. The great artists are the artists who were great not just for a moment, but even after the fervor for a given trend has passed into memory. The great artists exist not for one society, but for all societies.

I would therefore take the view that the art that forms the most relations is most beautiful, but dismiss the cynical conclusion that this leads to a view of art as a popularity contest. I am not speaking here of momentary relations, but of enduring relations. What is momentary is always cheap and disposable even if it seems particularly influential. What matters in art is not popularity, so much as endurance.

This was how aesthetics, growing up as it did, being intertwined with myth and ritual, helped to preserve religious feelings and ideas. This is the reason why our descendants will eventually forget about the slew of pop stars of today – there are too many to count, and really, I don't want to mention any of them at risk of dating this work – but we still remember classical, romantic, and baroque composers from hundreds of years ago: Bach, Mahler, Beethoven, Mozart, Chopin, Tchaikovsky, Vivaldi.

This even allows that we might remember one or two of the big names that are around today, but we can never say who was truly one of the greats so long as we are speaking of our contemporaries. Only history can reveal this. True Beauty is – *that which survives*.

***

Alex stopped the van. Nick and I got out of the vehicle, and began the walk to Nietzsche's room. The van proceeded up a winding road on the hill leading to Villa Scott. It was a continuous drizzle by now, and Nick told me that it would be a fifteen-minute trip or so by foot. I hoped it didn't come down any harder, since I had my phone with me and didn't want to risk getting it wet.

It wasn't long afterwards that we heard shouting coming from the stopped traffic on the street next us. There was the van. Alex was yelling for us, waving us to come get in. The cars were all stopped. We glanced at the light, which was still red, then hurried into the street, walking between the autos. We jumped inside just as the light turned green and the angsty Italian motorists began speeding forward.

"Villa Scott is closed for the day," Steve reported, sadly. "Me and Alex got up to the outside of it, took a picture, and that was it."

"I'll drop you off in the center of Turin," Alex said. "That way you can go, take a picture or whatever, I'll just circle around and pick you up again in twenty minutes."

"I'll go with ya'll," Steve said.

"You coming, Penny?"

"Nah man, I'm just gonna sightsee from the van."

We stepped out into a large, open square, near what looked to be a war memorial. I recognized the plaza from The Italian Job – the one from the 1960s. Nick's phone guided us along the crosswalks that would ferry us over the streets and tramlines, and then down a pedestrian alleyway, which led us to the edge of a piazza. Nick came to a stop, just before we got to the end of the street which opened up into another square. Towering over the square was what looked to be a courthouse, with regal stone pillars and triumphant verdigris statues. All of the statues were wreathed with flowers – there was a flower market open that day, and there were dozens of shops and stands beneath white tents, flowers and potted plants everywhere.

It started to rain a bit harder. Nick said the destination was right here, but none of us knew what to look for. We search for some kind of sign. Suddenly, I saw it. The memorial was set right into the wall next to us. It looked like it was still a residential apartment building just as it had been more than a century ago. We were standing right in front of it.

There was a profile image of him, with the name, "Frederico Nietzsche", and an Italian dedication explaining that it was here that he authored the book Ecce Homo. Steve took our picture in front of it. It had only been a few minutes getting there, so we set out to wander the market a bit before heading back.

We split up, and eventually met up again on the other side of the piazza. All around us were couples, holding umbrellas, perusing the selections of plants, jewelry, woodcrafts. There was such an interesting contrast: between the unchanging, stone architecture and monuments, and the living, vibrant, impermanent plants. The colors of the living flora, set against the ominous gray-black of the sky. The rain and the rumbling of thunder in the distance – and the peaceful ease of the people of Turin as they shopped and carried on.

***

A few hours before sundown, we pulled up to the bed-and-breakfast outside of Vercelli, twenty minutes or so away from the venue. Great Electric Quest arrived shortly after we did. We were greeted by a portly, older gentleman, who ran the bed-and-breakfast with his wife. He was mostly bald, wore a sweater vest, spoke softly. His English was impeccable. He said that he'd lived in America for a time. The old man told me a few stories about his own music career, when he was younger, playing jazz in the U.S., while Alex sorted out the details of the reservation with the innkeeper's wife. We were apparently the only guests at the moment. They seemed somewhat intrigued by the novelty of two rock bands staying with them.

Inside the bed-and-breakfast, the window overlooked the courtyard in front of the building, which was separated by a brick wall and a locking gate. There was an inground pool. It was nothing special, but a swim sounded nice. Below, I watched Nick wandering the grounds. He took a seat at one of the picnic tables, surrounded by the yard art, statues and planters. He pulled out his own notebook and began writing. I wondered what he wrote about, and if I'd ever have the chance to read any of it.

Beyond the yard was an empty field. In the very distance there looked to be a factory or warehouse of some kind. We were facing away from the small town behind us. The view from our room spilled out into idyllic nothingness, with the unmistakable reminder of industrialization lurking beyond. It was not an ugly reminder, not exactly. If anything, it looked lonely. A lonely island of modernity beyond the tall grass.

I do not recall anything particularly interesting about Vercelli. If there was any antiquarian architecture or historical buildings, I did not have the chance to notice them. The surrounding countryside was nice, but Vercelli itself seemed to be a nondescript, modern city. To Gero's credit, the venue was a real venue. There was a big, respectable stage, a bar, and plenty of standing room. That part of town had a yuppie vibe, however, and there didn't seem to be much foot traffic.

I met Gero in person for the first time. As with Valerio, I found I had little to say to him, both due to the language barrier and the fact that I did not have much that was positive to say about his management of our tour. He introduced me to a woman whom he said was a music journalist. I said hello and tried to be nice, but I didn't know who this woman was, and I couldn't bring myself to care at the moment. I was somewhat guarded with my expectations, given that this show had been talked up so much as being a big "label showcase." I was more interested in finding food, getting beer, and learning what time we were going on. I don't know how long the journalist stayed, how important she was, or what she thought of doom metal. But I sincerely hope she wasn't there for the show.

They initially gave a first set time of around nine pm. Great, this whole thing would be done around one 'o'clock in the morning, and then we could go back and hang out with Great Electric Quest on our last night together, before they parted ways and headed north. It could have started even earlier, in my opinion, but whatever. Gero wanted to start it later to get more people inside. We got a few drink tickets each, but that was all the venue did for us. There was no meal or accommodation provided. The venue staff didn't seem all that thrilled to have us, quite frankly.

Something I'd been far more concerned about was getting our records. We'd finally receive the vinyl pressing for Mors Aeterna that night. When Gero had contacted Steve to let him know, we were all excited. Even though the pressing had run late, we were excited to finally have the records. It's wonderful to hold the wax in your hands.

But when they showed us the vinyl, the art was a reversed version of the art on the CD. I had no idea why this was. The CD was a mirror image of the art on the records. Great. Just great. It wasn't the end of the world. But the label was proving to be incompetent in the one way that a record label must not be incompetent: in manufacturing records.

There were also little typos in the liner notes that I noticed. A whole two lines in one of the verses on the lyric sheet was missing. I didn't say anything to Steve. I didn't say anything to Gero. I just drank my free alcohol and then went out to the van. I didn't want to be around any of the people from the label.

Penny was already out in the van when I got there, nursing a beer. He was also livid. He and I stewed about it. Eventually, Nick showed up, and joined us in the van as well. All three of us just gave up for the night. We mostly just sat in silence, drank, and looked at our phones. I think Nick read a book.

There was that same gnawing feeling. Smoldering, was more like it. I don't remember exactly what was said between the three of us out in the van, if anything. But none of us had the strength to put on a good face and mingle that night. We all just wanted the night to end.

But it didn't end quickly. It was agonizing. Apparently, Gero had no ability to pull an audience in his own hometown. But since this was supposed to be "the big show" Gero and the other bands continuously pushed back the start time for the event, trying to drag things out as long as possible in the desperate hope that people would turn up. They didn't. I don't think we went on stage until about two or three in the morning. When we did, we played for the other bands.

I'd hoped the tour was about to finish on a relative high note, but the night was ruined. Now, as we all had to leave early in the morning, we had virtually no time to spend with Great Electric Quest that night. We'd be getting back to the bed-and-breakfast after four in the morning, at the earliest.

Nick passed out early; he'd been furious all night with the delays, and was really starting to crack in a way I'd never seen before. Penny went to bed shortly after him, because even though he wanted to hang out, he was too tired. Steve and I decided to stay up anyway, ignoring the late hour and disregarding what would've been responsible to do. We went up to G.E.Q.'s room with them. They were in the upstairs loft. We drank wine. We tried to celebrate the moment. To relish the crazy fact that we'd spent so much time together on the road, in situations like this one, in the unlikeliest of places. Even at shows that weren't always technically "worth it."

I supposed that I admired the ethos that Steve and Tyler lived by: the simple mantra, *rock n' roll*. Even as I've criticized this understanding of art as thoroughly un-philosophical, it is admittedly a thoroughly *artistic* understanding of art. It is dishonest, obfuscating, backwards. It is not self-reflective or critical. But perhaps it is the superior point of view for an artist, and why I have already been so conflicted about the artistic life: I am torn between the reflective mode of life, and the active mode of life. The active person doesn't require self-knowledge, doesn't act based on a theory. They're completely immersed in the moment, in their goals, in their feelings.

They have a certain demand for how their life is going to be, and they're going to live that life, no matter what. That is a special kind of pleasure, even when it requires enduring privation and disappointment.

As Nietzsche says in *Birth of Tragedy*, "Knowledge kills action; action requires the veils of illusion: that is the doctrine of Hamlet, not that cheap wisdom of Jack the Dreamer who reflects too much and, as it were, from an excess of possibilities does not get around to action. Not reflection, no – true knowledge, an insight into the horrible truth, outweighs any motive for action…"

What is the horrible truth? The near-certitude of the failure of the artistic life. Struggle towards no purpose, struggle with no improvement. If an artist gets too philosophical, and starts to reflect on this, it destroys the beautiful artistic illusion that he is living in. It threatens his ability for action.

However foolish it may seem to devote yourself to rock n' roll, with no regard for how things will turn out or whether one will ultimately be a success, that foolishness itself is a beautiful illusion that keeps the artist active. He forgets about the meaning or purpose of art, just as the birds do not think about the meaning or purpose of their songs. They just fly about, *vogelfrei*, and sing happily. Perhaps we artists are always destined to return to a naïve, foolish view of art, since the best artists have always been naïve and foolish.

***

I woke up around eight, forewent a shower that morning, and jumped into the pool instead. Before long, Jerry and Buddy were both awake. Jerry thought it was a great idea, and joined me. There were some leaves lingering on the surface, and it probably hadn't been vacuumed in some time. But the water smelled clean enough. Afterwards, I stretched out on the warm stone surrounding the pool and dried in the sun.

Our hosts set out a continental breakfast for us. There was traditional Italian coffee, made in a percolator, pastries, nutella, honey, two or three other kinds of bread, fresh fruit, yogurt, cheese, juice, and milk. There was perhaps enough for nine people, but for nine Americans it was a bit slight.

About half of us ate, and everyone who ate got their fill. We eventually said our goodbyes and hugged. I promised them that Switzerland would be a beautiful drive. They had a show that night at Hirschneck, the same place we'd played. It was another last-minute affair, like our show had been. We musicians are always saved by the skin of our teeth. We wished each other luck. The adventurers parted ways.

CHAPTER EIGHTEEN
VERCELLI - BELLUNO

As we drove through this old and beautiful country, my finite nature was nakedly apparent to me. Every little village we passed through was some artifice of the old world, everywhere were people who were themselves old and antiquated. Their faces were ancient, their manner of living was ancient. Every town was an enclave of people whose ancestors had long, long, long ago settled the question of how to live, and they had ceased in trying to figure any improvements on this model.

As I watched the faces pass by, between orchards and risotto fields, they appeared to me as those who lived and die like their crops, like the seasons. The rhythms of life recur again and again. You are one link in a long, spiraling chain. I yearned for something like that: some sensible place in the world, a place in a community, a culture. I guess doom metal is something like that. A culture.

XII. The Will to Eternity

What is my quest for artistic gratification? Can I finally answer it? It is the quest to survive. But let us say what survival is *not*. The quest to survive is usually associated with self-preservation. To speak cynically again, we might call this feeling synonymous with "death anxiety". Some might boil it down to the physiological urge to reproduce, from a naturalistic perspective. There is something incomplete and dissatisfying about all of these explanations. And they do little to actually explain the urge for artistic gratification.

While it may be convenient to chalk up all of our tilting against entropy as attempts to overcome "death anxiety," we should consider why it is that human beings might have such a thing as death anxiety at all. It is popular in some circles to attribute the motivations behind nearly everything human beings do to fear – as the primary motivator. In this type of theory, fear comes first, and the other motivations second. Something like greed, therefore, could be reduced to "fear of losing what one has," or "fear of not getting what one wants."

But I object to these kinds of descriptions of human nature. How can someone fear to *not get what they want* until they first *want something*? How can one fear to lose what he loves if he does not first have a love? Is it not clear that the desire comes first, and the fear second? Fear cannot be the primary motivator because something must be valued before fear can enter into the picture.

Here I am speaking of psychological fear, "anxiety" as we might put it, and not the mere physiological reaction to adrenaline, or an instinctual response to danger. Assuredly, even animals with no concept of self-consciousness can experience an instinctual feeling of danger, but this is not what I mean by the word fear. What differentiates humans from all non-self-conscious animals is the understanding of mortality. The fear we talk about in our human languages is therefore a distinctly human fear. We should look to the origin of our perception of mortality, rather than giving the phenomenon the completely un-explanatory label "death anxiety". *It is from the love of life that the fear of death springs, and not the other way around.*

All animals love life, but only human animals fear death. The understanding of mortality is only possible through the perception of time. This perception emerges through the realization of self-consciousness. The self's finitude reveals and is revealed through the revelation of our temporal nature.

In humans, this came about through the advent of the twin faculties of memory and imagination: these must have arisen simultaneously, in mutual interdependence. As to why humans developed these faculties, our very large visual cortex has something to do with it. Perhaps, so did dreaming. Whatever the case may be, humans acquired brains that could bring to mind images – pictures of things they'd seen in the past. And yet, while these pictures are indeed shaped of raw sense data, when we remember, that sense data is itself only a mental reproduction. Furthermore, it is a reproduction that the rememberer's brain alters. We alter our memories of the past to bring them into accord with information we learn in the present. Our remembrance of people and events is subject to the power of suggestion (as Loftus and Palmer demonstrated in their experiments). Meanwhile, what is imaginable to us draws from the sense data that we've taken in; we cannot imagine a color we've never seen, or a sound we've never heard. Even if memory can mix, match, and warp that sense data, there must be some raw material for what we're able to imagine.

To imagine is *to render an image in the mind*. Imagining is far less distinct from remembering than we like to imagine, just as our memories are less than safe from our flights of fancy and motivated reasoning. One could not have developed without the other, as they arose mutually.

In being able to imagine events unfolding differently than they actually unfolded, or imagine futures that have yet to come to pass, we thereby gained an understanding of time. As such a thing dawned on early man, we recognized, from past memories of all our departed loved ones, the reality of death and the fact that it eventually comes to every living thing. One would not simply realize the eventuality of one's *own* death, decontextualized from the rest of the world: impermanence must be reckoned with insofar as it governs all mankind. It is here, at the discovery of mortality as presiding over all human beings, that we can discover the ultimate motives behind art – for these are part and parcel with the ultimate motives of all human action. *The will to eternity, or to immortality: the desire to eternalize a feeling.*

Arguably, all life possesses the will to eternity, for the word "life" refers to the self-generating patterns we call organisms. Organisms all attempt to replicate themselves, to preserve themselves, to enforce their particular pattern, their particular reality on existence to the greatest degree possible. It is commonly known that Nietzsche located the primary human drive in the "will to power," but I have come to believe that the essential nature of the fundamental human drive is not correlated exclusively with the seeking of power. Nietzsche, admittedly, expanded the meaning of the term power, and offered insights in proto-psychology. He explained, for example, how power could motivate supposedly selfless or self-abnegating acts. But in doing this, Nietzsche did not get to the bottom of things. He expounded the doctrine of the will to power as *a means to an end*: in order to impose his own particular value system on the world.

Nietzsche understood this himself, as he explains in Beyond Good & Evil: "It has gradually become clear to me what every great philosophy up till now has consisted of—namely, the confession of its originator, and a species of involuntary and unconscious auto-biography; and moreover that the moral (or immoral) purpose in every philosophy has constituted the true vital germ out of which the entire plant has always grown. Indeed, to understand how the abstrusest metaphysical assertions of a philosopher have been arrived at, it is always well (and wise) to first ask oneself: 'What morality do they (or does he) aim at?' Accordingly, I do not believe that an 'impulse to knowledge' is the father of philosophy; but that another impulse, here as elsewhere, has only made use of knowledge (and mistaken knowledge!) as an instrument."

Nietzsche's description of all human action as motivated by will to power was a product of his own physiology: the fact that he was a weak and sickly person, who did not want to be pitied, and wished to affirm life even if meant affirming suffering. His ethical assessment of his society and culture is therefore concerned with the weakening of his country, the degeneration of Europe, and increasing sickness he saw around him. He was interested in finding a new source of *strength* for the continuation of life: his individual life just as much as the culture around him. It was toward these instrumental ends that he philosophized.

I believe that there is something deeper. Beneath the will to power, there is something more fundamental: this *will to eternity*. There is another in the history of philosophy who talked about the fundamental drive of all life: as a longing for immortality. This is Diotima, who comes to us through Plato's *Symposium*. Diotima is perhaps the most significant and influential theorist of "the will," understood as a force governing human action, though she is rarely discussed because of her obscurity.

Diotima was the High Priestess of Eros, the God of romantic love, in Athens. Socrates, in Plato's *Symposium*, recounts a conversation with her. Given that Diotima's lines were heard, and then repeated by Socrates, recorded by Plato, and then handed down through the ages, we cannot really know if the real Diotima believed the words attributed to her, or even if she actually existed. Whatever the truth may be, Socrates cites Diotima and the description she gives of *eros*, or the principle of loving.

Diotima expands the concept of love beyond biological reproduction, romantic love, or love between friends. She even takes into account the concept of loving an art or craft: the way we might talk today about one's "passion." She argues that the principle of *eros* is far deeper than any of these, which are just its particular manifestations. Eros here becomes synonymous with the deepest desire of mankind, its "will" in the sense that Schopenhauer or Nietzsche might have used the term.

Diotima brings up not the feelings of lust one has for a lover in order to describe this feeling of the deepest love, but rather, the feelings that one has for their children. She argues that we can even perceive this in nature, in animals. "They are ready to fight to the finish," she says, "the weakest against the strongest, for the sake of those they have generated, and to die on their behalf; and they are willingly racked by starvation and stop at nothing to nourish their offspring."

Diotima alludes to the fact that we can source our anxiety about death to our self-consciousness. But what of the animals? The animals do not calculate, and do not have the same understanding of death that we do. What we share in common with the animals is our mortality, yes, but also our deep instinct to preserve and expand our form of life. This precedes any kind of calculating rationality or death anxiety.

Diotima: "The mortal nature seeks as far as possible to be forever and immortal. Mortal nature is capable of immortality only in this way, the way of generation, because it is always leaving behind another that is young to replace the old. For while each one of the animals is said to live and be the same (for example, one is spoken of as the same from the time one is a child until one is an old man; though he never has the same things in himself, nevertheless, he is called the same), he is forever becoming young in some respects as he suffers losses in other respects: his hair, flesh, bones, blood and his whole body. And this is so not only in terms of the body but also in terms of the soul: his ways, character, opinions, desires, pleasures, pains, fears, each of these things is never present as the same for each, but they are partly coming to be and partly perishing."

What Diotima finds at the heart of loving, I find at the heart of artistry. Both love and beauty must be understood together, as manifestations of the same drive: the will to eternity. This will to eternity is the task of all life: to wage war on the law of entropy, and to create more and better patterns with increasing complexity – and increasing *survivability*. Nietzsche was right in rejecting the fundamental human motivation as self-preservation: for *self-preservation* is not one of life's goals, and never has been. It is the survivability of the *species* – the pattern, or rather, on the physical level, the 'selfish gene' as Dawkins put it – that allows the continued propagation of life, not the individual.

In the thinking individual's cognition, he perceives his own finitude. He perceives time, he perceives the self, and he perceives death. But the fear of death is not primary, the love of life is. *Like all living things, the thinking being wants eternity instead.* This is life's general struggle against all of reality. But whereas this struggle had heretofore been conducted strictly in the darkness of abject ignorance – of sheer, blind, stupid willpower against the unthinking, brutal indifference of nature – now there is a mind that possesses a concept of mortality, and can therefore imagine immortality.

Where we find both potential advantage and potential difficulty in this struggle, that the other animals do not, is insofar as we have associated our *selves* with our *minds*. A modern person conceives of the self as synonymous with their thoughts and self-consciousness. While other animals only have the option of battling against impermanence by having offspring, and preserving the pattern in that fashion, we now have the option of taking up the battle on another front entirely: through the preservation of ideas, images, symbols, histories, monuments.

The world of nature as driven by the will to eternity is still an all-out war, as nature always has been. To preserve oneself often involves destroying opposition as a matter of course. But the pleasure does not come, at the most basic levels, from "the feeling that opposition is being overcome" as Nietzsche describes the feeling of power. It comes from the feeling that immortality is being achieved.

This preservation through warfare exists in the realm of artistic expression as well. The famous or influential artist produces expressions that "colonize" the psyches of others. One might even say that one's artistic expressions can even *dominate* the psyche of an audience, or fellow artist. The greatest artists in history had this effect, reaping the whole sum of the cultural artistic capital and leaving all who followed in their wake to grab after their scraps: Goethe, Shakespeare, Miles Davis, Alfred Hitchcock, The Beatles, Black Sabbath, etc. By creating more powerful artistic expressions, one becomes more influential.

Yet again, however, the ultimate goal is not power, but survival: the battle of infinity against entropy. The emotional resonance of art is a strategy for preserving a certain feeling or play of feelings – across generations, epochs, even whole civilizations.

This satisfies our will to immortality, the same way achieving a reputation or a legacy satisfies it for a statesman or soldier, or bringing up offspring satisfies the family man or woman. The fact that *actual* immortality is never reached is quite beside the point: infinity is a limit that can never be reached. No one is actually immortal until they actually live forever; and no one actually lives forever until "forever" is over and done with, which can never happen (or else eternity wouldn't actually be forever).

As Diotima is quoted as saying near the conclusion of her speech: "For in this way every mortal thing is preserved; not by being absolutely the same forever, as the divine is, but by the fact that that which is departing and growing old leaves behind another young thing that is as it was. By this device... the mortal shares in immortality, both body and all the rest, but the immortal has a different way. So do not be amazed if everything honors by nature its own offshoot; for it is for the sake of immortality that this zeal and eros attend everything."

By being strongly felt by as many souls as possible, art survives. Art endures beyond the lifespan of any one organism. It is studied and interpreted. We speak about it and argue about it. It lives on in future minds and hearts.

Gradually, over many years, the meaning of an artistic work can grow more intense. Certain things are emphasized, and other artistic choices are ignored. Interpretations rigidify. The greatest art becomes cultural capital. Some of it becomes colored with religious or political interpretations. This might even be a problem for an individual artist, since it can lead to a distortion of the pattern they wished to express. I recall a story I read about a Buddha statue at a temple somewhere in Asia, where it was customary for pilgrims to rub just a bit of gold onto the statue when visiting. One Buddhist author wrote of visiting the temple that housed the statue, having heard so much about this golden Buddha. He reported that it had become warped beyond recognition by countless layers of gold that had been caked onto the thing. Its surface was now an irregular blob of gold vaguely resembling the outline of the Buddha it had been globbed onto. It was now monstrous and ugly.

Metaphorically speaking, this is what happens to all art. Everyone rubs his or her own interpretation on it. Societies come to identify with their art, come to see their artistic works as exemplifying their own cultural values and beliefs. Eventually, the original message is unrecognizable in ages to come.

But this is no lamentation. It is a simple truth that no artist is powerful enough to resist historical forces. You become part of a vast tapestry of culture, and are never separate from it. The individual artist does not survive, just as the individual organism does not survive. In the case of the organism, it is the genes that must be preserved; in the case of the artist, it is his style, his aesthetic. If we could atomize an aesthetic into all its different aspects – and imagine the molecules, or the "genes of an aesthetic" – we might say that the artist lives on through his aesthetic genes. This is to say, in those who the artist influences, who take his aesthetic, and pass it on in a modified form. The mortal partakes of immortality not by being absolutely the same forever, but by generating offshoots.

This is perhaps why the will to power idea becomes stretched too thin. Eventually, when examined closely enough, it loses its meaning. The will to eternity is not a will to colonize, to dominate, or to overcome. One could describe it as a desire to bring other things within the power of your artistic expression, for as long as possible – but this is not its driving essence. It is the will to have some offshoot of oneself endure through the ages. It is not required that one aesthetic dominate all others: in fact, it is only to the pleasure of the beautiful that it stands in contrast to all the less beautiful things around itself. It wants the other aesthetics to endure.

The artist endeavors to endure, not as an ideology, or as an individual, but as one thread of the tapestry. He wishes to enter into an artistic, and thus emotional dialogue, with audiences for ages to come. The quest to achieve the greatest beauty is the quest for the eternal relation: the artist's unending communion with mankind. The artist makes us glimpse eternity – for eternity is always in the back of the artist's mind.

What does this make the unsuccessful artist out to be? Rather than the *archetypal artist*, the one we might call the *typical artist?* – the starving, struggling, not-notable creative. He is a fool, if a noble one. He is resisting the great historical and cultural forces that will either erase him from the annals or else appropriate him for their own ends. He will be swept up in the flow of time, woven into the fabric of the tapestry, which is itself so large and all-encompassing that he will likely appear as mere fiber in it: a detail. A rest in the measure, rather than the emphasized note.

The typical artist is a fool trying to become a king. No, wait.... not a king, exactly. Perhaps prophet is a better word? No? Curse these words! Perhaps no word really exists for what the artist archetype signifies: except for the word itself, artist. But my problem with the word "artist" is that the connotation has become too sedate. It is a declawed term. It is too broad, too nebulous. Signifying everything and nothing to people. Subjective. I've tried for so long to wrestle with it, to make it reasonable, in order to understand myself.

We may call the unsuccessful artist a fool… but what of the successful artists? Those artists who eventually make something of themselves are just as certain to become fools – emperors with no clothes, divas drowning in fashion and opulence. How many develop addictions? Act out their strange psychological complexes? Give in to their basest instincts? How many go broke, get sued, fade into obscurity, or lose sight of the art and become addicted to adoration?

It may be easy, in light of those considerations, to declare vanity an enemy of art. And yet here I have said that vanity is, in some sense, the motive behind art. The ascension to something immortal, something important for all time. To resonate through the ages. What could be less vain than the quest for immortality? So, I suppose that vanity must get its due some way.

Art's paradox is that it is necessarily self-absorbed and necessarily other-absorbed: it is an interaction between the artist and the entire rest of the world. Art wants the largest possible reach. It wants the biggest impact. It wants to be different, to be novel, to capture the imagination and the soul. But this quest for an audience can override the quest to further the expression: that is to say, *the substance of the expression*, the emotional world made manifest. The artist must always be in a constant battle between the raw demands of their drive for expression, and its counterpart – the desire to seek an audience, to entreat with the largest number, to burn their soul's longing deeply into the psyche of others.

The desire for expression requires both *what is expressed* and *someone to whom it shall be expressed*. These forces are centrifugal. While both requirements depend on one another for art's very existence, these drives once fully understood and brought into conscious reflection can come to oppose one another. A famous musician may become aware of their need for the audience's validation, and try desperately on that account to alienate them, as part of a quest to make the most "authentic" music possible. Or, on the other side of that coin, one may find he enjoys the sense of validation far more than the act of artistic creation – which every artist knows can be difficult or painful. If either element of art is out of balance, beauty is inhibited.

Giving an audience what they want just to get their validation stands in relation to art the way someone pretending to love their partner during a long, unhappy marriage stands in relation to love. One might do so for practical or financial reasons, or simply out of comfort or familiarity, and we might even understand why such states of affairs happen: but such a state of affairs is *not* love. Beauty – or artistic quality – is not possible when the supposed artist is just feeding people something they find easy enough to swallow. Art loses its novelty when it is done by rote, and becomes mere entertainment.

When we absorb mere entertainment, which is the most debased form of art, it is so familiar, so predictable, so easy, that it is almost like we have not come into contact with anything at all. We forget about it; it passes from us. We do not incorporate it into our being. The emotional resonance in the case of mere entertainment is therefore counterfeit, an intense experience of lights and sounds and strong sensations, which seem significant at the time but which make no lasting impact.

Mere entertainment is ever popular, of course, and will always be produced in mass quantities so long as there is a financial incentive for doing so. But the stronger the ulterior motive for producing art, the worse it becomes. Art is a divine madness, after all: the more rational, the more utilitarian, the more self-interested we are in creating it, the more it is distorted. On the other side of that coin, all those experimental and avant-garde types who fail to resonate with anyone will also eventually die off, and be forgotten. Those works of art that fail to resonate at all – perhaps produced by artists who claim not to care a wit for the audience – will never be woven into the tapestry. The real argument against becoming a counterfeit artist or charlatan, then, is not to attack the vanity of the artist, but to point out that being a counterfeit will not truly serve one's vanity, in the end. By becoming a purveyor of mere entertainment, one lessens oneself, diminishes his legacy.

What is beautiful is what captures and bewitches us: which is why the question of beauty cannot escape questions of cultural relativism. What a culture thinks is beautiful is what it loves, what it wants, what it seeks, what it desires and wishes to have. The Greeks were profoundly irrational in correlating what is good with what is beautiful and what is true – and yet, on an emotional and artistic level (which is *by definition* irrational), they were completely correct. What is beautiful *is* good. This is the honest truth for us when we truly desire something. Beauty is its own justification of the existence of something, which makes it a form of the good, so long as we define good in any way that makes descriptive sense. Artistic expression, driven as it is by the will for immortality, is good because it is part of our campaign against entropy.

What is beautiful to someone is also therefore dangerous to him by that very token, and what we love is that which destroys us. That is the greatness of beauty, the power that beauty holds over us. We will even let it destroy us, like Icarus flying into the sun, like the crews of hapless ships casting themselves into the water, driven to madness by the beauty of the sirens' song. Beauty is more important than any one individual, whose survival has *never* been important in the grand scheme of life anyway.

The survival of that which is beautiful is, in fact, the *only* thing that is important. This has been a law of nature since time immemorial, and one need look no further than the peacock to substantiate the syllogism. The truly beautiful is a well for the thirsty and ambrosia for the hungry. All great music, painting, and poetry: all of it has this power. One grows a craving for it, and feels rejuvenated upon basking in it. One feels as though he has encountered an undiscovered land, or a rare gem, and wishes to share his finding with the world.

One feels a beautiful feeling, and thinks, "Does anyone else know of this? I must make sure that they do!" – and becomes an evangelist for his aesthetic, to spread it throughout the world. In this way: the strong survive, the beautiful survive.

***

That morning, Steve found his phone dead and unresponsive.

"I must've dropped it, spilled something on it," he said.

It was now an expensive paperweight. He tried doing a hard reset, charging it, fiddling with it every which way he could think of. Nothing worked. Hours passed, after he should have recognized that doing the same thing over and over again was the definition of insanity, he continued trying to fiddle with the thing.

"It's not going to turn on, Steve," I said to him.

"Just let me fuck with it, dude," Steve said, offering a smile.

It was jarring to be severed from satellite communication with the rest of the world. I thought of Amberly, and the prospect of suddenly not being able to talk with her. Even though there were only two days remaining before we'd be reunited, the prospect sounded terrible. So, he kept on compulsively fiddling with it, and I stopped judging him for it. Just as I'd had to rely on Steve to withdraw money while on tour, Penny offered the use of his phone for Steve to keep in touch with Suzy via Facebook messenger. It wasn't the end of the world. But I could tell that it sucked.

Tonight, the final show. Originally, it had been booked for Treviso, but the details of the show had been rearranged at the last minute. Now, it was in Belluno. Belluno was a bit further away, deeper into the mountains. It was a six-hour drive from Vercelli. Based on our experiences with playing small towns in Italy so far, and the overall track record of the tour, I braced myself for complete disappointment.

As we drove, Alex pointed out towards the mountains that overlooked the region. His hometown was in their direction, he said. We passed field after field of crops. I asked him what they grew here. He said they mainly grew fruit – kiwis, pears, stone fruit – otherwise, it was all rice. The wine was mainly cultivated up in the mountains where the temperatures were cooler.

We had a long stretch of driving between the fields of risotto. The road narrowed to a single lane, flanked on either side by the glossy sheen of a submerged rice field. Alex said he'd never been on this exact route before. We stopped at a convenient store for sandwiches, espresso and sparkling water on the way, and the shop seemed almost to be on an island of sorts, as the rice fields were on all sides.

Hours later, the route took us over the Belluno river, whose shallow, pristine waters rushed beneath the bridge. The road followed alongside it as the route began to climb upward. I asked if we were in the Dolomites; Alex told me that these were just "common mountains". We ascended, and the river below became further and further away, and the mountains pierced higher into the clouds. Within a few hours, we took in the sight of the

Dolomites. Truly, they were altogether more aristocratic than the common mountains we'd passed before.

Mists gently flowed over and beneath the peaks. We passed village after village, positioned on the slopes, most of them no more than ten minutes apart. All of them had their own little ristorante or tavern. There were mostly older constructions, and some newer-looking apartments. What I would have given to have even the cheapest apartment in one of these little mountain towns!

Belluno was, at a glance, of no greater size or importance than the rest of these settlements. We pulled up to the absurdly named Koala Werewolf Bar. It faced the main highway, away from a breathtaking view of the mountains behind it. The place was tiny. There was a raised patio in front, a bar inside, and a nook in the back for the bands. There was some seating room, but they were clearing space for the show when we arrived.

The soundguy and the owner spoke a little bit of English. We relied somewhat on Alex to help with the translations. They said that we were the first band from Texas to ever play a show in Belluno. Well, that was something. They also said that people didn't come out to shows so much in those parts. They seemed to be warning us against disappointment. But there couldn't have been any worse disappointment than the night before.

***

We met Messa two years previously, shortly before Jeff quit the band. It was their first tour of the United States, and somehow or another, they'd found Steve Colca of Heavy Friends Booking, and hired him to book it. Their debut album had come out a few months prior and had been well-received amongst those in the know.

I hadn't heard of them until the tour was booked, but I was an instant fan upon listening. There was something magnificent and primeval in their music. They alternated between sparse, desolate sounding passages and sections that exploded into pounding, distorted rhythms. Their vocalist, Sara, had that witchy, entrancing quality that every doom singer wished they could capture in those days.

Jeff drove Messa on that tour. We hired out our tour van. They toured with Witchcryer, fronted by Suzy Bravo, Steve's fiancé at the time, and now wife.

When Jeff joined the band, he and Steve were newly friends. During the four years that Jeff played with Destroyer of Light, his relationship with Steve deteriorated. By the time of the Messa tour, Jeff and Steve had been at one another's throats for quite awhile. To make matters worse, Jeff and Suzy clashed pretty hard on that tour. It made the relationship even more strained.

Both Jeff and Suzy came back from that tour with very different stories about what happened. Suzy said that Jeff was drunk all the time. He turned around and accused her of the same. He said she was unreasonable; she said he was irresponsible. After that tour, both Jeff and Steve talked a lot of shit behind one another's backs, but couldn't bring themselves to talk to one another. Same with Jeff and Suzy. Everyone involved just stewed, and let the anger seethe within them.

On the night of Messa's final show of that tour, however, you wouldn't have known it. Witchcryer opened the night, at Hotel Vegas on the east side of downtown Austin. Steve arrived late for load-in, having just come from a performance with Bois, Bois, Bois. He was therefore in costume: newly clean-shaven, with make-up and lipstick. Messa played second. We closed out the night. Given how lame and fickle Austin audiences can be, it was a great crowd. People packed in, the sweat flew and the heads banged, all the bands crushed it. We all hugged and partied and got drunk.

The next day, Steve and Suzy took Messa around town. Sara and Suzy became close friends. Marco told us that if we ever came to Europe to let him know.

Messa's tour was about the same length as our 2019 run in Europe. They seem to have had many of the same experiences, if the photo and videos they posted from that tour are any indication. They too were taking their first step into international touring, being driven around in a foreign country in a van with another doom band. We'd tried to make their final show as awesome and successful as possible, and in spite of our little inter-band drama, I think we gave them a good send-off.

Belluno was Messa's home region – they lived a few towns away. In the two years since we'd seen them last, they'd made big waves in the metal scene. Now we could finally oblige them and play a show in *their* hometown, as they would be headlining tonight. Messa arrived just after sundown. There was Rocco, the loud, party-animal drummer, Marco, the bass player and composer behind the project, Sara, the voice of the band, and Alberto, the classically-trained guitarist (I hadn't met him before, as he hadn't been able to make the tour to America).

Sara's fiancé told me I was speaking "the kingly Italian" when I ordered from the bar. which I suppose is what they teach in foreign language courses. I took it as a compliment. At least my Italian sounded like some kind of Italian.

Marco asked me privately how the tour had been, about Gero and the record label. I told him the truth. Perhaps I was a little too candid; perhaps I was a little too emotional given the events of the previous night.

"It was a shitshow," I said.

"Really?" Marco said.

"Well," I said, hedging. "It could have been a lot better, but it could have been a lot worse. We had two shows get cancelled, a couple busts. The label showcase was a joke."

"Mmm," Marco said, nodding. "I didn't really know anything about this label, or about this booking agent, so when I heard you were working with them, I wondered about it."

"Not good," I said. "I will say... do you know Davide Stracchione?"

"Yes," Marco said. "Yes, I know him."

Of course he did; everyone knew Davide.

"He was great. Alex is great too. But the label is garbage."

I'd probably said too much – and not enough. It was so much easier to focus on the negatives than on the positives. Besides, Steve didn't like it when I talked shit like that, especially to people outside of the band. Oh well. Fuck it.

Why could I say this to Marco and not to Steve? It's easy to talk shit when you don't think there will be a conflict as a result, that was why. That's why we "vent" to other people, rather than confront the actual social challenges that face us. We rarely take the time to appreciate just how difficult communication can be. I'd even had thoughts of leaving the band again, thoughts I'd expressed to Amberly to some extent, but mostly kept to myself. It wasn't as if leaving the band was what I really wanted. What I wanted was for things to change. But what did that mean, and how could I say it?

***

There was a local opener, then we performed. By the time we took the stage, the place was filled to the brim with people. They were spilling out onto the patio. I'd imagined that the place could hold maybe fifty people at most, but there had to have been more. They were surely breaking whatever fire code they had in Belluno.

I spoke to a couple that told me they'd driven fifty kilometers to come to the show. Messa were local heroes in their scene, and they didn't play in small local venues like this very often. Apparently, the novelty of a band from Texas didn't hurt. The show drew people from the small towns all over. The soundguy and the bartender seemed blown away at the attendance. The warning he'd given us had been incorrect.

In the tightly packed room, in the dead of night in an otherwise quiet mountain town, we blasted out booming tones of darkness and doom, banged heads, wailed, weaved soaring melodies, and elicited cheers and yells. Messa took the stage then, and beneath harsh red light, alternated between a plodding roar and an ethereal, dreamlike reverie. Sara dedicated one of their songs to, "Our brothers in Destroyer of Light," and the crowd cheered for us. It all felt better somehow. None of it felt pointless.

I stood atop one of our cabinets at the back of the room, giving myself a vantage point above the crowd. Bathed in the crimson, molten light of the stage lighting, Messa's performance became the sum totality of my existence – save for the brief reflection that the crowd had just communed with Destroyer of Light, in exactly the same way. Songs that we wrote – that I wrote – were now etched into their hearts, if for a brief moment.

These are the high moments, the stupid moments. High moments are always stupid moments, actually. How could it be otherwise? *Self-forgetting, self-emptying, unhistorical fucking Being.* That's why we all do this: for a taste of that state. A ritual that takes you above the din of the self's unresolved contradictions and endless, circular arguments with itself. This is Dionysian, yes, but the central element is still that beautiful, undeniable communion. Tolstoy's joyousness! It makes us Disciples of Divine Madness, and makes the practical concerns seem like ashes and dust.

But something else had emerged into the periphery of my consciousness now, over the past couple of weeks... an understanding of what that mad state was a taste of. The burning will that pushes the artistic mendicant. The taste of eternity. That night was eternal. The answers seemed almost more mysterious than the questions. What did it all mean? I don't think we ever truly appreciate our best memories until years later, though in some numinous moments we get an inkling that we are living a "life memory."

At the end of the night, the bartender came and gave us a very fancy bottle of wine, with a wax seal on it and a stamp indicating that it was part of a small batch.

He asked Alex to translate what he was saying.

Alex said, "He says not to *do a Penny*."

He gestured like he was slamming back a glass of wine in one gulp. We all burst out laughing.

The bartender said, in heavily accented English, "I don't think he is saying what I mean him to be saying," or something to that effect.

We all laughed and tried to explain the reference, which took in itself a lot of translating. I don't think any of it really got through. It was difficult to translate when drunk.

We carried on into the early hours of the morning once again. Normally, I'm with Penny and Nick in the van at the end of a night like this one – but not on that final night. I was one of the irresponsible ones that night, along with Steve. Nick began to get a bit frustrated, after we'd loaded everything and were still lingering on, laughing and drinking, while he and Penny sat in the van. He'd decided he was done with it, and wanted to head to wherever we were staying and get some sleep. It seemed like he was at the end of his rope.

Two young men who'd attended the show offered their apartment. We drove for about thirty minutes to get there, thankfully in the direction we were going the next day, climbed the stairs to their flat, and crashed out. I slept on the couch, with one of their cats rubbing at my feet as I struggled to get comfortable. It was just cold enough to be uncomfortable, and I had no blanket with me.

***

I tossed and turned, searching for the perfect position: on my side, on my back, with my legs on the armrest. Nothing worked. My mind turned back to two years previously. After the Austin show with Messa, when I'd first met them.

We didn't rehearse for three weeks in a row after that. Practice kept getting canceled. Someone would have an obligation last minute, we'd tried to reschedule, nothing would be forthcoming. So, we'd put it off for the next week.

Finally, after a month of not seeing each other, Jeff cancelled practice abruptly yet again, on the day of. As I read his text, even though he didn't indicate it with his words in any way, I remember immediately thinking, *He's going to quit.*

I texted him to ask how he was doing.

He sent me a picture of the view from the porch, his feet up on the railing, a glass of whiskey in his lap.

"I'm doing great, I'm out at the lake."

I told him that wasn't what I was asking.

"Is everything okay with the band? Between you and Steve?"

"To be honest man, I'm done. "

"You're done?"

"Not feelin' it anymore. Steve just wants to stay at the mid-level forever. So I'm done with this shit. I'm out."

I asked Jeff not to make any snap decisions, and that I was going to call him when I got off work. He told me okay. Less than an hour later, he messaged everyone in the band text and quit the group. When I finally got off work and called him, he was hammered. He slurred his words. He seemed to forget what he'd only just said, and would repeat himself. The conversation was going nowhere. Eventually, I hung up. He was done, and the bridge was burned. A lot of insults were sent in the group text, the kind of shit you say to someone you don't ever want to see again. Steve and Jeff didn't talk for a long time after that.

As the conflict had been brewing for weeks before that, I'd felt like I was stuck between the two of them. I didn't want to take a side because I wasn't there, and I was friends with both of them. I didn't feel like I needed to side with one against the other. Steve saw Jeff always focusing on the negative, always phrasing his criticisms as an attack, almost making things personal, getting drunk and loud and picking fights. Jeff saw Steve clamming up and not relating information to the rest of the band, swallowing his anger and not releasing it until it exploded in a fit of rage. This only really happened once or twice, but when it did, it was bad.

I'll always remember the last text Jeff sent, the night he quit.

"If you guys don't communicate, you'll die."

It was somewhat ironic, given that he hadn't exactly done the best job himself of communicating. But he was right about the problem. We'd failed. There were legitimate grievances fueling the conflict. But I never believed it was inevitable. That incident was not our finest moment. Steve and Jeff had let their anger stew, withheld their feelings, hadn't been able to talk about it until the resentment had overflowed and it was too late. Penny and I had stood by, not quite sure who to believe, what to say, or how to mend the situation. All of a sudden, it blew up, and a relationship was irrevocably changed.

It's pretty easy to cut people out of your life, to just walk away from someone and never come back. It's a more popular solution now than it has ever been. You get to avoid conflict. Finally, an end to all those inconvenient or abrasive things about someone that you'd put up with, for the sake of friendship! If ghosting a party is leaving without saying goodbye, this is ghosting a friendship. I've certainly done it. You don't abandon the other person out of a particular malice, even though ghosting someone is a fairly hurtful thing to do – it is always out of a need to be free of a tension, of an unbearable irritation that comes along with a friendship, which one can no longer tolerate.

I wonder if we take this kind of thing far too lightly. Part of why family is so important to people is because you remain loyal and loving towards your family members even when you find them annoying, when you disagree, or when you feel disrespected. Obviously, there are things people can do to alienate even their own families, but in general, we are supposed to learn to live with our frustrating family members because ties of blood are worth preserving. But why limit it to ties of blood, the genetic relationships that no one chose, and which happened out of dumb luck? If your bandmates are like family, you can't just abandon them when things get difficult.

Or maybe you can. People do it all the time.

What happened, happened. I don't regret it, not exactly. If Jeff hadn't quit, I'd never have met Nick. Whatever music we'd have made would have been different to some degree, and so Mors Aeterna might not have been made. It wouldn't have been the same, at least. What happened had to happen. Nothing can change it. But I wondered about the future. If we can't communicate, we'll die.

CHAPTER NINETEEN
BELLUNO - MILAN

Next morning, I woke up, and wandered onto the balcony. Three of the cats who lived in the house followed me outside. Steve woke up shortly after me. We looked out at the mountains together.

"I can't believe it's the last day already," I said.

"I know," Steve said, nodding. "Crazy couple weeks, huh?"

I laughed and rubbed my neck. "Can't argue with you there."

We went to a late lunch with our hosts at the only ristorante that was open that day, or at least the only one for miles around. It was a few towns away, but it was on the route back to Milan.

Nick and I had talked about doing some souvenir shopping in Milan. I'd mentioned it on our first day there. So far, we'd never had the time for that kind of thing. It would also be difficult, since anywhere we'd want to go, Alex would have to drive us, which meant that all of us had to go. With another five-hour drive or so, and after waking up at such a late hour, it probably wasn't in the cards. I probably wasn't the best at communicating this thinking, but I figured Nick would get the picture. Besides, he didn't speak up either.

We spent a few hours longer than we should have at the ristorante. Then again, how long was too long? We could have tried to squeeze in some shopping or sightseeing, but I was content to spend it with our Italian friends: our hosts for the night and our driver Alex. Italian time.

***

With the complete understanding that future interpreters will take it from us and make it their own, build it into their own psychic personality structure, we continue to create art. In that case, is the artist really understood? Is the work of self-expression, the attempt at communicating the truths of one's soul certain to eventually fall upon deaf ears? A person only really knows his or her own mind and experiences. Is all knowledge simply self-knowledge? Is the ulterior motive in understanding a work of art always to understand ourselves and ourselves alone? Does this mean that the communion we hope to find in art is a farce? This would be a tragic view of art: that it is an attempt at communication that is never fully realized.

But if we accept that our emotions arose communally, as essentially communicative, then our fears are unwarranted. Philosophically, we may never have a definite logical basis for proving that we experience the same emotions as others. But artistically, we take it for granted that we do experience the same emotions, that these emotions are communicable, and that the chasm between the inner worlds of different minds can be bridged.

And furthermore, we do not need to speculate, but know for a fact: *that which is beautiful survives!* Even if it is re-interpreted, re-purposed. Something of the artist still survives – some image, some melody, some phrase – something that leapt out of the depths of him now endures in the hearts of others. Like our children, our works of art take on their own personalities and their own lives, and we cannot own them. But we must understand that the "child" – the communion, the unity, the emotional resonance – is the offspring of both artist and audience. We cannot ever be divorced if the artistic experience is to continue. The author is not dead. The audience is not irrelevant. Their offspring is alive and through it, both endure.

These are uncomfortable thoughts. It means that the concern of the artist *is* more than "just the music." This means that my hemming and hawing over whether my artistic attempts have been worth it becomes a serious question. The artist is only as significant as the audience he communes with. This means there are real artistic failures and artistic successes, and that it is not a matter of self-satisfaction or subjective assessment. One might want to seriously consider whether he is an artistic failure or not, and factor those considerations into his continued artistic career.

Imagine that someone decided to create an anti-resonant form of music – meaning, that a musician might intend to create something that *no one* would enjoy listening to or find worthwhile outside of himself and himself alone. Is such a thing even possible?

On the road, I have heard every attempt at dissonance and harshness possible. I have heard the loudest bands in the world. I have heard black metal that sounded like an ice pick stabbing into my brain; I've heard tones that were so loud, perpetual and shrieking. I've heard the most experimental electronic noise projects, some of it intended solely to hurt the ears. I've heard the lowest and most rumbling guitar tones produced by doom bands, the most blood-curdling screams. I've seen the most aggressive performances and seen the most terrifyingly wicked self-portrayals. I've seen the bleeding edge of the avant-garde and the most avowedly traditional-to-a-fault "genre" bands.

In every case, there were other people there who enjoyed it and wanted to listen to it. If for novelty's sake alone in some cases, someone found it interesting, and paid attention long enough to respond to it. In almost all cases, there is some kind of scene around some number of bands attempting these artistic endeavors.

I can only conclude that there is nothing a human can do in an artistic sense that no other human being on Earth will be interested in or find to have merit. We all draw our aesthetic sensibilities from the same primate brain. Not everyone has the capacity to love or understand every type of art, but in every case, there is also someone else, some group, however small, that *are* interested.

We may look at this situation any number of ways. If we are to end on a cheerful interpretation, we may note that this means that, however unsuccessful an artist may be, perhaps he can be assured that so long as he is genuine, there will be at least *some* audience. Tolstoy seems assured of this. The hunger for communion seems sufficiently strong in humans in order to claim this. However strange, however weird, however abrasive: there is someone there, waiting to commune with you. In even the most obscure niches, beauty exists: it is created in every emergent relationship between artist and audience.

The paradox of the will to eternity is that we wish to preserve something of *ourselves*, but ultimately *the self* is the one thing we can't preserve. We can preserve the ideas, we can preserve our image, we can preserve our DNA through our descendants. But ultimately, the self is a subjective experience. Arguably, ever since the advent of self-consciousness, the subjective experience is what really matters to us. To recapitulate: experience is precisely what we're talking about when we talk about the self.

The only way to come even remotely close to preserving an experience is through art: and that is why we continue in the Sisyphean task, constructing ever-higher artistic edifices upon ever-shifting sands. Perhaps this washes those last, bitter dregs of pessimism: the understanding that the collective eventually swallows up the artist's work. Most artists never become a significant part of the artistic memory.

But even the most significant artists did not really own these artistic experiences. This is the kernel of truth in Barthes: the person as merely a conduit. The artist inhabited a body that underwent experiences, and then tried to hold onto them in his memory. Ultimately, as all mortals discover, they were not his to hold onto. The body dies, and the mind with it. Of all the experiences expressed in art, yes, it is only the most beautiful which survive. But they survive in the insignificant artist as much as in the influential artist, *because all artists are themselves part of the audience, and the audience part of the artist*: the multi-generational experience of art to which nearly the whole human race now has access.

Just as evolution preserves a genome, a species – and not the individual – so too does art preserve the subjective experience, the resonant emotions, the profound expression of that which came from above, as from a god or a Muse. These are common property and don't belong to anyone. To return to Socrates, the artist is merely someone who has gone out of his mind in order to speak the divine words of a Muse. Just as the father and mother, in their quest to preserve something of themselves, are really preserving their species and not anything of themselves, so too is art preserved in the same way. We preserve not ourselves nor our individual existence; we do not even ultimately preserve our legacy.

It is not for our own sake that the will to eternity exists, and not for our own survival that we seek artistic gratification. The feeling of artistic gratification is the feeling of creating beauty. It is simply the feeling of joy in the fact that there is *something* eternal, and that we have touched it with our own experience. Artistic gratification is reveling in the survival of the beautiful, of reveling in the memory of aesthetic history, of reveling in the hopes of our aesthetic future.

The creation of something that endures beyond the individual human life is at least a taste of eternity. We love beauty because we know what is beautiful will survive, even if we will not. By our very nature, as compelled by the laws of physics, that which is eternal cannot be ourselves, in our frail, human bodies. That was never a possibility to begin with. But we can still strike a blow against entropy, still take the fight to entropy so long as we are able. Art is the forefront of our war on reality, for whatever good or ill this battle may be fought.

Beauty is the recurring victory over entropy. It is for this reason that all art exists.

***

Valerio booked us a hotel that was close to the airport but pretty far from Milan – a good thirty-minute drive or so. Nick and I had talked about splitting a cab from the hotel to the city for souvenirs, but it seemed unrealistic now. Nick seemed pissed with me as I explained this. It didn't seem logistically feasible.

"Given the stress and the expenses of this tour," I said, "I've decided to forego gifts. This hasn't been a pleasure trip. So, I don't feel guilty about it. My friends and family can deal with it."

"Maybe if we hadn't spent all afternoon dicking around we would've had more time," he said, angrily.

The fact was, by that point, I had no desire to secure transport into Milan to do gift shopping. I was worn down. All I had to do for the evening now was drink the rest of the wine I'd bought, have a meal, and go to sleep.

Alex dropped us off at La Viscontina. It was a hotel about twenty minutes outside of Milan, on a working farm. Horses lingered and grazed in a field next to the gravel parking lot. Unlike every other arrival, we didn't have to unload the gear. This was the final stop, and Alex would be taking it all back to the rental company. We took out our luggage. We'd be taking a shuttle to the airport the next day.

We left the records with him. We had all the other merch to bring back, and the CDs, not to mention the guitars, pedalboards, cymbals and kick pedal. With one bag each full of luggage, we'd be pushing the limits of what the airline would let us check anyway. Alex said he'd get in touch with Gero and Valerio and ship the records to Austin.

We all hugged Alex before he left. With a final thanks, we said one more goodbye, to the first and last person who had been immensely hospitable and helpful to us on that tour.

Steve, Penny and I went out to the tables in front of the hotel's ristorante. It was twilight. I had an entire bottle of wine to finish myself. We could have shared, of course, but everyone had their own wine. I couldn't count on any help. Steve and Nick were both set on checking a bottle or two and bringing them back home. I had a vision: of opening my bag up and seeing a bunch of shards of glass and clothes soaked with red. Maybe it was an irrational fear, but I didn't trust baggage handlers. I resolved to finish all of it.

Eventually, Steve went up to the room. Penny and I talked more, reminiscing about the weeks that had just passed. Then he got a call from his wife, Merriet.

I wandered the grounds of La Viscontina. There was a little pathway leading from the hotel to a quaint, wooden bridge over a flowing stream. On the other side of the bridge, I passed under an archway covered in creeping vines and followed the dirt path into the woods. I could hear water rushing, more and more clearly, the more I walked. The wooded section didn't last long, however, and I soon emerged on the other side of the thicket. There was a man-made canal of some kind. There was a dam over to my left side, the source of the sound.

I climbed the concrete steps and walked out onto the middle of the dam. On one side, the canal flowed on and on, curving off around a bend and disappearing behind the wall of trees. I remembered we crossed the river when Alex dropped us off. On the other side, there were a few cranes bobbing lazily on the glassy surface of a deep, azure lake. Occasionally, one of them dipped into the water, grabbing at a fish with its beak.

I was just drunk enough for it to be pleasant but not debilitating. My head was swimming only slightly. I was a bit wobbly, but I could still walk fine. And so, I just kept walking, over to the other side, where the trail continued. It didn't matter how long I walked or how long it would take me to get back to the hotel. I didn't have anywhere to go or anything to do until tomorrow morning. Twilight was coming, and the golden light of the afternoon failing. The sun, already choked by clouds, was slowly sinking behind the treeline.

I thought about my inquiry. It was going to take years to edit. I didn't know how much of my musings were even usable. The notebook itself was not pretty any longer. All those ripped out pages... crossed out phrases... scribbled ramblings and prosaic observations... streams of consciousness and studious copying-down of quotes. It was a mess.

And yet, it felt like a breakthrough! Beauty is that which survives. We love the beautiful because it means we've lived to fight another day against entropy. Art is a way of transferring and preserving our inner states, of communing with future generations! I'd made sense of myself!

But it was all so ponderous. I'd included the whole anthropological history of man in this thing: all our attempts to communicate, to make the inner world known to the outer world, to understand our emotions, to speak, to sing, to dance, to worship. The whole fucking meaning of life had to be in it in order for me to make my silly point.

All of that, just to come to this: Why am I doing this? What did it mean to me, for me? What did it mean for my own understanding of my artistic project, for my understanding of what it is we're doing out here? I was still not sure I fully understood it, in practical terms.

We came seeking an audience. A new and different audience. Why? The Muses demand to commune with the souls of all the world. Troubadours, outlaws, fools, kings, monks. Any word used to describe the lifestyle didn't really come up to it.

Consciousness itself is about sharing, about transmitting, about unifying. Nothing that I think, feel or create is just for myself. Nothing anyone thinks, feels or creates is just for themselves. Community is the meaning of life for humans. The social life is our gift, it is our curse, it is our nature. Sharing is how we survive. Nothing in this whole game of life is worth anything to us unless we share it. Nothing...

We were looking for something greater than ourselves, something eternal and enduring. I supposed that this was also why I'd written this troublesome inquiry in the first place. I realized now that I simply could not stop. I couldn't argue with the Muse. Art is irrational. The thoughts that had troubled me throughout these weeks recurred, as they always do. You will not find final happiness. Not here, not anywhere. When you are here, you want to be there, and when you're there, you want to be here. You know this is foolish, but you can't stop. You always choose this, because you have no choice.

***

Eventually, I found my way back to the hotel room. The room we had was split into two separate bedrooms, with a single bathroom between them.

Nick was cloistered off in his room. Penny was still downstairs. The only person in the room with me was Steve.

He was counting up the money we had. We had a couple thousand dollars in hand.

"Technically, we broke even," he said, excitedly.

"Not if we include the price of the plane tickets," I said, referring to the tickets we'd each purchased out of pocket for a trip to Milan with a return trip.

"Well, sure," Steve said, hesitating before saying anything else. "I'm just saying..."

"Yeah, I know," I said. "It could have been a lot worse."

"We did pretty well for a first trip."

"Yeah. At the same time, man... you have to include the price of the tickets. That's a cost. It puts us in the red."

"Yeah, I just don't count that," he said. "The price of the plane tickets, I don't count that."

"Okay, you may not count it," I said. "But we all had to pay it. And none of us are getting paid out. After all the expenses, we did worse than break even."

"So...what," Steve asked, "You don't think it was a good tour?"

"I didn't say that."

Steve was silent, waiting for me to elaborate.

"We can't work with this label again. They fucked us. We got in bed with the wrong people."

"I don't think it was that bad..."

"They fucked up the vinyl. They fucked up the tour routing...."

"It was our first time here... we have to play the shitty plays, do the long drives..."

"No one knows who these guys are. Marco didn't know who the fuck they were..."

"Valerio still took care of us, he got us this hotel out of his own pocket..."

"Steve, it's a miracle that this tour went as well as it did. Which was... not good."

He looked at me with an expression with which I was familiar. He was frustrated. He wanted to focus on the positive: the conversation always had to circle back to something positive, something constructive. I looked back at Steve, wobbling ever so slightly where I stood, wine in my belly and on my breath, the tipsiness warming my limbs and flushing my cheeks. I sighed. The difference in perspectives was not about to be reconciled. I'm someone who, out of habit, always wants to put the conversation off until later. And yet, sometimes later is exactly the right time.

"I'm not saying..."

"I know."

"It was a good tour, man," I said. "We've done something that only a handful of other bands has done."

"That's what I'm saying, man," Steve said. "We made it through. Next time will be better."

Next time will be better. Always, next time will be better. If I've shown anything in this book, it is that artists like myself are, above all, blind. When I call art "irrational," and call the artist's quest quixotic, these are polite ways of saying that the path of the artist is a stupid one. But it is an admirable form of stupidity, sort of like the stupidity of hope.

You have to tell yourself that next time will be better. Always, next time will be better. Even when experience tells you that, more than likely, next time will be the same or, at best, a negligible improvement. You have to fight the artistic fight with the same blind, stupid hope of a commander ordering his men to fight to the last man: that if you hold on a bit longer, reinforcements are coming any minute. You press on with the same foolish optimism of an unrequited lover, trying to court after beauty even though she hasn't returned your calls. You just keep putting one foot in front of the other, and keep your eyes fixed on the horizon.

The minute you start glancing backward, wistfully yearning for days that have long since passed, you've lost. You've started dying. Life demands a balance. You can't forget the past, and you can't ignore the existing problems. But you *have* to keep looking forward. To the next one. Steve was, in the end, entirely right. And I was wrong.

And so, I said, "Yeah man. Next one will be better."

EPILOGUE
HOME

Another impossibly long day at the airport. We had to wrap some of the parcels together to get all the checked luggage home. The clerk who checked us in and printed our boarding passes told us he'd meet us at the gate to help us get the guitars on board. Lo and behold, there he was when we arrived. The attendants let us board before anyone else this time. We got the "rock star treatment"! To our surprise, they boarded us before even the first-class ticket holders. The crowd watched us skip the throngs of people queuing up, and a couple of yuppie moms asked us if we were band with big smiles on their faces. This time, the staff had room for the guitars upstairs. Things went smoothly.

Penny requested wheelchair assistance when we reached the gate at JFK. It's not as if Penny needs a wheelchair: as should be clear from the events recounted in this book. But it was the correct decision. It helped us and made it so we didn't have to worry about him injuring himself trying to keep up. When you come into the U.S. on an international flight, you have to go through customs of course, but you have to reclaim your bags and then check them again. He could only walk so fast, and this way we were able to make our connecting flight.

At JFK, that meant switching terminals. The staff member who helped us aided us with every step of the process; he told us exactly where to go, where to check our luggage, fast-tracked us through customs, and did his best to put us on that plane on time.

The cops at the airport certainly didn't help. Two of them stopped us, and hassled us about our guitars. Wanted to know if we'd documented that we'd taken them with us to another country, because if not they could be seized and held until we paid an import tax. Then he acted as if he was "helping us" by implicitly threatening us in this way but not actually following through. He let us go on after a brief lecture, and we quickened our pace as this little distraction had us perilously close to missing our boarding time. It took us almost the whole three hours of our layover to reach the gate for our connecting flight to Austin, but we made it. We probably would've missed our flight if Penny hadn't asked for help.

***

We arrived in Austin around one in the morning. The Austin airport felt quaint in comparison to the monstrosity in New York City, and it was virtually deserted except for passengers disembarking from our flight. We collected our luggage. I was informed by a little, white note that my pedalboard had been opened by the TSA, apparently in the rain – little beads of water covered the pedals and the power supply. I hoped nothing was damaged. We then discovered that Nick's pedalboard didn't make the journey there at all. He went to sort it out at the luggage desk. The airline promised to send it to his address.

"At least they didn't lose it on the flight *to* Europe," I offered, shrugging.

"I'm sure it'll be alright," Nick said, looking discontented. But he said nothing more of it. Maybe he was just too tired to care.

We stepped out of the automatic doors into the sweltering, muggy night. I'd truly forgotten how much more unpleasant the night was in Texas during summertime, and May is already summertime in Texas. The humidity never really goes away this time of year; the heat doesn't truly dissipate at night. I was covered with a dirty film all over my body from the day's travels. Sweat dripped down from my forehead. We must have smelled awful. Same as the day we arrived in Italy.

We were picked up by our loved ones, one by one. Each left in turn, with a simple, "Bye."

Amberly picked me up. We kissed. She was so naturally beautiful, even after having gotten up in the middle of the night to come get me. As she rolled down the window, lit a cigarette and took a drag on it, I asked her for one.

"I thought you quit?" she asked.

"I started again," I said, shyly.

She couldn't say any more, as she hadn't quit either.

I was tired, but also wide-awake from the jet lag. We'd talked almost every day that I'd been away; such is the marvelous technological world that we live in. I'd already regaled her as to the events of the tour, in real time. She read along with all of you reading this now, and knew the story just as well as you do now. Other than our day at the airport… there was nothing much to say. Similarly, I'd already heard from her what was going on in her life – with friends, with family, with work. We were both already caught up after almost three weeks of being parted.

There aren't really any words that can convey the joy of being reunited. Schopenhauer tried, when he said that every parting is a foretaste of death, and every reunion a foretaste of resurrection. I like this coinage even though it is too conceptual for its own good.

We just drove. It is a wonderful privilege of a long relationship to be comfortable in silence with one another. This is when the awkwardness in silence has disappeared completely, and the two of you are silent not because you have things you want to say and can't say them, but because you have pretty much said everything already. The longer you know someone, whether in a romantic relationship or a platonic one, the more your communication becomes non-verbal. The better you get to know someone, the more deeply you get to know them, the less needs to be expressed in terms of language. And so it is also a communication which is non-conceptual. The deepest communication is silent communication. The deepest love is silent love.

AUTHOR'S NOTE
"A TRUE STORY"

Due to the nature of our onetime deal with the record label, we were under no future obligation to them and didn't work together again. Their hearts might have been in the right place, but they were not up to the task. A word to prospective financiers in the music industry: don't get into the game if you can't deliver. It's a fucked-up thing to do to musicians.

Case in point: another band that we know, War Cloud from San Diego, had an absolutely horrific tour booked by Valerio a couple months after we got back. In essence, they faced many of the same problems that we had. But rather than making it work by the skin of their teeth, it was a complete disaster. Shows were canceled, badly promoted, under-attended. Promoters informed them that the booking agent had been so non-communicative and unprofessional that they were blacklisting him, and apologized to the band for their unfortunately having found themselves in that situation.

In our case, Stracchione had saved the tour. Meeting Hell Obelisco and becoming friends with them saved the tour. Three or four decent shows saved the tour (Dresden, Aalborg, Stockholm, Belluno). Over the course of two weeks, around three nights made all the difference. If we hadn't had Davide to make the tour schedule work, and we missed one of those shows, for example, the tour would have been an unmitigated failure.

Shortly thereafter, another band of Austin locals, Monte Luna, who were also on the same label, had their tour canceled at the last minute. They'd already bought their plane tickets, and Valerio contacted them to ask if they could "postpone the tour" by a few weeks. If you understand how much planning goes into booking a tour, and how every date must line up down to the day, and every venue must be booked months in advance, then you realize how batshit crazy that is. Monte Luna lost a shitload of money because of these assholes. The tour was canceled after they'd bought their tickets.

As mismanaged as our tour of Europe was, we were the lucky ones. Meanwhile, we waited for the records to ship. Valerio had promised to send them. We waited a month. Then another month. After three months passed, he said they'd been returned to him. Said he'd send them again. Finally, Gero, the owner of the label, had to drive over to Valerio's neck of the woods, pick up the records, and FedEx them to us. All in all, the process took six months.

It was strange, frankly. We'd done this whole underground touring thing for seven years before signing a record deal. We'd put out three vinyl releases ourselves, only one of which we partnered with a small indie label to release. We'd been careful in choosing who to get in bed with. And then this is the label we end up with? When we'd signed, the contract was so flimsy that we figured we could easily walk away if we didn't like the outcome. We underestimated how much it sucked to have our first tour of Europe mismanaged, to have our album release be mismanaged, to have typos on our CDs and reversed art on the vinyl records.

Ultimately, with the combined sales in Europe through the label, and in America through our own website, it was one of our most successful releases. We sold them on the road during a few short regional tours after we finally received them, most notably on a short run with Pallbearer near the end of the year.

We became friends with Hell Obelisco, and we still keep in touch with them to this day. Davide as well. It's easier than ever to keep in touch, in the age of social media. For all its faults, that is one upside of technology.

Actually, we all have very fond memories of that tour. We didn't end up following our European tour with a Japan tour, or with another, better tour of Europe the following year, but that was due to unforeseen circumstances. It turns out that the tour in this book was one of the last tours we did before the coronavirus pandemic hit in early 2020. The coronavirus scuttled all touring that next year for both ourselves and everyone else. You can't make this stuff up: a pandemic shows up at the end of the decade, as if to clearly demarcate the "end of an era."

***

When I first set out to write this book, I wondered if it was even significant for me to talk about any of my personal experience. It's not like I've toured Europe more than anyone else; I'm not an expert on it. I'd say that my touring experience is beyond the vast majority of underground musicians, but that's all back in America. As of this writing, I've only toured Europe the one time. I wondered, I suppose, what *right* I had to write about all this. And why did I find this tour in particular to be so compelling, when arguably I had encountered more outrageous events and perilous situations over the years touring in America than anything that happened in Europe?

I eventually concluded that it was the confusing mix of emotions and experiences that made it the perfect tour to write about. In some ways, it was a high point for us, but from another perspective, it was a low point. It was disappointing and yet fulfilling. It was life changing, and yet ultimately of little consequence.

And now, with a bit of retrospect, it is a sort of glance at what a certain music scene was at the end of that era, not from the perspective of the macro-historian, looking from a bird's eye view at the overarching trends, at the most famous and influential figures – but a report from the ground by someone living it. A micro-history. A snapshot.

I started writing about my experiences on the road during the pandemic. It was both a way to pass the time, and to cope with the fact that this whole world had been taken away from me. In the course of doing so, I recognized something about the frailty of my own memory. Over the years, I did so many tours that they all started to blend into one another. In some cases I had personal journals; in most cases, I didn't. There were usually pictures, sometimes videos. But the documentation is never complete. I realized that the experiences themselves – *the stories* – would be eventually lost to time. We're not famous or influential enough for there to be all sorts of witnesses following us around wherever we go. To the extent that we document our own lives and our own career, it will be preserved. To the extent that we do not, thinking, "Well, who cares anyway?" – well, that prophecy will be self-fulfilled, and no one ever will care.

It's the same thing that motivates our grandparents to compile photo albums, watch old family videos, tell stories to the family around the dinner table. You eventually become a walking history book. We don't sufficiently appreciate how valuable all these walking history books are, or ought to be, because we think that all history will be preserved on the internet, or in books, or in universities. We don't sufficiently realize that the kind of history that gets preserved over the years by institutions and in encyclopedias is macro-history. But what we all become in old age are historians of a micro-history: history on the local level, on familial level, on the personal level. These are histories that would otherwise get swept up by the tides of fate, if not for these micro-historians. The people who carry all your family's micro-histories are likely your grandparents, and if you don't preserve those stories, they die. Don't feel bad about it though. It's probably more likely than not for your story to die out.

So, I committed to finally write down not just mere scribbles, but a real tour novel. It proved challenging in ways that I hadn't considered. How does one write about tour? Perhaps the first challenge one encounters is the narrative structure. There is not any clear narrative structure that forms when one recounts the events of a tour. Yes, there will be one or two funny or unusual anecdotes, but these can be told separately from the story of the entire expedition. Such short anecdotes were not my goal: I wanted to write an actual story, a non-fiction novel out of my experiences. I plan to compile something like a collection of tour stories in the future, but my attempt to communicate my theory of art had to be contained in a novel. I felt this deeply, for personal reasons which are both obvious and obscure to me.

The live performance itself, which is the most interesting part of the tour experience, is probably the worst part of the tour to write about. How many times can you find ways of describing your own performances? Most of the time I am not even self-conscious during my performances. They are mostly a blur in my memory. That is the whole point of the live music experience: to lose yourself, *to not be self-reflective*. So, one must write about the surrounding experiences. After all, it is all the day-to-day experiences of the tour lifestyle that reveal what the tour life is like, more so than the show itself.

When it comes to the day-to-day events of a tour, one quickly realizes how repetitive the events are. Most of the day consists of driving. Then, waiting. It is one thing to write badly, but it is quite another to write boringly. The last thing I wanted to do was to write something boring. And yet, in trying to construct a narrative out of a tour experience, one is faced with the reality that *nothing really happens on tour*.

So – *how does one tell a true story?* I did not wish to sensationalize, to force the progression of events into a three-act structure, to exaggerate character traits or contrive a moral to the tale. I suppose there is nothing wrong with any of that, but the extent to which a story is exaggerated is the extent to which it is untruthful. I didn't want to dress up my memories with forced drama so that they could be more entertaining. It would also be disrespectful to the other people who lived them.

David Lynch, one of my favorite directors, has sometimes spoken of his love of the ordinary: of the rich, aesthetic value of the regular occurrences within daily life, of small and apparently unremarkable events. Lynch goes even further than this, however, and attacks the conventions of narrative structure as we know them. In one interview, he criticizes the idea of "closure": the fact that the audience has certain expectations for how a story will end. The audience has certain needs that must be satisfied: for example, there must be a big confrontation at the end, the bad guy must be defeated, the hero gets their love interest, and so on. To Lynch, these narrative contrivances that we all expect actually make the story *boring*.

To give an easy example of this, we may consider the countless crime dramas on television today. In every episode, the detectives investigate a crime, gather evidence, chase suspects, usually have a shoot-out or a fistfight, the criminal is apprehended. Finally, the suspect breaks during interrogation, admitting their guilt. To take a Lynchian view of this format, we might say that the formula has removed the tension from the narrative. However competent the filmmaking, the fact that we know how every story will progress – and how it will end – ultimately deprives the story of the ability to surprise us. And once there is closure, you file away that story in your mind as resolved. And, in the words of Lynch, "you forget you've seen the damn thing."

I share a fondness for the ordinary, and Lynch's words provided the license I needed to embrace that aesthetic. I learned to write this book by learning to recognize the simple beauty in most ordinary moments and scenes. To the extent that driving to a different city every single night to perform is outside of the ordinary for most people, the events in this book are interesting. Therefore, the setting, the very concept of the book is where the novelty is to be found. The characters and events, on the other hand, are not outlandish or fictionalized. I tried to keep them as ordinary as possible, in fact.

My journal was the other aid in finding a direction for the book. On this tour, I'd thought of keeping a journal where I recorded the events of the day, but insofar as I did so, the notes were fairly minimal.

One example is the entry from May 19th: "7:15 AM. Driving to Fredrickshavn, catching ferry for Gothenberg. Wild show last night, lots of dancing – stayed up late and got a little drunk. They played Boys Boys Boys! Finally had some fun last night. We smoked the last of the hashish this morning. Aalborg is a magical but dreary place, the weather has been dreary everywhere. It's so early that the sunlight is stinging behind the eyes ... "

Some good phrases and paragraphs survived from my writings on aesthetics on this tour, but a lot of it was re-written from the bottom-up. I'd first sketched out the basic points of the philosophy on art that I put forward in this book, through the philosophical ramblings that interlaced the autobiographical. And so, I came back to the old trick of inserting my philosophy into my memoirs. Perhaps I should mention Robert Pirsig as another influence in that regard. It is not such an original thing to intersperse a philosophical argument with a story of traveling on the open road.

I suppose I broke my share of rules. The road story is the quintessential American story, and yet, this was a road story set in Europe. More alarmingly, told from the perspective of someone who isn't even driving.

None of us were therefore "in control," which is a key part of the road story, and what being the driver signifies to us in a road story. We set the tour in motion through our own volition, but during the events of the tour one's individual will becomes sublimated entirely to the project of touring. Thus, this is a story where the characters do not really exercise their volition in order to affect the plot.

There is therefore a very subtle meaning to the analogy of musicians being "free" on the open road, brought out through the concept of *vogelfrei*, "free as a bird": the freedom one experiences on tour comes in some part from the total absorption of one's will into the project of touring. Freedom does not mean to have no constraints, for constraints are the human condition: freedom means unity of purpose, no conflict in what one does and wishes to do. In fact, we always find freedom in constraint.

By spending so much time on the road, spending weeks traveling to a different city every night, I've learned to be an observer. When you spend one night in a place, you hardly affect anything. The city doesn't even notice your presence. You're there, and then you vanish. All you do is observe. You observe a slice of life there – a very particular slice – and then are whisked away again. Everywhere you travel, people are living lives just as intricate as your own, and just as important to them as yours is to you.

Nietzsche wrote, "If we could communicate with the gnat, we would learn that he flies through the air with the same solemnity, that he feels the flying center of the universe within himself." Everyone is the center of his or her own universe, to whom every experience is the sole reality. The grandiose and contrived narratives of modern storytelling exist primarily so that we may distract ourselves, or create a moral illusion to worship. More to my taste are the little stories, for the little stories comprise life. The little stories redeem life.

DESTROYER OF LIGHT'S
2019 EUROPEAN TOUR DATES

With Hell Obelisco:

May 10th Bologna, at Freakout
May 11th Genoa, at Lucrezia Social Bar
May 12th Lyon, at Le Farmer
May 13th Toulouse, at Usine De La Musique
May 14th Strasbourg, at [unknown]
May 15th Dresden, at Chemiefabrick
May 16th CANCELLED (Hamburg)
May 17th Aalborg, at 1000fryd
May 18th Stockholm, at Copperfield's
May 19th CANCELLED (Copenhagen)
May 20th DAY OFF (Kassel)
May 21st Basel, at Hirschneck

With Great Electric Quest:

May 22nd Milan, at [unknown]
May 23rd Vigone, at a farmhouse
May 24th Vercelli, at L'oficina Musica

With Messa:

May 25th Belluno, at Koala Werewolf Bar

"No, life has not disappointed me. On the contrary, I find it truer, more desirable and mysterious every year – ever since the day when the great liberator came to me: the idea that life could be an experiment of the seeker for knowledge – and not a duty, not a calamity, not a trickery. – And knowledge itself: let it be something else for others; for example, a bed to rest on, or the way to such a bed, or a diversion, or a form of leisure – for me it is a world of dangers and victories in which heroic feelings, too, find places to dance and play. 'Life as a means to knowledge' – with this principle in one's heart one can live not only boldly but even gaily, and laugh gaily too."

– Friedrich Nietzsche, (1844-1900)

ABOUT THE AUTHOR

Keegan Kjeldsen is the host of The Nietzsche Podcast and the Untimely Reflections YouTube Channel, and the guitarist in bands Destroyer of Light and Slumbering Sun. Born and raised in Austin, Texas, he spends whatever time he can with his family in the Colorado Rockies and the Sandias of New Mexico. He has been a touring musician since 2012, when he set down the path of outlandish dreams, financial ruin, and the most gratifying and exciting experiences of his life. He married his wife Amberly in 2016, and lives with her in Austin to this day, with their cat, Deforest Kelley.

Note from Keegan Kjeldsen

Word-of-mouth is crucial for any author to succeed. If you enjoyed *The Ritual Madness of Rock & Roll*, please leave a review online—anywhere you are able. Even if it's just a sentence or two. It would make all the difference and would be very much appreciated.

Thanks!
Keegan Kjeldsen

We hope you enjoyed reading this title from:

BLACK ROSE writing™

www.blackrosewriting.com

Subscribe to our mailing list – *The Rosevine* – and receive **FREE** books, daily deals, and stay current with news about upcoming releases and our hottest authors.
Scan the QR code below to sign up.

Already a subscriber? Please accept a sincere thank you for being a fan of Black Rose Writing authors.

View other Black Rose Writing titles at www.blackrosewriting.com/books and use promo code **PRINT** to receive a **20% discount** when purchasing.

Printed in Poland
by Amazon Fulfillment
Poland Sp. z o.o., Wrocław

35402716R00184